Beautiful

I would like to dedicate this book to my surgeon Mr Mohammad Ali Jawad: an innovative and forward thinking man. Without his skill and expertise this book would not have been written because there would not have been a story to tell.

Beautiful

A Beautiful Girl. An Evil Man.
One Inspiring True Story of Courage

Katie Piper

37

First published in 2011 by Ebury Press, an imprint of Ebury Publishing
A Random House Group company

The Random House Group Limited Reg. No. 954009

Addresses for companies within the Random House Group can be found at www.randomhouse.co.uk

A CIP catalogue record for this book is available from the British Library

The Ra ... rdship
Council® (... nisation.
Our books ... er. FSC is
the only fo ... nmental
organisati ... y can be

Prin ... YY

ISBN 9780091940768

To buy books by your favourite authors and register for offers visit
www.randomhouse.co.uk

Contents

Disclaimer

This book is a work of non-fiction based on the life, experiences and recollections of the author. The names of some people, places, dates, sequences or the detail of events have been changed to protect the privacy of others.

Prologue

It was just a normal mirror, a round sheet of glass encased in a white plastic frame, but as I reached for it, my hand trembled.

'Take your time, Katie,' my psychologist Lisa said gently. 'Look at your chest first, then work your way up slowly, inch by inch.'

But I didn't do things by halves – I never had, and a few purple blotches on my cheeks weren't going to change that. I mean, how different could my face be? It might be red and scarred a bit, but it would still look like me, right? Taking a deep breath, I held it up to my face.

All of a sudden, that normal little mirror became a window into hell.

Staring back at me was the most awful sight I'd ever seen. My skin was red raw and weeping like meat hanging in a butcher's window. My eyelids were puffy, and underneath, my eyeballs protruded like two cartoonish globes. My lips were swollen like sausages and my eyelashes and eyebrows gone. I reeled, unable to recognise the face peering back at me.

'*That's not me,*' I thought, unable to understand what I was seeing. '*Have they given me a broken mirror? Or are they showing me a picture of someone else?*'

Staring at the stranger in the mirror, I sat frozen, studying every tiny part of the disfigured face. The way my left eyeball looked milky and opaque. The circle of raw flesh surrounding my left ear. The small, shrivelled mound my nose had become. The way my cheeks had sunk into my skull: my face had melted into my neck like candle wax.

My hitherto disbelief and desperate denial shattered. I wasn't a model and TV presenter any more. How could I be, looking like that?

'No,' I whimpered, my chest heaving with sobs. But no tears came: my ravaged eyes couldn't even cry.

'*What have you done to me?*' I wailed inside. '*Where's my face? Get it out of the bin, and give it to me right now. I'll fix it myself.*'

'It's early days, love,' my dad said, soothingly.

'You won't look like this forever,' Lisa added.

But all I could hear was the thump of my heart, and the whoosh of blood in my head; their voices sounded far away. Even though I sat there in silence, in my mind I screamed and screamed. I screamed for my beautiful, stolen face, but it was gone forever.

Chapter One
Head Full of Dreams

Gold plastic tiara clamped round my feathery blonde hair, I whooshed my red cape in a circle around me.

'Say cheese, Katie,' Dad said, peering into his camera.

'I'm not Katie, silly, I'm She-Ra!' I giggled, as he snapped away. 'I'm He-Man's twin sister. The Princess of Power!'

It was a bright spring day in our leafy back garden, and I was trying out my brand-new dressing-up costume.

'Will you take another picture please, Daddy?' I beamed, whirling like a dervish as my cape danced around me. Round and round I twirled, the daffodils and daisies whizzing by in a blur of yellow and white. Even though I was only three or four years old, I already loved having my photo taken.

Born in a quiet village in Hampshire in 1983, I had had an idyllic childhood. My dad, David, owned a barber shop and my mum, Diane, was a teacher. They doted on my older brother, Paul, my younger sister, Suzy, and me.

An impish little chatterbox on a constant quest for adventure, I was mad about dressing-up. My beloved She-Ra outfit,

Mum's old clothes, my cowgirl costume, plastic bangles, glittery hair clips, smart dresses with lace collars. 'You're such a gorgeous little thing,' people would always smile when I emerged from my bedroom in all my finery.

Not that I ever thought much about that – I just relished being the centre of attention, and I was forever putting on shows for my parents. Every Christmas, I drafted Suzy and Paul in for a nativity play, then absolutely refused to let them do any of the main parts: I cast Suzy as a donkey and Paul as an angel draped in a net curtain, while I took the plum roles of Mary, Joseph and Jesus for myself. When my cousin Louise came to visit, she was roped in to my games, too. Armed with a sticky mixture of flour and water, I'd tell her we were going to pretend we worked in a beauty salon and then slather her in gloop as we giggled uncontrollably. As for my poor dolls, I chopped their hair and caked them in Mum's best make-up until they looked like badly shorn drag queens.

But I didn't just love anything pink and glittery. I was a daddy's girl with a tough tomboy streak, and any time Dad embarked on DIY, I was hot on his heels with a paintbrush in my hand. I spent hours dangling like a monkey from the roof of our shed or careening around on my bike, and if I ever fell, I never cried. Instead I just picked myself up and carried on. I was the sibling who lead the way to the school bus and handed the fares to the driver. I was the one who chucked myself in the deep end at the swimming pool, and I was the one who scampered to the top of the climbing frame without a backwards glance. Even back then, I was independent and sassy and fearless. I never suspected there was any badness in the world.

As the years went by, this little show-off grew into an ever bigger one. By the age of eight, I was a die-hard Michael Jackson and later on a Spice Girls fan, and Mum and Dad became my captive audience. One afternoon, with my blonde hair in bunches, I struck a pose in front of the fireplace and, flanked by Louise and Suzy, started belting out 'Wannabe'.

We were hopelessly out of tune with the music blaring from my CD player, but in my mind, I was Baby Spice and we were storming the stage at the Brit Awards.

'You missed your line!' I giggled to Louise, whom I'd transformed into Scary Spice by backcombing her brown locks into a pretend Afro.

'Whoops!' Louise smiled sheepishly, and we started giggling again.

We strutted across our front room with Suzy, who was draped in a Union Jack flag so she could be Geri.

'Girl power!' we all screeched as the song ended, and Mum and Dad started clapping and cheering.

I bowed, my little cheeks flushing with pride.

It wasn't that I longed to be famous like my heroines; I just loved entertaining people. I relished their smiles, as well as the knowledge I'd made them happy. I basked in the warmth of their approval. Still too young to have clear ambitions, I wanted to be a vet one day and a policewoman the next. Meanwhile, I ping-ponged from one hobby to the next. Tap-dancing, horse-riding, Brownies, Judo; I attacked them all with my customary gung-ho enthusiasm, then lost interest usually just after Mum and Dad had bought the kit. Still, they never stopped encouraging me.

'You can be anything you want to be,' Dad used to tell me, and I believed him. I felt that I was invincible and, as I moved into my teens, my confidence didn't waver once. Not even puberty could shake my self-esteem: as my body changed, I became more aware of my appearance. My face lost its childhood chubbiness and I started blossoming. *'I'm quite pretty!'* I thought in delight, examining my new cheekbones, my wide-set blue eyes and my big, goofy smile in the bathroom mirror.

At primary school, I'd always had lots of friends, and at secondary school I made even more. Constantly cocooned by a gang of mates, I didn't suffer any teen angst. Life was a giggle, even if the teachers were constantly telling me off for chattering in class, or wearing the high heels I used to sneak out of the house in my school bag and then change into. 'She's a lovely girl. If only we could get her to stop talking,' my poor teachers always sighed to Mum and Dad on Parents' Evening. There was no malice in my mischief, though – I just wanted to have fun.

By the age of thirteen, just as I did when I was little, I still loved doing my friends' hair and make-up, even when we were limited to the cheap lipsticks that came free with *Sugar* magazine, or mascara we'd all clubbed together to buy from Boots. Every

Saturday, my best mates Michelle, Carly, Nikkie, Vickie and I got dressed up in our smartest tracksuits and trainers and headed into the nearest town. As we sat in a café over a single plate of chips, we would gossip and giggle about anything and everything. I also used this time to plan garage sales for charity. Mad about animals, I was forever raiding Mum and Dad's cupboards for things I could sell to raise money for the World Wildlife Fund for Nature. 'Think of the poor little seals,' I'd smile winningly, pilfering old clothes and tennis rackets.

Before long, we started to talk about boys, too.

'Everyone fancies Katie,' Michelle teased one afternoon. I chucked a chip at her. Sure enough, however, in the next few months, plenty of boys at school got their friends to ask me out. Confident and chatty, I didn't mind the attention one bit, and after sharing some kisses by the tennis courts, I started dating a boy called Stephen when I was fourteen. Mum and Dad were quite strict, but they didn't need to worry. It was only ever holding hands on the way to school or slow-dancing at the disco.

'You're so beautiful,' Stephen told me one day, as he gave me a present. It was just a yellow cover for my mobile, but at the time it seemed like the most precious thing in the world. Of course, like most first loves, our romance fizzled out within a couple of years, and Stephen and I had broken up by the time I left school at sixteen, but I wasn't the type to mope or give into melancholy.

I decided to follow in my dad's footsteps and take a three-year course in hair and beauty therapy at college in Basingstoke.

As it wasn't too far away, it meant I could live at home and commute there by train. Even though I could drive, Basingstoke was just a half-hour by train from our sleepy village, which seemed like the easier option. And when I arrived I was completely overwhelmed – the bright lights of this big town seemed like another world entirely. It was time for me to spread my wings, and I couldn't wait to taste freedom.

I took to college life straight away, and the other girls in my class were lovely. We had a ball using each other as models, experimenting with wacky hairdos and going to events like the Clothes Show. As the weeks rolled by, we learned how to do everything from waxing and styling to bridal make-up and massage.

At the end of term we staged a segment of the show *Grease* for the whole college. Working behind the scenes, I helped with costumes and styling, then I took to the stage as Sandy to mime and dance to 'Beauty School Dropout'. My singing was as shocking as ever, but as I sashayed in front of the audience dressed in a 1950s skirt, white shirt and matching cravat, I felt that old familiar thrill of performing. The applause for our efforts brought the house down; as I squinted into the bright stage lights, I glimpsed Mum and Dad clapping hard, too.

'Well done, darling,' they said afterwards.

'Thanks,' I smiled, flushed with pleasure.

When it was time to sort out a few weeks' work experience, I took the bull by the horns and wrote to the beauty department at Harrods. What was the harm in aiming for the top? Dad drove me to the interview, and to my amazement I got the job. It was like another world there – all champagne and oysters and Crème de la Mer face cream.

'They have velvet cushions for women to put their jewellery on before they get their hair done!' I relayed to Suzy, breathless with excitement. It was my first taste of the high life, and I loved it.

Unleashed in the big smoke for a few weeks, my social life suddenly took on a new turn, too. My friend from college, Heidi and I would spend ages doing each other's hair and make-up, before dancing the night away in cheesy nightclubs. We were never short of male attention.

'You should be a model,' lads would tell me, but I never thought much of it. At 5'3", I knew I was much too tiny and besides, I loved beauty therapy. I loved helping other women feel good about themselves and seeing their delight when they looked in the mirror after a treatment.

In my third year, I moved into a flat in Basingstoke with another friend, Jo, and life became even more of a blur of going to class and clubbing. Jo and I spent at least four hours getting ready each time before hitting the town. We bought cheap frocks from H&M and shrank and sewed them, altering them to emulate our boho-chic idol, Nicole Richie. I was forever changing my hair, styling it into curls or chopping at my blonde fringe.

I was as confident as ever, although one thing did bother me: my tiny chest. Like two Jelly Tots on an ironing board, my boobs were less than impressive and showed no signs of improving. I was so out of proportion that I struggled to get clothes that fit me properly, and even the AA bikini tops I wore on holidays sagged pathetically. For someone who loved fashion as much as I did, it was really annoying.

'*Maybe I'll get a boob job some day,*' I thought, in typical Katie style: there was a solution to every problem; you just had to find it, and then make it happen. What was the point in sitting around complaining about something?

After I qualified as a beauty therapist, I began working in an upmarket salon, in Basingstoke, giving facials. Popping in and out of London for training, I began a well-informed regime to look after my own skin, too. After all, it was my livelihood. Before long, I was the salon's resident Brazilian waxer, and I saved up enough money to get my boobs increased to a modest C cup, which made me more proportionate. The procedure only took three hours, with two weeks' recovery time – the worst thing was having to try and cut down on my beloved Marlboro Lights during that time! I didn't tell Mum and Dad because I suspected they'd disapprove of any kind of plastic surgery, but since I always wore padded bras, anyway, they never noticed the difference. I did, though, and I loved it. I was now totally happy and confident in my body.

Working in the salon was great. I had perks like free fake tans and manicures, and my clients were so much fun, they became like proper friends. I really cared about them all, and I used to listen to their problems and dish out advice as I waxed and smoothed. But after a few years I started to get restless. I wanted to try something new so, against Mum and Dad's advice, I jacked in my job and moved to Southampton. There I studied to be a beauty therapy teacher, and worked part-time in a raucous Spanish bar where dancing *Coyote Ugly*-style on the bar was encouraged. I also started seeing a student called Steve, and decided to take part in a local beauty pageant. When I was named second runner-up to Miss Winchester 2006, it was a wonderful feeling. It planted a little seed in my mind, too. I was twenty-two, and for years, people had been telling me I should be a model. What was stopping me? I loved the limelight, and it appealed to my sense of adventure. Jet-setting between photoshoots, wearing amazing designer clothes, meeting loads of cool people, doing different things every day ... To a young girl from a village in Hampshire, it sounded so exciting. Even if it was a cut-throat industry, I was savvy enough to take care of myself. I'd always loved a challenge, and I was prepared to work as hard as it took. Why didn't I just go for it?

Over the next few weeks, I trawled through pages and pages of advice and information on the internet. I didn't know the first thing about launching a career in modelling, so I needed to do my homework. I was definitely too petite for catwalk work, but I could still do things like catalogues and adverts.

It became obvious that I needed some test shots I could email to agencies and photographers, so I found a photographer online. For a few hundred quid he would take some proper pictures of me. '*I wonder what my best side is*,' I thought nervously, practising my smile in my bedroom mirror the night before our appointment and, '*Am I doing this right?*' as I posed in a fancy black evening dress in front of the photographer, trying not to blink every time the flash popped.

After that, I spent more hours online, going on forums, investigating auditions and applying to join agencies. You often hear about models getting discovered on the high street and two weeks later they're gracing the cover of French *Vogue*, but the reality is usually very different. Luckily, I was under no illusions. I knew success wouldn't be handed to me on a plate, so I was constantly hunting for work, going to castings and meeting photographers for unpaid shoots to build up my portfolio.

My experiences of photoshoots were mixed: some of these sessions were great and some were a bit sleazy, with the photographer asking if I wanted to stay for dinner or a drink after the shoot. One even emailed me the photos afterwards with little hearts and flowers he had superimposed around my head like a halo, while others had more 'out-there' ideas for the shoots. For one, I had to pose holding a kitchen knife covered in tomato ketchup, as though it was blood. And for another I had to perch on a motorbike, looking windswept. The only problem was, the photographer only had a tiny desk-fan. It barely ruffled my fringe. And another time, the photographer told me there'd be clothes there I could change into, but when I arrived all I found was a pile of manky old underwear. I decided to keep my own clothes on, instead.

It was all good experience, though, and, after a few months of constant hustling, paid gigs started coming in. I earned money by lounging on sofas for furniture catalogues, talking on the phone for stock shots and posing for lads' mags.

'*Nudity's nothing to be ashamed of*,' I thought as I pulled on some fancy lingerie for a *Maxim* shoot. Striking sexy poses and smouldering into the lens, I didn't feel exploited or manipulated. I was young, I was beautiful, and I was making a living – what was wrong with that? It could actually be a right giggle. The photographers would usually show me what kind of pose they wanted by demonstrating it for me, and it would be all I could do to keep from giggling to myself as they struck the poses themselves, their generous beer bellies straining over the waistband of their jeans.

Luckily, my boyfriend Steve, who was now working for his dad, didn't feel threatened by the glamour shoots. But I knew Mum and Dad wouldn't be so understanding. They were pretty old-fashioned and conservative, and I didn't think they'd like to know their daughter was flashing so much flesh. I knew it would upset them, and I certainly didn't want to do that so, just as with my boob job, I decided it was better to keep quiet than risk their disappointment.

As the months went by, my modelling career gathered momentum. Okay, it wasn't quite as glamorous as had I hoped it would be, but I loved it. No two days were the same, and that suited me down to the ground, while the the click of the camera shutter still made me happy, just like it did when I was a little girl.

Even though I didn't realise it at the time, I was starting to get sucked into this world. It was such a whirlwind, I barely even noticed when I stopped contacting Mum and Dad so much and started spending more and more time with my glitzy new friends. I was too naive to see it, too caught up in the thrill of it all.

In mid-2006, I landed a job presenting a satellite show called *Your Night on TV*.

'I've made it! This is the big time!' I squealed, and texted everyone I knew to tell them the good news.

Your Night on TV was a low-budget, late-night programme filmed in nightclubs around Southampton. As the host, I had to convince clubbers to accompany me into a makeshift booth called the 'love shack', then interview them about going on the pull. Babysitting drunken students who mostly wanted to swear or be sick wasn't easy, but I loved every messy second of it.

'*I can't believe I'm on telly!*' I thought on my first night, as I weaved my way through the sweaty throng in a nightclub. Spotting a gang of guys, I made my way over.

'So, is there anyone here you've got your eye on?' I asked, smiling brightly for the camera.

'Your mum!' one of them shouted, and they all started whooping and cackling. Another was so drunk, he toppled off the sofa mid-sentence, but somehow I managed to keep my composure.

'You're a natural, Katie,' the producer told me afterwards, and I blushed with pride. This was even better than being photographed – I had to think on my feet, improvise and talk to people. I had to use my brain instead of just grinning into a camera, and I was hooked. I was going to be a proper TV presenter no matter what it took. In the autumn of 2006, I headed for London with Steve, two suitcases and a heart full of hope.

Chapter Two
Fame

I knew London would be a tough city but I also knew that I was a tough cookie. As I unpacked in our poky little one-bedroomed flat in the north London suburb of Hendon, I felt a rush of optimism: I just had to keep on plugging and hustling and hoping, and I'd get there in the end.

Sure enough, a few weeks later, I landed a job hosting a TV dating show called *The Lounge*, where lonely hearts texted in to be matched up with other viewers. My job was to encourage them to send texts and to dole out relationship advice if they phoned in. Even though it wasn't exactly my dream role, it was still a step in the right direction.

Within a few weeks of my debut, presents had started to trickle in from admiring viewers. 'These are for you, Katie,' a smiling assistant said to me one day, as she handed me a little pile of packages. I opened them to find chocolates, teddies, Avon make-up and even a packet of Oats So Simple porridge. 'What the hell?' I giggled. 'Someone must think I need fattening up!'

As the weeks went by, more and more mail flooded in. Middle-aged men, in particular, sent in photos of themselves, with letters about how much they liked me. They sent perfume I'd never heard of or compilation CDs with 70s music I didn't have a clue about. Others were a bit kinky – like the foot fetishists who wanted to know what shoe size I was, or the guy who liked having sex with balloons. It wasn't something I'd come across before and I found it a bit odd, but still, it was fan mail, and surely this proved I was on the right track!

As one of several presenters who hosted *The Lounge* in shifts, I was able to keep up with the modelling, too. London living was expensive compared to what I was used to, and I reminded myself that any exposure was good exposure. The day I got signed up by a prestigious agency called International Model Management, I jumped up and down in excitement. Through them, I went on lots of commercial modelling jobs, promo work, and yet more lads' mag shoots.

January 2007 saw me on one such shoot, for *FHM*. Dressed in a barely there white bikini, I posed with six other girls in front of the Houses of Parliament. We brandished placards about the government and tried not to shiver as baffled and bemused tourists looked on.

'God, this is boring. And I'm bloody cold, too!' I smiled at one of the girls.

'Me, too,' she replied. 'But it's all in a day's work, isn't it?'

She was right – modelling was a tough profession, and not for the faint-hearted. You had to take the good times with the bad, and go with the flow of the rejections, the bitchiness and the jealous girls who put you down to make themselves feel better. You had to accept being told you weren't the right look for a certain job, or that you were too fat.

I certainly didn't want to fail, so I started putting even more time and effort into my appearance. I banished chocolate and crisps from the kitchen cupboards so I could stay a super-slim size six, I got hair extensions and fake nails, and I scrubbed, exfoliated, moisturised and plucked like never before. This industry wasn't going to grind me down, no way. I was stronger than that!

I had started making lots of friends through work, and over cocktails in Soho bars we'd bitch and moan, gossip and giggle. During one job to advertise Swedish cake at various exhibitions, I met a lovely guy called Pete. We were both decked out in traditional Swedish dress, and bonded over how silly we looked. An aspiring film-maker, he helped me make a showreel to send to TV companies and, in return, roped me in to star in a short programme he was making for the satellite channel, Current TV, called *Smoke Swap*.

'You'll quit smoking for ten days, and I'll take it up,' Pete explained. 'We'll keep video diaries, visit a health clinic for check-ups and get some experts to comment on it. It'll be fab!'

And it was, even though ditching my Marlboro Lights was torture. 'I need nicotine,' I groaned on day three, sniffing random strangers on the street as they puffed on cigarettes. I'd always known smoking was bad for me, and I intended to give up one day; but I was only in my early twenties, and more interested in having fun than my health. I certainly wasn't worrying about what might happen twenty years down the line …

With so much going on, I was really neglecting Mum and Dad. I didn't visit nearly as often as I should have, and when they rang me, I was distracted and disinterested: 'Gotta go, Mum,' I'd breeze. 'Got an audition.' Steve and I had started growing apart, too. He was working nine to five while my schedule was haywire, and with all my new modelling friends, we were moving in completely different circles. So we called it a day and, in mid-2007, I moved into a six-bedroom houseshare in Golders Green, in north London. It was full of dancers, models and other TV people and, as we opened a bottle of white wine on my first night, I knew I'd love it there.

My new accommodation and all the friends I made on photo shoots pulled me still further into that glamour-fuelled world. It was like being inside a bubble – making it as a model became my whole existence, and everything else dimmed into insignificance. I forgot all about the way I used to hold those garage sales for charity, and even though I still gave money to beggars in the street, I didn't really think about people in need. It was all about the next audition, the new showreel I was making, the latest club opening. I was losing sight of what was important.

As for my presenting job with *The Lounge*, it was losing its appeal. Fans were still posting in pictures of themselves, and random presents – one man had even sent in an engagement ring, while another had recognised me in the pub one Friday night: 'Aren't you that girl off the telly?' he had asked, and I had nodded happily. It was happening; I was making it! But still I wanted something bigger, so I packed in my job there.

What followed was a round of endless emails, phone-calls, castings … I kept on doggedly pursuing better work. I started working as an extra too, and it was just as hilarious as Ricky Gervais's comedy made out. On the set of *The Bill*, I was well and truly put in my place: 'We're not extras,' a snooty woman corrected me. 'We're supporting artists.'

After that, I appeared on *Hotel Babylon*, *EastEnders* and *Ashes To Ashes*. I really savoured the buzz of being on set with famous faces like Keeley Hawes, even if I was only a blur in the background. 'It's not for long,' I kept reminding myself. 'Some day, the camera will be on me.'

I also landed a job on another satellite show called *Fit and Fearless*, where three other models and I travelled to paranormal hotspots all over the UK in a luxury Winnebago, like a troop of glamorous ghost-busters.

One episode, we were filming in a supposedly haunted castle in Wales. As darkness fell, we ventured inside with a camera crew and a medium, in the hope of capturing some paranormal activity on tape.

'*What a load of codswallop,*' I was thinking sceptically, as I wandered down into tunnels said to be haunted by the ghosts of children who had died there centuries earlier. But then, all of a sudden, a great wave of sadness washed over me. The feeling was almost tangible; I felt I could reach out and touch it. I didn't see any ghosts, and I wasn't even sure what that feeling was. But it stayed with me for a long time.

A few months and two series later, I finished on *Fit and Fearless* and was back hustling for work. I was posing in my undies for *Dear Deirdre*'s photo casebook from *The Sun* newspaper, working as a presenter for a satellite channel called Smart Live Casino, pitching documentary ideas to production companies … It was a constant battle, and for the first time ever, I started to doubt myself.

With every rejection, my ego took a battering. Was I bad at what I did? Talentless? Not pretty enough? Every time I flicked through a magazine, I saw other models I knew in ads, or fashion and beauty features. Was everyone working but me? It felt like that.

Surrounded by beautiful people and racked by doubt, I started to focus on my appearance even more. I began spending hours in the gym, stressing about my abs or the shape of my bum. Before, I'd just accepted I was attractive and been grateful for it, but now, as my self-esteem wavered, I became more and more obsessed with my looks. If I had a spot, I refused to leave the house, and if my hair extensions weren't sitting right, I fretted all day. The more immersed I became in this world, the more my self-confidence turned into vanity. I was totally self-absorbed, but I was too dazzled by the promise of the bright lights, the glitz and the glamour to even realise.

Four nights a week, my flatmates and I hit the town. For hours, we'd paint our nails, apply false eyelashes and curl our hair as we sipped vodka and soda, then slip into our fanciest Top Shop dresses and head for London's swankiest nightclubs. Chinawhite, Movida, Pangaea … We'd get on the guest list through the model agency, as the club owners would like it to be full of pretty girls, and swan past the envious queue like we were *bona fide* celebs. Inside, it was always a poser's paradise: a place to be seen and make contacts rather than have a good time. One night, in Chinawhite, one of my flatmates, Tania, pointed excitedly to some Chelsea footballers.

'Look, there's Frank Lampard and Ashley Cole,' she squealed, as I squinted across the crowded room.

'Oh, yeah,' I shrugged. Those places were always full of famous blokes and girls who would try it on with them but I didn't want to sleep my way to the top. I wanted to earn my success through hard graft and talent.

Flat-out with work, I didn't have much time for romance, but I went on dates now and again. My career was still my top priority and I wasn't looking to settle down any time soon, but what girl doesn't want to fall in love?

I was getting more male attention than ever before. It seemed as though every time I went out, men tried to chat me up. They wolf-whistled when I walked past; they stopped me in the street to ask me out; they tried to buy me drinks in bars. Photographers sent me flowers, and random guys asked friends for my number. If I agreed to go on a date with them, they whisked me to fancy Japanese restaurants in Mayfair, or posh wine bars in the West End. But they were almost always the same kind of guy: silver-tongued slimeballs who just wanted a trophy girlfriend to impress their mates; a pretty little dolly-bird who'd look good on their arm.

One night, an affluent property developer, with whom my friend had set me up on a blind date, insisted I meet him at his car rather than inside the pub. '*That's a bit weird*,' I thought, until I got there and realised he had a bright red Ferrari he wanted to show off. And that wasn't the worst of it. As we sipped the champagne he had insisted on buying, he told me how the work on some luxury apartments he'd been developing had been held up after the builders found some human remains.

It was a shocking story, and I felt sorry for the person who had come to die in such a lonely, out of the way place. But I was more shocked by my 'date's' reaction to it: 'Why did they have to go and die there? Now I have to sort out all the paperwork. It's really going to hold my entire schedule up.'

I stared at him in disbelief. What a selfish, arrogant scumbag.

The more dates I went on, the more I started to despair. Was I never going to find a guy I really liked? A genuine, down-to-earth guy who liked me for who I was inside, rather than what I looked like on the outside? People assumed I must have had the pick of the bunch, but my looks just seemed to attract the wrong kind of men. Where was my Mr Right? My new world just wasn't set up for nice guys.

During our rare nights in, my flatmates and I would sit in the front room with our laptops, endlessly trawling the internet for work and uploading pictures and comments onto Facebook and other social network sites. In my naivety, it never occurred to me that any of the friend requests I was accepting could be possible sources of danger. I was always careful never to accept completely random strangers, but as long as they had some connection to my work, or other mates, I was happy to sign them in to my page.

One evening, towards the end of 2007, I spotted an ad looking for presenters for the Jewellery Channel, a new satellite channel that was being set up. I emailed in my CV and, a few days later, I drove up to Birmingham for the audition.

The next day, back in London, I was despondently drifting round some shops in Islington, eyeing up clothes I definitely couldn't afford. I had been so nervous in the audition I was certain I had blown my chance.

My mobile rang. It was Sarah, the owner of the production company. 'We'd love to have you on board, Katie,' she said. I yelped with excitement, doing a little victory dance in the middle of the street. Of course, I treated myself to a new jacket and dress to celebrate.

The job was based in Birmingham so I'd have to spend four days a week up there, but I wasn't worried about that. It was another adventure, and I packed my bags with a real sense of anticipation for the next phase in my life.

There were six other presenters on the show, and we all shared a house as we prepared for the launch, which was to happen in a few months' time. In between all the training, practising and researching, we guzzled wine and got to know each other. As part of our training, we also travelled to Bangkok to see jewellery being made. As we wandered along narrow little alleys, lined with street vendors and simmering pots of mysterious local stews, I thought about how lucky I was.

'Hello, pretty girl,' one of the Thai men smiled, and I beamed back at him.

Back at home, with Christmas approaching, I headed to Mum and Dad's as usual. I hadn't been to visit them in ages: apart from having Suzy to stay now and again, I'd been too caught up in my glittering new life to think about my family.

As soon as I arrived, I was itching to leave again. It didn't help that Mum and Dad kept nagging me about parking fines I'd carelessly received and, even more carelessly, not paid.

'Kate, you got three in one month alone! You owe them £300,' Mum sighed as I rolled my eyes. 'You just need to be a bit more responsible'.

After a few days of this, I'd had enough and I snapped. 'Just leave me alone,' I shouted, grabbing my bag. 'I'm going back to London.' They had no idea how hectic my schedule was; I was much too busy to worry about bloody parking fines. They just didn't understand.

As 2008 dawned, I pushed the row out of my mind and told myself this was my year. The year I was going to make it.

A few days later, however, Sarah at the Jewellery Channel phoned to say their company was locked in a legal battle and that it couldn't launch the show I was due to present on for at least another twelve months.

I was gutted, but with my bank balance dangerously low, I couldn't afford to sit around complaining. Every morning, to keep my spirits up, I would tell myself my day would come as I played Christina Milian's 'I'm a Believer', singing along into my can of hairspray. Before long, I was working for another interactive television show called *Fame TV*, where viewers sent in YouTube-style video clips, and also worked as a ring girl at Cage Rage Mixed Martial Arts contests. This basically involved walking around the ring in skimpy shorts and a crop top in between each round, but we got to travel, stay in nice hotels and even performed in Wembley Arena. The people were all really nice, and it was a great little earner.

To fill my days, I decided to up my fitness regime even more. With the help of a personal trainer, I started doing weight-lifting and boxing and, as I grew stronger, I felt safer too. I always tried to be sensible, never walked in any dodgy areas on my own or used an unlicensed taxi, but you could never be too careful in London.

'*If anyone ever attacks me, I'll be able to defend myself*,' I thought as I pummelled the punch bag. And at the time, I really believed it.

Chapter Three
Boyfriend

You know how a silver bangle starts to tarnish? Or a twinkly stone in a ring grows dull? By the end of January 2008, my glitzy new life was starting to lose its sparkle, too. I was fed up with living hand to mouth, and not knowing where the next pay cheque was coming from. I was tired of chatting rubbish on a TV show no one watched. I was seasick from the endless merry-go-round of castings, and the rollercoaster of rejection and success. So, in typical Katie style, I decided to do something about it.

'I'm going to scale back the modelling, and just focus on getting better TV work,' I said to myself, my determination brewing with my growing excitement. 'Maybe I could even do a journalism course, or work abroad for a while to beef up my CV.'

As for my social life, partying and posing in glam clubs didn't excite me anymore, either. I sometimes wondered if some of my friends liked me for me, rather than because of how I looked or what industry contacts I had. Was this life more shallow and superficial than I'd realised? It would be nice if I had a boyfriend, I thought. Someone who wasn't involved in that world, someone

I could go on holidays or to the cinema with. Someone who liked the person underneath my pretty, polished exterior.

One night in February, as I lounged on the sofa, I flicked on my laptop. In between looking for jobs, I logged on to Facebook and saw I'd received a poke from a guy called Danny Lynch.

'*Who's he?*' I thought, squinting at his profile picture. It showed a good-looking, mixed-race guy in a blue martial arts uniform, doing some impressive karate-style pose. I didn't recognise him but we had thirty mutual friends: people I'd met through my work as a ring girl at the Cage Rage fights. Had I met him at one of those? I couldn't remember him, but it was definitely possible. I didn't think much about adding him to my friends list – especially since he looked cute. A quick glance at his profile showed he had lots of friends, too, and as I read the message he'd sent, introducing himself, a smile spread over my face. He explained that he was really into his Mixed Martial Arts and a grappling champion.

I already knew grappling was a bit like wrestling and I couldn't help being impressed that he had the self-discipline and tenacity to become a champion in it. Perhaps a sportsman like him had more substance than the guys I normally met? I typed a quick reply to say hello and, over the next few weeks, we messaged back and forth.

Danny asked about my job and showered me with compliments, telling me I looked gorgeous and had a beautiful face. Of course, I was flattered. He'd leave really sweet comments underneath pictures in my photo albums, saying I looked especially pretty.

Full of intrigue, I sent him a message back. '*Are you going to be at the fight in Reading this weekend? I'll be there. Would be great to see you,*' I wrote.

As soon as I walked into the ring that Sunday in my white hot pants and crop top, I glimpsed Danny sitting at one of the ringside tables that were usually reserved for VIPs. When the show finished I headed out to the foyer, and he was hot on my heels.

Hearing someone shout my name, I spun around – it was Danny.

My breath caught. He was so good looking. Over 6' and well muscled, he was smartly dressed in a Dolce and Gabbana sweater and expensive jeans. I grinned back at him.

'Are you having a good night?' I asked.

We got chatting and my cheeks blushed as Danny nervously stammered out one compliment after another. How sweet!

I really wanted to talk to him some more, but knew I had to get on with work. 'Look, I'll get in trouble if the organisers see me chatting to a bloke, but we're going for some drinks when we've finished here. I can put your name on the list of the bar where we're going, if you like?' I asked.

He agreed and walked off with a huge smile on his face.

I didn't get to the bar until an hour and a half later as we'd been busy packing up and getting changed. '*I wonder if he's got bored with waiting and left,'* I thought, having a look around. But he was perched by the bar, and when he spotted me, his face lit up with relief. Sipping a beer, Danny told me he was twenty-eight and living in Hammersmith. We chatted for the next hour or so, and then I glanced at the clock and slipped off my stool.

'I'd better go,' I announced, grabbing my bag and as I left we agreed we'd talk more on Facebook.

Shy and awkward, Danny wasn't the most charismatic guy I'd ever met. Even though I did fancy him, he hadn't blown me away – still, there was no harm in keeping in touch, was there? Maybe we could go on a date, and see if anything came of it. He seemed genuine, down-to-earth and attentive – listening to me prattling on, rather than shooting big lines about himself. He was a world away from the flashy guys I normally attracted, and I really liked that.

The next morning, I logged into Facebook and saw he'd sent me a message containing his mobile number in the early hours of the morning.

'*Jeez, he's keen!*' I thought with a smile.

After that, we began chatting every day, and we really clicked. Danny revealed that as well as being a professional fighter, he was studying computing at college and owned some properties in Kent and Manchester. I was impressed – this guy sounded like he had his head screwed on, and I liked the way he was so driven and ambitious, just like me. I started to warm to him even more, so when he asked if I'd go on a date with him, I agreed happily.

I suggested we go to the Comedy Club in Leicester Square – it would be fun and relaxed, and we wouldn't be under pressure to make small talk.

We arranged to meet at 8 p.m. outside the venue, and the excitement I felt in my stomach fluttered as I got ready, and caught the tube into central London.

I waited for half an hour before he arrived, flustered and out of breath, hurriedly explaining he was late because he got lost.

'*That's a bit weird,*' I thought. What Londoner doesn't know Leicester Square? But I forgot about it as we walked into the Comedy Club and Danny snaked his arm around my shoulders. Out of the corner of my eye, I could see him smiling shyly while he told me what a lovely outfit I had on.

'Thanks!' I looked down at my skinny black jeans and silk camisole top. 'You do, too.'

Inside, we took our seats as the first comedian came on. Danny kept his arm round me constantly, and it struck me as a bit forward. It was only our first date, and already he was acting like we were a proper couple.

'Let me tell you about my mother in law ...' the comedian in front of us began, when I suddenly noticed out of the corner of my eye that Danny was staring at me instead of the stage. What was he doing? Had I something on my cheek?

At the interval, I stood up to go to the loo.

Danny stood up too and insisted on escorting me to the Ladies. He even waited at the door until I came out. It seemed chivalrous and old-fashioned, and I smiled at him as we sat down again.

After the show, we headed to the Jewel Bar in Piccadilly Circus for a drink. Danny told me some more about his grappling career and explained he'd even done a tour around the UK, while I filled him in on my modelling and TV work. Around 11.30 p.m., I got up to get the last tube home.

'I had such a nice time,' I said, smiling, as we said goodbye at the entrance to the tube station. There weren't any fireworks when we shared a lingering kiss, but it was still nice.

Danny seemed disappointed it was over so quickly and tried to get me to stay out.

'I have an audition tomorrow, but let's hook up after that,' I replied, grinning, before heading through the ticket barriers. '*Wow, he seems really into me*,' I thought happily as my Northern Line train whizzed towards Golders Green.

By the time I got out of the tube, he'd already texted, saying he couldn't stop thinking about me. Talk about a good catch – Danny was hot, he was successful, he was genuine, and he didn't seem to be playing any games with me. What a refreshing change that was!

We met up again for dinner and drinks the following evening, and Danny was as attentive as ever. He kept telling me how happy he was to see me again.

Generous with money, he insisted on paying for everything from a big wad of cash in his wallet, and I noticed he was wearing the most expensive-looking Cartier watch I'd ever seen, as well as £400 loafers. He seemed loaded; but when we went to his place for the first time, I was a bit surprised. It was a small council flat in west London, and his mother and brother lived there, too. I didn't care at all that it was in an estate, but it just seemed odd considering everything he'd told me.

Danny explained he was just staying there for a while because it was near the gym where he trained, but I didn't totally believe him. Maybe he wasn't as successful as he had been making out? Still, I didn't want to be as shallow and superficial as those people I had met modelling, only concerned with money. If he wasn't as rich as he made out, this didn't change the fact he was a nice guy. After all, who was I to judge?

As that first week together passed, we went out for lunch, wandered arm in arm around the shops, and shared a Chinese takeaway at my place. Danny never seemed too fussed about going out or clubbing and, as we sat on my sofa with some chow mein, I thought about how this was what I'd been missing. Someone to cuddle up with at home; someone gentle, affectionate, and completely devoted, who made me feel like the most beautiful woman in the world.

Danny and I were in constant contact. He sent a never-ending stream of texts and Facebook messages, and phoned my mobile constantly. If I was at work and couldn't answer, he'd just ring and ring and ring, asking me where I was and what I was wearing. He always seemed to be genuinely amazed that we were together.

It was overwhelming, but I liked him a lot, and my head was turned by all the attention. Any time he spotted our reflection in the mirror or a shop window, he smiled in delight and commented on how perfect we looked together. He even asked me to autograph a picture of myself, so he could stick it on his wall beside his bed.

He also seemed really impressed by my career and when I told him about a new job I'd auditioned for, he was really supportive.

'It's a reality programme called *Candy Crib*, where lots of models live together in a secret location and people get voted off each week. It could be a great opportunity for me,' I explained excitedly.

Danny smiled and hugged me, his chest puffed with pride.

He told me his father had been a famous wrestler, but his parents had broken up and he'd had a difficult childhood. My heart filled with compassion. I'd had an idyllic childhood, and I knew not everyone had been so lucky. Then he told me that his best friend had recently died in an accident on a building site.

'You poor thing,' I said, throwing my arms round his big, muscle-bound torso. I wanted to look after him, and take his hurt away.

One afternoon, Danny took me to the gym he belonged to. As I climbed onto the exercise bike and started pedalling away, I noticed he was spending more time staring at me than lifting weights, and that if any other bloke so much as glanced in my direction, his face clouded with suspicion. It was as though he thought I might start kissing someone else right there in front of him.

'*Hmm, I hope this doesn't develop into jealous-boyfriend syndrome*,' I remember thinking, as he came over and tried to kiss me.

'What are you doing?' I pushed him away playfully. 'This isn't the place for that!' Did he just want to prove to all the other guys that I was his?

That first weekend, as I picked him up in my car, he handed me a little teddy bear and a single red rose. I smiled and said thanks, then he suddenly turned to me. And, to my surprise, he told me that he loved me.

'Aw, thanks!' I giggled, trying quickly to diffuse an awkward situation. We barely even knew each other! Danny hadn't even met any of my family or friends, and already he was declaring his love. It seemed a bit full-on, and I started to feel uneasy. I was also starting to wonder how much of what he'd told me was true. There were no grappling trophies or computer course books in his bedroom, and he seemed to have a lot of free time on his hands to ring me and email me. It seemed strange – wasn't he supposed to be a property developer, student and pro-grappling champion? It seemed like he was just sitting at home on his computer all day. Had he exaggerated to impress me? Did he think I wouldn't like him for who he was? And when Danny suggested we move in together, I really began to be alarmed.

Because I lived in such a big houseshare, my housemates and I had an unwritten rule not to have people back to stay. This gave Danny the perfect excuse to suggest we get our own place together, despite the fact that we had only known each other for twelve days.

He'd got it all worked out, explaining how we could put it in my name but he'd cover the rent. He had a vision of it being our love nest where we would be able to be together, away from the rest of the world. It was like he wanted me all to himself.

'I don't think so, Danny,' I said gently. 'I really like my independence. I enjoy living with my friends.' Thinking about it afterwards, I put his behaviour down to first-flush enthusiasm. We were both really happy to have met each other, and he was simply getting beyond himself. As long as I was the sensible one, he could dream for us both!

As the second week of our fledgling romance passed by, however, my little doubts started growing. One night, I was out in a gay bar in Soho where my flatmate Tania worked when Danny phoned. I asked if he wanted to come and meet us, and he was happy to agree. But the second he walked through the door, he scowled in annoyance, his fury written all over his face as he realised that it was a gay bar. He made it crystal clear that he didn't want to stay.

I pulled him down onto the seat beside me. 'There might be gay guys here, but that doesn't mean they're going to try it on with you. C'mon, Danny, just get a drink and relax.'

But there was no reasoning with him. He jumped to his feet and walked out. I have always hated any kind of confrontation, so I went out after him to calm him down.

The instant he realised he'd got his own way, Danny went back to his easy-going self. I wasn't happy, though. Deep down, I was seriously questioning whether or not I wanted to be with someone like that. Lots of my friends were gay, and I hated any kind of prejudice. But Danny had such a nice side, too. He was so sweet, complimentary and generous, and he wasn't just another vacuous party boy.

Later that week, I called in at his flat after I finished my shift on *Fame TV*. As Danny pottered about in his bedroom, I sat in the lounge chatting to his mum about my work on TV. But then she said, almost warned me, about being careful as there are a lot of strange people around.

Just then, Danny walked in and hearing what his mum was saying, he flew of the handle. He told her to mind her own business.

Danny ushered me into his bedroom like nothing had happened and then, seething, he ranted about how he felt like throwing her off the balcony. I just nodded in silence. Was he like this because he'd had such a troubled upbringing? Growing up without a dad on a rough inner-city estate can't have been easy – no wonder he was angry at the world. Perhaps he just needed someone to love him, and then he'd be okay. Or, it could just be a throw away comment that you end up saying in the heat of the moment.

'Maybe I should try to help him, instead of writing him off,' I thought.

Cooling down, Danny made a suggestion in light of the situation, saying we should perhaps stay in a hotel one night to get some privacy.

'Yeah, maybe,' I said, not wanting to commit Danny to something so expensive when I wasn't sure about him.

I saw more evidence of his temper when we went shopping one afternoon. Wandering through a shopping centre, we stopped to buy some Krispy Kreme doughnuts.

'I'll have a chocolate one, please,' I smiled to the old guy behind the counter.

'Here you go, darling,' he said, handing me the little bag.

All of sudden, Danny erupted. He was livid that somebody else had called me 'darling'.

The man and I both gasped. Mortified, I quickly apologised then led Danny away by the arm.

'What was that about?' I demanded, horrified. Just as quickly, he flicked back to his normal self and apologised. He smiled sheepishly, before slinging his arm around me, telling me he couldn't believe how lucky he was to be with me.

My patience was starting to run out. Sure, Danny was thoughtful and romantic, but he was also extremely jealous. I was also starting to feel smothered by the constant texts and emails and phone calls: when I came home from work one day, he'd sent me thirty-seven messages in the space of a few hours. I laughed in disbelief as I told my flatmates.

'He's getting a bit stalkerish,' Tania said.

'Yeah, he's more like an obsessed fan than a boyfriend. It's starting to do my head in,' I sighed.

By now, I'd found out I'd won a place on *Candy Crib*. It meant I'd be away for at least a week, and I started thinking about cooling things off with Danny after I came out. I'd see how it went over the next few days, and then make my mind up. Life was full of possibilities and my future was wide open, but I was starting to suspect Danny wouldn't play a part in it.

How wrong could I be?

Chapter Four

The Nightmare Begins

Over the next couple of days, I continued to chat to Danny. And, despite my doubts, when he invited me to dinner at his one night I decided to go, thinking it would help me make a final decision about the future of our relationship. Danny was on his best behaviour as we enjoyed a roast his mum had made, full of smiles and politeness. And, afterwards, we settled in his bedroom to watch a crime film DVD.

'You like really macho movies,' I said, flicking through his DVD collection. They were all martial arts flicks or testosterone-fuelled gangster capers, but I wasn't surprised or concerned. Lots of blokes like those, right? As we cuddled on his bed, I remembered why I'd liked him in the first place. He was someone who liked just sitting in and spending time with me, instead of trying to impress me with Cristal champagne in expensive London clubs. Maybe there was hope for us after all.

Not long afterwards, we decided to go shopping in Hammersmith, and Danny insisted on buying me a pair of jeans by 7 for all Mankind that I was eyeing longingly in a fancy boutique. They cost £180.

'No way, they're much too expensive,' I protested, but he wouldn't take no for an answer. Pulling his bulging wallet out of his jeans, he paid in cash and handed me the plastic bag.

'Thank you so much,' I said, and we linked arms as we wandered round the shopping centre.

In a shoe shop, Danny spotted some trainers he liked, and decided he was going to buy us matching ones. I laughed and told him not to be so daft, but his mind was made up. The shop assistant brought two pairs in our size to the till, but when Danny spotted a tiny scuff on one of them, in the blink of an eye he had flipped.

This time he was angry as he felt the shop assistant was trying to show him up in front of me. He started swearing at the top of his voice, hurling all kinds of abuse at the shop assistant. I blushed beetroot with embarrassment as everyone in the shop turned to stare. What the hell was he doing? He was making such a scene.

'I'm so sorry,' I apologised to the shop assistant as Danny turned on his heel and stormed out.

Following him outside, I asked him what was up. His face contorted with anger, Danny told me to drop it, and I knew from the tone of his voice that there was no point in arguing. But why had he lost his cool over something so minor? Not wanting to push him, I didn't press the issue as we made our way to the barber's, where he'd made an appointment to get his hair cut.

When we walked in, the barber told us he just had to finish another client first. For the second time in half an hour, Danny kicked off.

He started screaming again, just like he had in the shop, furious he was being made to wait, before stomping out. This time I didn't follow him. He was acting like a spoilt child instead of a grown man, so I just sat on the sofa in the reception area and waited for him to come back. A few minutes later, my phone rang. It was Danny, demanding to know why I hadn't followed him.

'Just calm down and come get your hair cut,' I told him, and he stomped back in.

As the barber cut Danny's hair, I fiddled around on my phone texting friends. Every time my mobile beeped, he shouted over to ask who it was. Why did he have to be so possessive? I told him it was just my mates, but he insisted I come over and sit in the seat beside him.

Then, much to my embarrassment, he started boasting to the barber about how I was a model and TV presenter. The barber looked distinctly uninterested, but that didn't deter Danny. He proudly listed all the shows I'd appeared in.

My heart sinking, I suddenly started to wonder if he was like all the other blokes after all. Did he just want a trophy girlfriend, too?

As we wandered to a pub nearby, I thought about ending things with him. His behaviour had been terrible, and I realised I'd made too many allowances for him.

'*I think I'll stop seeing him,*' I decided as we wandered to a nearby pub. '*I'll go into the* Candy Crib*'s house in a few days' time, and things will peter out after that.*' After all, Danny and I had only been dating for two weeks. It was hardly the love affair of the century. I'd just spend the rest of today with him as planned, then that would be it.

Danny suggested we get a hotel in town for the night. As he spoke he persuaded me: it meant I could have a few drinks over dinner as I wouldn't have to drive back afterwards, and it would be handy for my hairdressing appointment at Lee Stafford's hair salon the next morning. Plus Danny seemed to be back to normal: all sweet smiles and charm itself. What was the harm?

After dumping our shopping bags, we headed to an Italian restaurant nearby, where Danny laughed and joked as we tucked into our food. He even suggested we went on holiday together.

'Maybe,' I smiled, though I was pretty sure it was never going to happen. After the waiter brought us complimentary coffees with our bill, we wandered back to the hotel.

It had been a nice evening, but when we got into the hotel lift my happy smile quickly slipped. Danny looked at our reflection in the mirror and suddenly snarled: 'You're not even all that in the flesh, are you?'

I was shocked, and looked away. Danny was trying to put me down, I decided, to make me feel bad because of his own jealousy and insecurity, but I was sick of his childish behaviour. I'd had plenty of that from models over the years, and I certainly didn't need it from someone who claimed to love me.

Back in our room, my flushed cheeks grew even redder. Despite what he'd said Danny assumed he could still get intimate with me. I fobbed him off, making it as clear as I could that I didn't want to sleep with him.

And that was when it all began.

His face flushed red with anger and he started accusing me of not wanting to be with him any more. He launched into a tirade of abuse. I froze as I watched his face twist with fury, his dark eyes glaze over.

He was so close I could feel his hot breath stinging my cheeks. With his lips curled in a snarl and his teeth clenched, he looked like a wild animal.

'*What do I do?*' I panicked, desperately searching my mind for a way to calm him down. But I couldn't think quickly enough. Danny's ego was dented and there was no stopping his rage – with all his body weight he pushed me and I hit the door. As the back of my head cracked against the fire exit sign, terror surged through me. Then everything faded to black as I slumped to the floor.

'*What's that noise?*' I thought, woozily. I could hear an angry voice shouting, but it seemed fuzzy and far away. '*What's happening?*' My eyes flickered open and I stared, dazed and disorientated. But then catching sight of Danny looming over me, my chest tightened as the horror of what had just happened hit me. The man who was meant to be my boyfriend had attacked me.

Through a haze of shock, I instinctively reached for the back of my head and felt blood pulsing from it, like warm water from a garden hose. My heart pounded as I held my hand in front of my face. It was covered in thick, crimson blood, as though it had been dipped in a pot of paint. My shock exploded into panic.

'I need to get to hospital,' I sobbed hysterically, but Danny simply ordered me to stop crying.

I struggled to believe this was real. I felt sick as I tried to anticipate what Danny would do next. Who was this man? And, what was he capable of?

My head throbbing, my vision fuzzy, and my limbs as heavy as lead, I fought to stay calm. '*He'll let me go*,' I kept telling myself. '*He'll calm down any minute now. Don't worry Katie, everything will be fine*.'

As I quivered like jelly, every moment that passed seemed like an eternity. I flinched as I felt the blood from the gash on my head trickle down my back. *Drip, drip, drip*. Gasping for breath, I tried to ignore the sight of my blood-soaked hair and think fast.

'*I have to try to reason with him*,' I thought blearily. '*I need to make him see sense. I need to get to hospital*.'

But before I knew it I was being forced on to the bed. I began to whimper as cold dread filled my veins. Instinct told me what was coming next. '*Surely not …*' I thought. '*He wouldn't …*' Yet, his body language told me otherwise. It was true. Danny was going to rape me.

I started weeping. 'Please, no, not that. Anything but that,' I begged, hysterically. How could he do this to me? Hadn't he injured me enough already?

But, Danny ignored me and continued to hold me down, while screams tore my throat.

'*Please don't do this. Please stop, please*,' I sobbed inside, unable to get my words out. All I could do was try to comfort myself. Surely deep down, he knew how wrong this was? Surely there was some shred of humanity underneath that brutish, cruel exterior? He'd come to his senses. But I was so, so wrong.

Danny started raping me.

It seemed to go on and on, like some nightmare I couldn't wake up from. Screaming seemed to make no difference and I couldn't move. I was Danny's prisoner. Completely trapped, all I could do was try to zone out; all concept of time slipping away from me as I prayed for it to end.

I kept looking at the door that Danny had just smashed my head against. Why was no one coming to help? We were in a hotel – there were people all around us. In the room next door, right across the hall, above and below us. Where *were* they?

As Danny persisted, I could feel blood seeping from the wound on my head, as new, fresh pain exploded in every tiny part of my body. My throat was constricted with fear, and my chest heaved with desperate sobs.

What was I going to do? Why wasn't he stopping? My eyes wide with horror, I frantically looked around the room. The door was too far away: even if I could get out from under him, there was no way I could make it. Then I spotted a phone on the bedside table, but it was completely out of my reach, too. And, at some point, Danny had smashed up my mobile phone, as well.

In a sudden moment of clarity, I realised there was no escape and Danny wasn't going to stop. He wasn't going to have second thoughts, climb off me and apologise. There was nothing I could do or say to make that happen.

'*When is this going to end?*' I asked myself. '*When am I going to get out of here? When? When?*' It was all I could think as I lay there on the blood-stained duvet, completely helpless while Danny grunted away.

Then, most chillingly of all, I thought: '*What if Danny doesn't just let me go afterwards? What if he actually murders me? What if he strangles me or beats me to death?*' My mind raced, delirious with pure terror.

'*Oh God, he's going to kill me,*' I panicked, my heart thumping and thudding so hard I thought it might burst. Adrenaline pumped through my body: I'd never see my friends or family again. Someone would find me dead, naked and covered in blood. They'd know this was how I died, humiliated and terrified.

'*I don't want to die,*' I wailed inside. But then suddenly, something else infiltrated my frantic mind … silence. Danny was suddenly still.

Paralysed by shock and fear, I just lay there and he moved away from me. As he skulked across the room, I stared at him, trying to understand what he'd just done. He'd battered me then raped me. Why?

This, then, was the real Danny. The shy, reliable and sweet guy who told me I had the most beautiful face in the world was a facade, and now I saw what was underneath. He was dangerous, unpredictable and capable of doing absolutely anything.

Convinced, he had finished with me for now, I tried to stand up but my body was so frail, I flopped back down again. Eventually, I managed to climb off the bed and staggered passed him towards the bathroom. For a fleeting moment, I looked at the room's door. But what was the point in even trying to run away? I could barely stand up, and if I took even a step in that direction, Danny would be on to me. And then he'd kill me for sure.

I stared at myself in the bathroom mirror. Who was this girl, covered in red, angry marks? The blood on her face was brown and crusty, her make-up was all gone and her hair was sticking up in all directions. I hated her.

I felt so dirty, like I'd never be clean ever again. I wanted to wash it all away, destroy every trace of him on my body. Then the door burst open, and Danny came in to find me trying to wash myself of him. It infuriated him. Once again, he started swearing at me, calling me all the names under the sun.

My nerves shattered and I screamed. How was this going to end? Was I ever going to get out of this alive? Danny had completely lost it. He threatened to kill me and my family if I ever told anybody about what had happened. It was like he was possessed.

With every word he uttered, my panic skyrocketed; my stomach lurched so violently, I thought I was going to be sick. My whole body went rigid, from the tips of my fingers right down to my toes, and I could scarcely breathe. This wasn't something that happened in real life. Not to me. I was trapped in a room with a complete maniac. Even if I did make it out, Danny was right. He knew where I lived and worked – there was no escape. Ever.

Grabbing a disposable razor from the sink, Danny ripped the cover off it and held it in front of my face. I froze.

'*He's going to cut my face to ribbons,*' I thought, my skin prickling.

The blade glinted in the bathroom light. He had already stripped me of my dignity and broken my body. But I could hide that. If he mutilated my face, however, my life would be over. My career would be ruined, and I would see his evil handiwork every time I looked in the mirror. Bracing myself, I said a silent prayer.

'Please, not my face.'

Chapter Five
Living in Fear

I held my breath and waited for the razor to slice through my cheek like butter. Was Danny going to ruin the face he'd claimed to love? Was this the end of my career, everything I'd worked so hard for, in tatters? Seconds seemed like hours, then he turned away, slapped the blade on the sink and walked away.

As soon as he was gone, I grabbed the razor and tried to hide it under some towels.

'No, that won't work. He'll find it. Where should I put it? I have to get rid of it. Think, Katie, think.'

In a flash of inspiration given my hazy state, I chucked it in the loo and flushed. The blade disappeared with a whirlpool of water, and I almost cried out in relief. But it was a fleeting victory. At the sound of the flush, Danny reappeared.

Choking on silent tears, I tried hard not to cry as I knew that just infuriated him even more.

'Why are you doing this to me? What have I done to deserve it?' I thought, my soul crumbling inside me. Beaten and bruised, raped and humiliated, I didn't know how much more I could take.

Then when Danny started babbling about how he'd done this sort of thing before, fear almost made me vomit. How was this going to end?

Suddenly, I noticed him looking back into the bedroom, his eyes darting around the room. I began to shiver with cold dread as I heard him ask me where my belt was. Struggling to hold it together, I gagged as nightmare visions of Danny beating me with it flashed through my mind.

'No, please, no,' I shrieked. But he wasn't listening. He pulled my black leather belt from my jeans. Only instead of whipping me with it, he walked over to the door, and hooked it around the arm of the metal hinge at the top. It dangled down like a noose, and a realisation hit me like a punch. Petrified, I watched as he grabbed a chair from the desk and placed it under the belt.

Then in a voice so cold and inhuman it made me shudder, he ordered me onto the chair. Adrenaline shot through my body once again, and I knew this was it: if I was ever going to make it through the night and get out of the room alive, I had to talk him out of it. I had to fight for survival.

'You don't have to do this, Danny,' I blurted. 'I won't tell the police, I promise.' And it was true. I didn't consider reporting him for one second. He had threatened to hurt me, my family and my friends if I did. And he had already raped me, so I knew he was capable of it.

Danny paused. He was considering it, I knew he was. But then he shook his head and again told me to get on the chair.

'Please, Danny,' I kept on babbling.

But he ignored my pleas and instead offered me an ultimatum – either I get on the chair or he did and then I'd be left alone in the room with his dead body. Fear iced my cramping veins. 'You don't need to do that,' I said shakily, trying my best to placate him and calm the situation down.

I noticed that the sun was rising. Dawn light was spilling into the room, and Danny's fury was fading. Fight or flight kicked in like never before. I didn't want to die at the hands of this monster.

I kept talking, promising not to tell anyone, swearing I'd forgiven him, telling him it would be okay, saying anything to save myself. 'The chamber maids will be here soon,' I said. Trying to sound calm and reasonable, I did my best to convince him that he wouldn't want to face them, given the state of the room.

Slowly, the situation began to change. I think he began to realise he couldn't keep me in the room for much longer without someone discovering us and he decided we should leave.

Visions of my friends' faces, my flat, my bedroom, Mum and Dad, swam through my mind. I had to stay strong – I was almost free. On autopilot, I showered and got dressed. Like a zombie, I rubbed foundation over my cheeks, and flicked mascara over my eyelashes. The girl in the mirror looked just like the old me, but her eyes were so frightened. My body throbbing, I attempted to wipe the blood from the bathroom walls and floor.

Then, I held my breath as Danny opened the door and we walked into the hall. There was no surge of relief, though. I wasn't free yet, and I couldn't run screaming for help. I didn't even consider trying to run, I was so traumatised and frightened. As Danny had warned me, he knew where I lived, and he knew where I worked. I was still at his mercy. Side by side, we walked to the lift and travelled down to Reception. It was a picture of normality – the receptionist on the phone behind the front desk, tourists checking in ... How could the world still be carrying on, as though nothing had happened?

In silence, we made our way to the car park and into my car. I slid into the driver's seat, while Danny got in beside me. My hands were shaking so much, I could barely get the key in the ignition. Turning the key, I started to drive as slowly as I could, all the while trying to convince Danny to let me go to the hospital.

'I'll just say I fell over,' I swore, and eventually he agreed. He directed me to the nearest hospital, but as soon as we got to the door of the bustling A&E department, he suddenly changed his mind and refused to let me go in.

Back in the car, I cowered against the door as Danny's eyes flashed with anger. Looking at his watch, he announced he had to attend a parole meeting, and I was going with him. As I heard his words, surprise added a new dimension to my fear. Parole meetings were for people who'd been released from prison, but Danny had never mentioned being in any trouble with the law. What the hell had he done?

In tense silence, we drove through London. The journey was a blur I was in so much shock. I just couldn't work out how this had all happened.

When we arrived at the parole office, Danny turned to me and told me in no uncertain terms not bother to saying a word. I nodded dumbly, and sat down in the Reception area while Danny went to see his probation officer. By now, my head was really throbbing and I could feel fresh blood seeping from my wound. I felt so weak, so feeble and scared, I didn't even consider running.

Back in the car, Danny's aggression bubbled over again. Hopelessly trying to maintain normality, I said I needed to go get ready for work – I was due to start a shift on *Fame TV* that evening. By now desperation had left my nerves ragged, but somehow I found the words to persuade Danny to take me home.

Pulling into a parking space around the corner from my flat, I turned the engine off. Then for what felt like forever, we sat there as I pleaded and made promises, just like I had in the hotel room. My flatmates didn't work nine to five so we both knew they'd be in. And we both knew Danny couldn't lock me up in my own home.

When he finally said I could go in, relief flooded every inch of my body. But then Danny started ranting again. It seemed his biggest worry was that he'd lost me. Some kind of realisation had set in, but unbelievably all Danny cared about was that our relationship was over. He was deluded!

But then, another spark of realisation lit up Danny's face – he realised he'd smashed up my phone in the hotel. Wiping his face, he announced he was going to the phone shop on the high street to buy me another mobile so he could contact me and warned me not to drive off.

I nodded, rooted to the front seat with fear. For a second, I thought about running away. Just jumping out of the car and getting into my flat. It was only just round the corner. But what was the point? Danny would only come after me, or hurt someone I loved to punish me. No, I had to stay there. I had to do what he said.

When Danny came back a few minutes later, he gestured for me to get out of the car, and we walked round the corner to my flat. I was almost free, and Danny wasn't happy about it.

He started ranting at me in the street, and people turned to stare. His angry voice hurt my ears as he told me he would be out to get me if I breathed a word to anybody. Even though we were in public, I still didn't feel safe. This guy was a maniac. I had to get away from him.

'I won't tell anybody,' I promised. I backed away from him, reassuring him that everything would be OK.

Danny nodded, and I turned on my heel. '*Don't run, Katie, just walk slowly. Almost there …*' I slipped my key into the front door, expecting him to appear behind me. When he didn't, I walked in and slammed the door shut behind me. I was safe, but for how long?

My heart hammering, I ran up the communal stairs three at a time, dashed along the outside balcony and into our flat. I closed the door and leaned against it as my mind raced. Was it over? Had the nightmare ended at last?

Hearing voices in one of the bedrooms, I burst in. My flatmates were sitting there, chatting, and as soon as I saw them I told them what had happened, terror forcing each frantic word out of me.

'Danny attacked me,' I blurted out. 'My head's still bleeding. Can you take me to hospital?'

Their faces blanched and they ran to my side. Terrified Danny would be outside waiting, I ran into the front bedroom to look out of the window. And there he was, marching up and down the high street and shouting into his mobile. As soon as I spotted him in his pink Ralph Lauren jumper and jeans, I started to panic all over again.

The new mobile he'd given me started to ring. No one else had the number so I knew that it was him. And that if I didn't answer it, he'd come and kick the door in like he'd threatened.

'Hello?' I said as I pressed the button to connect the call. Danny started screaming down the line at me, asking whether or not I'd told my flatmates. They looked on in horror as I tried to placate him.

'No, Danny, of course I haven't. Please go home.'

Eventually, I managed to get off the phone. After a quick discussion, my flatmates and I decided to leave. Going out of the back door, through the alley where our bins were kept, we fled to my car. As I got behind the wheel and we screeched off, I started weeping and at some point I confessed that Danny had raped me too. I was too traumatised to go into any more detail, but saying that aloud for the first time made me feel even more disgusting.

After gasps of horror, I felt somebody squeeze my arm.

'You have to tell the police,' one of them said gently.

'No way! He knows where I live, and he said if I report him he'll kill me, or hurt my family,' I cried, my knuckles white from gripping the steering wheel so tightly.

'You can't let him get away with it,' they urged, their voices full of anger.

'I can't.' I had realised something on the drive back here: 'I've showered and washed away all the evidence, so it wouldn't do any good, anyway.'

When we got to A&E, I didn't even consider telling the truth. There wasn't a doubt in my mind that if I did, Danny would take his revenge.

'I was moving some furniture in my bedroom, and it fell on top of me,' I told the doctor as he examined my head. He shot me a sceptical glance, full of pity, and I knew he didn't believe me.

Two minutes later, after he'd taped the wound closed, the doctor disappeared, returning with a female colleague. She gave me the same concerned look, and asked me again what had happened. And again, I lied. It made me feel even more pathetic, but at the time I didn't think I had a choice.

Even though he wasn't with me, Danny was still controlling me.

Back at home, one of my flatmates called my work to tell them I was too ill to come in. We sat together in the lounge and everyone tried to keep my spirits up with a constant stream of chitchat, but I was like a zombie. The only thing that got through to me was my phone. It felt like it rang practically every ten minutes, and I'd jump out of my skin, then reach for it like it was poison, like it could kill me. It was Danny, always Danny, demanding to know where I was, who I was with, what I was doing, if I'd told anyone, whether or not I hated him.

'I don't hate you. I haven't told anyone,' I lied. 'Please, just give me some space.'

Locked in a cocoon of shock, I thought about how he had done the most awful thing that could be done to a woman. He had brutally raped me; he had forced himself on me as I begged him to stop.

I never imagined for one second there was worse to come.

Chapter Six
Goodbye Katie

The water trickled over my aching flesh, and I scrubbed every last inch of skin. But I still felt dirty, so disgustingly dirty. My private parts were aching, and it was a constant reminder of what Danny had done. It was as if that area wasn't mine, anymore: that part of my body didn't belong to me now. Danny had made it his, and I didn't know if I would ever get it back.

It was Friday evening, six hours after Danny had let me go. As I stared at the bathroom tiles, the memory of that other bathroom flashed through my mind. Then blood-stained sheets, crimson splashes on the sink …

I wondered how I was ever going to get over this, and I knew that I couldn't let it destroy me. I would block it out of my mind; never ever tell my parents or the police. I would keep placating Danny until I went into the *Candy Crib* house on Monday evening. I didn't know how I'd manage it, how I'd act normally around other models when I was falling to pieces inside, but I was determined to try. I would be safe there; it was in a secret location, and Danny wouldn't be able to find me. Then maybe I'd go abroad. He'd realise I wasn't going to report him, and he'd get bored and leave me alone at last. Decision made, I stepped out of the shower and wrapped myself in a fluffy towel, carefully avoiding my reflection in the mirror. I couldn't bear to look at it.

Back in the lounge, I tried to watch TV with my flatmates, but it seemed like every time they flicked the remote, sex appeared on the screen. I would have thought nothing of it before – sex had always seemed natural to me, nothing to be embarrassed about. But now, it just triggered a flashback. Being held down on the bed as Danny forced his way inside me. The agony between my legs, rippling all the way up through my tummy. I turned away and squeezed my eyes closed.

All day long Danny had kept on ringing and texting. It was always the same questions, and I parroted the same reassuring answers, even though the sound of his voice made me want to hurl the phone out of the window.

My flatmates didn't know what to say. They knew there was no point in trying to persuade me to tell the police, and there was no way I was telling my parents, either. It would hurt them too much; the thought of what their little girl had been through.

I tortured myself by blaming myself. I'd been so naive, allowing myself to get carried away with all the compliments Danny paid me and trust somebody I really didn't know.

'*But I never dreamed he was capable of something like this*,' I thought in desperation and despair. Danny wasn't some psychotic-looking madman. He was an attractive young guy, who could have had his pick of women. It sounds naive, but he looked too *normal* to have had that kind of a temper, that kind of character. What he'd done was so far removed from my life, I'd never even considered it was a possibility. How could I have been so trusting? So innocent? So *stupid*?

Another thought struck me with horrifying clarity. What if I was pregnant? Or worse, I had a sexually transmitted infection? Shuddering, I risked venturing outside and ran to the chemist with Tania to get the morning-after pill.

Back home, not able to handle watching anymore TV, I dragged myself into my bedroom. With its piles of shoes and unpaid parking fines notices, it was just as I'd left it. My Ugg boots on the floor, my collage of photos from nights out on the walls. Now, they seemed like relics from the past; an Egyptian tomb uncovered after centuries. That girl in the photos striking a pose, laughing into the camera – she looked carefree and happy. She could never know what it was like to feel this way.

In bed, I tossed and turned for hours, expecting Danny to arrive at any moment. He could force his way in, chuck a petrol bomb through the letterbox, come back with friends and kill us all.

The next day, I stayed in the flat in my pyjamas. My flatmates barely left my side, but Danny didn't give me a minute of peace, either. Too frightened to antagonise him, I answered almost every call and tried to stay on his good side.

He wanted to know my every move, he wanted reassurance that we were still a couple. It was like he wanted to know exactly what was going on in my head, like he was still trying to control me.

Too nauseous to even think about food, I managed to nibble on some toast and drink water, but that night I couldn't sleep once again.

I just kept reminding myself that I was going into *Candy Crib* the following evening, and that I'd be safe there.

I was due to meet my best friend Kay, with whom I used to work at the Smart Live Casino channel, at the pub for a quick drink. As I left the flat, I had a quick look round for Danny, but I didn't think he would attack me in front of people, and I had no intention of letting him lure me somewhere secluded. Somewhere he could hurt me again.

Over a few soft drinks, I told Kay what had happened. She gasped and asked if I was going to the police. I shook my head and told her I couldn't – that Danny would kill me or my family if I did. I could tell from the look in her eyes that she reluctantly understood, and she didn't push me.

'Maybe you should get away somewhere then,' she suggested, and I nodded. We'd talked in the past about going to work in Dubai, and it seemed like it could be a good solution. There was no way he'd find me there.

'When I finish *Candy Crib*, we should sort it out,' I said, feeling hopeful for the first time since Danny had thrown me against that hotel room door.

*

I also found myself confiding in my friend Michael when we met up in a Café Rouge in Hampstead. He was a photographer who had shot me dozens of times, and over the last twelve months we'd become close friends.

In a quiet voice, so the waitress wouldn't overhear, I relayed the horrific tale, while his eyes clouded with sadness and disgust.

'I don't understand how he could do that to you,' he said, and I shrugged helplessly. I didn't understand it, either. I would never know how Danny's mind worked, or how he could live with what he'd done. We sat in silence for a few moments, and then Michael reached across the table and took my hands.

'I'm worried something else might happen to you. I'm worried you could end up dead,' he said.

My heart started pounding, and my eyes welled with tears. Michael wasn't saying anything I hadn't already thought a hundred times myself – but hearing him say it out loud made it seem so real. I was in danger, real danger, and I had to keep Danny sweet till I could get far away from him.

Lost in our own thoughts, Michael and I barely spoke as we picked at our meal. When we got up to go, he hugged me close.

'You're my best friend and I really care about you. Please be careful,' he whispered, and I nodded.

'I will,' I told him. I drove home with Michael's warning ringing in my ears.

Back in the flat, the incessant phone calls and texts from Danny kept on coming.

In a barely controlled voice, Danny said he wanted me to give back the clothes he'd bought me, and a video camera he'd lent me so I could make a showreel for work. I quickly realised he wanted an excuse to get me to his flat, but there was no way I was falling for that. Instead, I offered to get a courier to bring them round in the morning, but Danny refused to give me his address and postcode. He told me he had a present for me.

After all he'd done, did he really think a present could fix things? What could he possibly give me that could change any of what he'd done? There wasn't a single thing in the whole world that would make me forgive him.

I was at the end of my tether. After the trauma of the violence and the rape and the relentless, endless contact with Danny, I was practically feverish with fear. What the hell was he planning to do? Was he going to try to hurt me again?

Lying in bed that night with the lights on, the flurry of texts continued, but something changed in his tone. He began to seem cocky and cool, almost as if he had a plan. His attitude and this bizarre promise of a present had scared me even more.

Then Danny sent one last text message, in which he simply said goodbye to me. As I read it, my blood ran cold. What did he mean? Was he going to kill himself, or me? He was so obsessive, surely this wasn't the end of it? Surely he wouldn't let me go so easily? But maybe it *was* a good sign. Maybe he had finally woken up to what he had done, and realised he couldn't torment me like this. I would leave tomorrow, and then I'd move away. It would all be okay.

I tried to sleep, but every time I closed my eyes, I pictured Danny holding that razor blade. I saw his lips curl with disgust and his dark eyes flash with evil. I felt his spit on my face as he shouted vile, obscene things at me. I smelled his rank sweat as it dripped onto me, and I relived the crush of his weight on my trembling body. It was like I was back in the hotel room, completely at his mercy. Trapped in a living nightmare.

After another sleepless night, I dragged myself out of bed on Monday. Unable to even bear looking at my reflection in the bathroom mirror, I was feeling lower than ever. The enormity of what I'd been through was just sinking in, and I couldn't wait to get into the *Candy Crib* house. It was my ticket to freedom; it was something the old Katie would do, and it would help me get her back.

As I despondently packed some clothes into a suitcase, I decided to go to the hairdresser's down the street with Tania. She was getting her hair dyed, and I didn't want to be alone.

As we made our way there, my mobile rang. Danny demanded to know what I was doing, and automatically I told him.

In the hairdressers, I sat in Reception and watched the stylists and customers chatting. Hairdryers whirred and the smell of shampoo comforted me a little. It was such a familiar scene, but I still felt so lost. As Tania got her hair done, Danny kept on hassling me. What was I doing? What were my plans for the day?

Was I going anywhere else before I headed off to *Candy Crib* that evening?

'*You really scare me,*' I told him, begging him to leave me alone. It didn't do any good, though. Danny kept on ringing, demanding to know what time I was leaving for *Candy Crib*. He threatened to come to Golders Green and find me, if I didn't tell him. His angry voice was so loud it made my phone vibrate as he roared down the line and I desperately tried to calm him down.

Back in the flat, I sobbed and sobbed until my throat ached. Then the phone rang again. It was him, saying he'd sent me an email that explained everything. He was insistent on me reading it. I sighed, mentally and physically exhausted.

'My internet connection's down,' I told him. It was true, and I was glad. I had no desire to read anything he'd written. It would just be empty words from a sick monster.

He suggested that I go to the coffee shop across the street where they have internet access. I thought about it for a few moments. If it would finally get him off my back, then maybe it was worth it.

Danny ordered me to get ready and then call him back, in a voice that brooked no argument. I dragged myself to my bedroom and pulled on a grey tracksuit, a hoody and some Ugg boots. I scraped my hair into a ponytail, and didn't even think about putting on any make-up. The old me would never have left the house looking so scruffy, but now I didn't have the energy to care what I looked like. In fact, looking sexy and feminine and glamorous was the last thing I wanted. The prospect of men noticing me and fancying me filled me with revulsion, and I wanted to look as unattractive as possible. I wanted to feel invisible.

As I shoved my purse and keys into my handbag, I took a deep breath and spoke to Danny again and told him I was leaving.

'What are you wearing?' Danny asked. It was the kind of question I'd ask my mates, but it seemed odd coming from him, especially considering the circumstances. I briefly described my outfit, and then he asked what style my hair was in. I told him. I didn't have the energy to even think about why he wanted to know. Then he said his other phone was ringing and hung up.

Slinging my bag over my shoulder, I said goodbye to Marty and headed out of the door of our flat. As I closed the door behind me, Danny phoned back, asking where I was.

'Walking along the communal balcony,' I answered.

As I made my way down the stairs, Danny wanted me to tell him my every movement. I was mystified, but up until now just going along with his sick games had seemed to work, so I played along.

I opened the door and blinked as I stepped out into the bright, busy high street. As soon as I did Danny quizzed me again, desperate to know if I was on the street yet.

'Yes,' I sighed, closing the door behind me.

And then that's when I spotted a young guy in a hoody, crossing the road and coming towards me.

Chapter Seven
Destroyed

With his arms outstretched and a coffee cup clasped between his two hands, the young guy made a beeline straight for me.

He was scruffy and unkempt, and his dark eyes stared into mine. They reminded me of Danny's – crazed and possessed, like a deranged killer in a scary film. I shivered, then told myself I was being paranoid and silly. He was just a druggy or a beggar, and all he wanted was for me to put some money in his cup. In that moment, I actually felt sorry for him. '*Poor guy*,' I thought, '*he must have an awful life.*' Still on the phone to Danny, I rested my mobile in the crook of my neck and reached into my bag to get my purse.

'Wait a minute, Danny,' I told him.

By now, the young guy was only an arm's length away from me. I was still trying to dig my purse out from in the depths of my bag when it happened.

Splash. The guy chucked the contents of the cup at my face and, in that split second, my life changed forever.

*

The liquid drenched my face and dripped down my neck, and for one brief moment, I didn't understand what had happened.

'*Has he just thrown his coffee over me?*' I thought in shock and disbelief, clinging on to my phone tightly. '*How rude! I'm going to have to go home and get changed now.*'

And then the pain hit me. It was an explosion of agony, unlike anything I had ever experienced before. It spread through my body like fire, hotter than hell. What had he thrown on me? It wasn't just coffee. This was something else. Something worse. From the top of my head all the way down to my feet, every inch of me was in agony. And my face ... I could feel it burning, burning so hot I thought it was going to burst into flames.

I lurched away a few metres, oblivious to everything around me, doubled over in pain. With every second, the agony clawed its way deeper and deeper into my skin. I heard a horrible screaming sound, like an animal being slaughtered. What was making that noise? Then I realised it was coming from me.

Desperate thoughts raced through my mind. Had that boy thrown bleach on me? Or was it acid? That was it! It was acid; it had to be.

'*Danny is behind this!*' I suddenly realised, horror and terror swirling in my mind in equal measures. '*This was the "present" he was talking about.*'

And he was still on the phone, listening to my screams.

I felt as if I was being burned alive, that I was melting like a candle. I tried to think clearly, but the pain was so excruciating it swallowed me whole. I thought I must be dying; it was impossible to feel this kind of agony and survive.

What should I do? I needed help so badly. I was staggering around the pavement outside my flat, screaming those awful screams, but people were just staring at me, their mouths hanging open in shock. Why was no one helping me? Was Danny waiting round the corner with the young guy in the hoody? Was he going to bundle me into a car, take me away somewhere and then rape me again? For brief, irretrievable moments, I was paralysed by indecision.

The acid had dripped down my forehead and into my eyes. They were swelling shut, and I could barely see a thing as I stumbled to the restaurant that I knew was next door. My hands felt as if they were on fire, as they had been covered in acid when I had raised them instinctively to try to wipe my face, but I battered frantically on the glass window anyway.

'Someone, please! Help me!' I screeched, but no one did. The passers-by on the street just kept on standing there, staring at me. Couldn't they see I was dying? Didn't they care?

My vision fading, I knew I had to get across the busy main road. There was a café on the other side and they knew me there; they would come to my aid. If I didn't move, Danny might appear at any second, while the pain was getting worse and worse, deeper and deeper.

With the feeling that every vein in my body was on fire, I careened across the road. A bus screeched to a stop and drivers sounded their horns. One of my Ugg boots fell off, but I barely noticed any of it.

Somehow, I made it to the other side of the road. My vision was getting fuzzier and fuzzier as I raced into the café. '*I must look like something from a horror film*,' I thought fleetingly, imagining my flesh bright red, bubbling and disappearing as the acid ate it up. I didn't realise that I had turned pure white. The acid had gone so deep, it had destroyed two layers of skin and seeped right through to the bone.

All I could think about was the pain. It eclipsed everything else. I didn't think it was possible, but it increased with every second. I never knew such agony existed.

'I've been attacked! Please help me,' I screamed, lurching behind the counter where I thought there would be a sink. The customers all froze, coffee cups in their hands, once again just staring at me. Noticing an ice bucket half-full of water in front of me, I started trying desperately to rinse my face in it.

'Are you okay? What happened?' one of the staff members exclaimed, rushing to my side.

'Someone threw acid on me,' I gasped, desperately trying to dunk my face. But the bucket was too shallow; I couldn't submerge myself properly. What was I going to do? The toilet! Still shrieking with fear, I staggered into the Ladies, and stuck my head into the loo. I flushed and flushed, but the trickle of water didn't do a thing. Why wouldn't the pain stop?

I blundered back into the café, where pandemonium had broken out. Everyone seemed to be shouting and running around in a panic. Someone sat me in a chair and started spraying my face with water. But sitting down made the pain even worse. The acid ran down my neck, onto my chest and legs, and I felt my clothes sizzling and burning as it ate away at the fabric, and then the skin underneath. I couldn't speak – I could only scream and scream as I writhed in pain.

'Breathe into this paper bag,' another person said, but nothing anyone could do helped. They didn't understand; the pain was too big. It was pure, raging agony, and it was fuelled by absolute terror, too.

Danny had done this. And he might come back at any time to finish me off.

Time seemed to stop as the agony grew and grew. My skin, my muscles, even my bones, felt like they were ablaze. Every blood vessel, every millimetre of tissue and sinew was shrieking in agony. I couldn't even scream any more. I just slumped there, my head bowed and arms dangling lifelessly.

'*I'm going to die here*,' I thought, and I could feel myself start to slip away. After everything I'd gone through in that hotel room, after how I'd fought for my survival that night, I was going to die in the coffee shop across the road from my flat.

'*Maybe it's better this way*,' I found myself thinking. '*The pain will stop. It'll all stop. I'll be at peace, and I won't be afraid any more.*'

But suddenly, my family's faces flashed through my mind. Mum and Dad, Suzy and Paul. I felt strength well up inside me.

I had to fight; I couldn't give up. All around me, I could hear people moving and talking, asking me if I was okay. Their voices sounded distant, as though they were far away instead of right beside me.

'It'll be okay, don't worry.'

'You'll be fine.'

I knew they were just trying to comfort me, but they didn't understand. I was going to die unless I did something. The pain was going to kill me. Somehow, I managed to remember my phone. By now, I couldn't see a thing, but I could operate my mobile in my sleep. Feeling the buttons, I remembered Marty was the second to last person I'd rung. I just needed to hit the call button, and scroll down once. Somehow I did it, and when I heard him answer, I found the strength to shout: 'Marty, Marty! Come to Mocha! Come to Mocha!'

'What?' he stammered in shock.

'I've been attacked! Come to Mocha.'

'What?'

'They threw acid in my face. Please come!' I begged.

Seconds later he raced in, his voice piercing my fog of agony. 'Katie, are you okay?' he asked, frantically.

'Danny, where's Danny?' I whispered, thrusting my phone at him. 'They threw acid on me!' I was delirious with fear and pain, but Marty's presence soothed my terror. He knew what Danny looked like; he wouldn't let him come in and take me away. He wouldn't let me die right here, in this seat.

Through my haze of pain, I heard Marty ring 999. I was barely able to move. I heard him tell the emergency services my name and my next of kin, and then the café's staff was leading me to the back of the shop.

'Come on, Katie, let's move you over here,' someone said, leading me by the arm. Every step was excruciating, every movement unleashed a fresh gush of pain.

'I need to get my boot and my handbag!' I mumbled, as if they mattered now. Talking hurt so much my throat felt like I'd swallowed razor blades. Marty darted away, and reappeared a few minutes later with my bag. It was soaking wet, splattered in acid.

'Ring the police!' I begged as someone doused my face in water, but after that, the pain swept everything else aside. It became my whole world, and I was trapped inside it.

Unbelievably, for the next hour I sat in that seat, as still as I could, while the ambulance weaved its way through rush-hour traffic. By now I couldn't see a thing and all noises sounded muffled, as though I was under water. I couldn't fight the pain – all my strength was gone, and I faded in and out of consciousness as the paramedics waited for the green light from police before they could treat me. Apparently, they had to make sure my attacker wasn't nearby still, but I'd lost all concept of time. It could have been two minutes or ten years – I was only aware of the torment, the burning.

The next thing I knew, I was being zipped inside something and wheeled out of the café into an ambulance.

'*I must be dead,*' I thought in relief. '*This must be a body bag, and those voices I hear are other souls who have died, too.*' Then everything went black.

When I came to the following morning, pumped full of morphine in a specialist burns unit at Chelsea and Westminster Hospital, I didn't know where I was. Was I dead or alive? Where was Danny? I couldn't make sense of any of it. Then I glimpsed a flicker of blue through my swollen eyelids, and heard Dad's voice. He always wore blue shirts: he had a wardrobe full of them and it had become a family joke. I realised he and Mum were there with me. Apparently the police had phoned them and they'd come as quickly as they could, but I simply assumed they were dead, too.

'*I wonder how they died,*' I thought. '*What an unlucky family we are.*'

By now, my head was the size of a football. After the attack, my face had gone so pale I was almost green, but with each hour that passed, it began to swell and swell and swell. I wasn't aware of it at the time, though; as nurses washed my face to try to neutralise the acid, I was barely conscious. Tests at the hospital revealed it to be neat, industrial strength sulphuric acid.

That night, I was put under heavy sedation. Luckily the drugs worked, and I was barely aware of anything.

Around dawn the next morning, I stirred, my mind still fuzzy with medication and panic. I heard Mum and Dad's voices again, trying to reassure me, but I couldn't seem to speak and my eyes were welded shut. I couldn't see Mum and Dad crying as they looked at my head, inflated to the size of a pumpkin. I couldn't see the skin on my face, black and brown and orange, and bubbled like burned plastic.

Someone handed me a clipboard and pen, and I started to scribble some messages. '*Help me. I can't breathe. Where am I? Am I dead? Am I blind? I'm sorry, I love you. Please don't cry.*'

When they had done their best to answer my questions and reassure me, Mum then asked if Danny had done this to me. I'd mentioned I was dating him in a text I'd sent her a few days earlier, and the very mention of his name made me want to scream. Gripping my pen clumsily – the acid wasn't so bad on my hands, but it still hurt to write – I wrote that he'd raped me. How he'd threatened to kill me. How I thought he was going to break into the hospital and kill me. At the time I didn't know what was going on, but I *was* certain of one thing: Danny was going to come and finish me off, and I was helpless to stop him. As far as I was concerned, I was better off dead. I scribbled another message: '*Kill me*', before the darkness swallowed me up again.

I faded in and out of consciousness for the next few hours. At some point that day, a family liaison officer from the police arrived, but I couldn't concentrate as he sat by my bed and asked me questions. His name was Adam and he seemed nice, but I was trapped in a shadowy world of morphine and confusion. Still blind, for some reason I imagined him looking like my childhood idol, Michael Jackson.

After he left, I kept trying to talk to Mum and Dad, but my voice sounded so weird. Raspy and deep, not like me at all. Why was that? I had better just sleep for a while …

The next day, I started to catch flashes of the real world as my vision came back a bit: my sister Suzy leaning over me; Mum and Dad, not leaving my side; an Asian man with warm brown eyes and a kind voice, who introduced himself as my surgeon, Mr Jawad.

'I'm going to help you, Katie,' he said. 'You're going in for an operation on your face.' I just nodded. I knew I could trust him.

Only two days after the attack, I had the first of what would prove to be over sixty operations to rebuild my face and internal damage to my oesophagus. In the operating theatre, under general anaesthetic, the medical team sliced away my entire face, removing the dead and burned skin there. I'd suffered third-degree burns, as well as losing most of my nose, my eyelids, and half my left ear. The acid had also damaged my eyes, my mouth and my tongue. It had splashed onto my arms, hands and legs, and burned right through my neck and cleavage. I had the worst injuries the medical team had ever seen.

After the operation, I was swaddled in bandages and moved into a high dependency room, with a single bed and a window that faced onto the nurses' station. I wasn't aware of anything, not even the police specialist rape team who came to see me. It was a blessing – after everything I'd been through, the shame of having my private parts examined would have been too much to bear.

The next day, I went back into theatre for another operation to remove more burned flesh. The top of my head was shaved in preparation for a mask made up of donor skin from corpses, which was stapled to my face to help it recover and prevent infection. I had to wear it for ten days and must have looked like a patchwork quilt and, if I'd known, if I'd seen my reflection, I'm sure I would have screamed in horror.

'Can you draw a picture of me, Dad?' I slurred afterwards, and he sketched a girl with longitude and latitude stitches marching across her face, like a human atlas. I just nodded, too out of it to really care what I looked liked.

Fear filled my whole world, and even when Adam, the police liaison officer, told me Danny had been arrested at the scene of the acid attack the evening after it happened, it didn't lessen my terror. Apparently he'd gone there, acting concerned, and told them he was my boyfriend. The police had immediately arrested him, but he had boasted to me about knowing bent coppers – he could get out, couldn't he? He could come here, and could wait until the police officer standing sentry by my door was distracted, couldn't he? Why didn't they understand that? He'd already carried out his threat to get me – why would he stop there? He couldn't risk letting me live.

The next day, five days after the attack, I was dozing in bed when Dad woke me up. 'Kate,' he whispered gently. 'The police think they've caught the guy who threw the acid. They need you to look at some photos on a laptop, and try to identify him. They're coming later. Do you think you can do it?'

A vision of the hoody's dark eyes flashed through my brain, and my heart skipped a beat. I never wanted to see that face again. I didn't even want to give evidence, something Mum and Dad had warned me I would have to do. They had also told me how important it was that I did it. I couldn't let Danny and his accomplice get away with it as they could do it again. They could rape and disfigure other girls, and I couldn't live with that on my conscience.

'Okay,' I croaked.

Worried about my eyesight, Mum and Dad had been testing me by showing me photos from magazines to see if I could recognise who the people in them were. Brad Pitt, Angelina Jolie – I managed to get them all right, so I knew I'd be able to see well enough to identify the hoody. If his picture was there.

When it was time for me to identify the acid thrower, a police officer and solicitor came into my room. They sat the laptop on the table, and explained I'd see nine pictures of nine different men. I shouldn't say anything till I'd seen them all twice. Only then should I say if any of them had been the one to throw the acid on me.

'Do you understand, Katie?' the policeman asked, and I nodded slowly.

It began. I looked at one man, then another, then another. No, no, no. What if they had the wrong man? What if he was still on the loose? Then, suddenly, his face flashed up. Same eyes, same nose, same mouth. I stared at it, more terrified than I'd ever been in my life. That was him, the young guy who'd marched towards me with his arms outstretched. Adrenaline flooded my system, my stomach flipped, and I lost control of my bowels and bladder.

'Dad,' I whimpered. 'I've messed myself.'

I had to carry on, though. This was my only chance to nail Danny's accomplice and so I went through the process twice, as asked. When it was over, trembling and sobbing, I pointed him out. I'd done it.

'Well done, Katie,' Dad said. 'We've got him.'

The hoody's name was Stefan Sylvestre. He was just twenty years old, and he'd only been caught because he'd been splattered by the acid as he'd thrown it on me. It had marked his face a little, and he'd told his mum he'd been attacked. When she'd mentioned it to someone else, they had remembered a police appeal for information about what had happened to me and put two and two together. Stefan had been arrested, and now I'd successfully identified him. He was with Danny, behind bars where they belonged.

The next day, Suzy and Paul came to visit, and I was euphoric to see them.

'Suzy, where are your curls? You've straightened your hair! It looks gorgeous!' I smiled.

'Oh, Katie!' she exclaimed, as tears ran silently down her cheeks. She thought I couldn't see them, and she was fighting to keep her voice steady.

'Don't cry! I'm fine, honestly.' Doped up on medication, I really hadn't a clue how severe my injuries where, despite all the medical equipment, feeding tubes, IV drips and monitors set up all around me.

The next few days passed in a haze: in between plenty of rest and sleep, I was cajoled into managing to sit in a chair for the first time; there was another operation to clean my wounds; I was able to swallow yoghurt for the first time; and I sat up to play Connect Four! I also had to give taped video evidence to Adam, the police liaison officer. Afterwards, Mum and Dad read out the messages from the dozens of cards I'd been sent:

'*We love you Katie.*'

'*We're thinking of you.*'

'*Sending all our love.*'

Underpinning everything, though, was *fear*. It was constant. In the early days, it could erupt like a volcano until the nurses were able to sedate me yet again. Even sleep was no comfort. Danny and Stefan stalked my nightmares, and I woke up screaming every night.

Nine days after the attack, my surgeon Mr Jawad came into my room and explained I would soon be having a major operation. They were going to use something called Matriderm, a new, cutting-edge dermal substitute that would act as a sort of scaffolding for my skin grafts, to rebuild my face.

'It's never been used on an area this large before, but I think it's the best option for you, Katie. It contains cow collagen, and it helps create soft and supple skin,' he said gently. 'Once we've applied that, then we'll take skin from your back and buttocks, and graft it onto your face, neck, chest and hands. Afterwards, we'll put you in an induced coma so you'll have better results, and the best chance of recovery.'

Sedated as I was, I barely followed what he was saying. All I knew was they were going to try to fix me, and I was in safe hands. Mr Jawad seemed like an angel to me, and I knew he would do his very best.

Two men had destroyed my face, and now this one was going to try to rebuild it.

Chapter Eight
Hope

I didn't know it at the time, but when I was wheeled into theatre on 10 April 2008, I was about to have truly pioneering treatment.

Mr Jawad fought for me to receive Matriderm, and insisted I be placed in an induced coma afterwards. The pain was going to be too great, he told them. It would traumatise me even more, and I needed to be perfectly still for the skin graft to heal properly.

During the six-hour procedure, my guardian angel worked hard to repair the damage Danny and Stefan had done. After he finished, I was wrapped in bandages like a mummy, and wheeled back to intensive care where, for the next twelve days, I lay in a drug-induced coma.

Even though the coma was the best possible option for my recovery, it wasn't, however, a deep and peaceful sleep. I was pumped so full of morphine, I started having horrific hallucinations, and I was plunged into a nightmarish world full of terror.

In this other world, I would be walking down a city street. It would be dark and cold and raining, and I would know I had a massive scab where my face had been. No nose, no mouth, no features – just a bright red, crusty scab that oozed pus. I would be wearing the tracksuit I had on when I was attacked, but my hair was in a Mohican, and everywhere I looked there were teenagers, pointing and laughing.

'Freak! Freak! Freak!' they chanted, everywhere I turned. Their cackles and taunts would get louder and louder, and then I would be running into a police station. But no one would help me. Why would no one help me? The gang of teenagers would then drag me out of the station, but I would manage to get away. I would run to a square, which looked just like Albert Square in *EastEnders*, where I'd worked as an extra. But they would always find me again, and drag me towards one of the doors of the houses on the square, knock on it and then run away. The door was always flung open and Danny would be standing there. I would run away, screaming, into the rain.

'Please help me!' I would bang on another door. A woman would answer and usher me inside. 'Shush.' She would put a finger to her lips. 'This is a squat.'

I would nod and lie on the ground, but a man would start trying to touch my boobs. I'd push him away – and then the police would burst in, and arrest me for being so ugly. They would think I was a boy, and they would just laugh when I tried to tell them the truth.

'I'm Katie! I'm a girl! I'm a model!' I would shout in this nightmare.

'Shut up, little boy,' would come the reply.

'*It'll be okay when they examine me. They'll see I'm a girl*,' I would think, but when I took off my clothes and lay on a cold metal table, my private parts would be gone. I was a man, and my own screams deafened me.

This dream would play out, with variations, but always pretty much the same way. Then there was another dream I had nearly as often, too.

In this one, I would be in a prison, wearing my orange tracksuit, desperately showing other women inmates photos of the old me.

'That's not you,' they would snort. 'She's beautiful, but you were born ugly. You were born looking like a monster.' They would punch and kick and batter me, until I was knocked to the floor.

A prison guard would then look in. 'Danny's here, you know,' she'd say nonchalantly. 'He asked if he could visit you, and we let him. He can do whatever he wants.' I would shriek in terror. He was here; Danny was here. He was going to get me.

The dream was so real, and seemed to go on forever. Every time, the inmates would sexually abuse me. They would slash my private parts with scissors, and when I looked down they would have vanished. There would be just an empty space where they used to be.

'*They've cut them all away*,' I would think, and part of me would be glad. At least now they couldn't hurt me there any more.

The dream made it seem like I was trapped in that prison for years. Naked because the prisoners took my clothes, starving because they stole my food, helpless as Danny raped me every night ... It was so real that I had no idea at all that it was all in my mind. I felt every blow, every punch, every surge of panic.

Eventually, I was brought out of my coma. But when the medical staff reduced my sedation and I started to wake up nearly two weeks after the operation, the hallucinations continued. On large doses of morphine, I was still lost in a strange twilight world, experiencing a horrifying cocktail of nightmare and reality. When the physiotherapists massaged me to prevent congestion on my lungs, I thought men were trying to abuse me. And the nurses – why did Mum and Dad not realise they were trying to kill me, too? When nurses washed me down, I thought I was lost and alone in the rain. When they tried to inject into a vein in my foot, I thought I was having my ankles broken.

'Get them away from me! They're trying to cut off my oxygen,' I begged, not realising they were only ever trying to help. I punched and kicked them away, certain they were going to hurt me.

'Mum! Was I in a car accident? I'm in prison, but I'm innocent. You have to get me out of here,' I babbled, pointing at my blue hospital gown. 'See? It says "HMS Prison Use Only".'

'No, sweetheart, it says "Hospital Use Only".' Mum said soothingly, but in vain.

'No! Why won't you believe me?'

I couldn't make them understand. Was I in the jail's hospital wing? Was that why Mum and Dad were allowed to visit? That was better – I was safer there, but Danny was still nearby. Oh God. Where was he? They had to stop him!

'Shush, love, Danny can't hurt you. The police have arrested him. You're totally safe now,' Mum would reassure me, and pure joy would seep through my body.

'He can't get me. I'm safe.' My heart would sing with joy and relief. These respites didn't last long, though. At night, I would see giant reptiles and bugs slithering up the walls of my room, and when I looked through the window into the nurses' station, there were men in scary Halloween masks on the other side of the glass. They just laughed and laughed, as I screamed and screamed, and soiled myself in fear yet again.

I was completely oblivious as the hallucinations raged on and on: Danny sneaking into my room at night and attacking me all over again; reliving the rape and the acid and the pain; monsters lurking in the shadows; the sound of my own screams. I had no concept of time passing, no ability to distinguish what was real and what wasn't.

In an attempt to stabilise me, doctors changed my medication, but it sedated me to the point that I was practically catatonic, and Mum and Dad thought I must have brain damage on top of everything else. I stared into space, slack-jawed and dribbling from the sedation as they moved my bed so I could see out the window, as they took x-rays to make sure I wasn't getting a chest infection, as they scraped cells off my eyes to examine them.

Within a few days, thankfully, the hallucinations gradually started to die down. I was still on the heavy medication, however, and I wasn't lucid. One minute, I was sobbing uncontrollably, and the next I was talking about how I was going to be a beauty therapist when I got out of hospital.

'I can't wait to get back to work, Mum,' I would chirp brightly. 'I stayed up all night thinking about it, and I've decided I'm going to stop modelling and go back to beauty therapy. I've got it all figured out. I can get another job in a salon, and it'll be great!'

'Sounds good, love,' Mum replied, even though she knew I had no chance. I couldn't use my hands properly, and I still didn't understand how badly hurt I was.

At one point, I even thought we were all on a film set, and the doctors and nurses were all actors and actresses. 'You're too late!' I cried to Mum. 'We've finished; you missed the show. I have to go home now, but you can come later.'

Another time, I hadn't a clue who was who. 'Who am I, darling?' Mum asked.

'You're Mum,' I tutted in frustration. Why was she asking me such a daft question?

'And who am I, Kate?' Dad said.

'You're our dog, Barclay, silly,' I replied.

One morning, I woke up in a panic. My bank cards hadn't been cancelled! What if someone tried to defraud me? I had to tell Mum and Dad, so I called them at 5 a.m. They raced into my room from where they'd been sleeping in the Patients' Hotel, a facility with rooms for family members of patients at the hospital, and I started ranting.

'You have to cancel my cards! What about my money? What if someone steals it? It needs to be done right away!'

It was gibberish – I was permanently overdrawn and had hardly any money, anyway, but in my confused and muddled state, I couldn't rest until it was done.

For some reason, I kept telling everyone about my old life, too. I was desperate for them to know I hadn't always been this way. 'Hello! My name's Katie, and I'm a model,' I said over and over to the nurses. 'I know you can't tell now, but I used to be pretty!'

'We know, it's okay, Katie,' they always reassured me.

'Honestly, it's true.' I was determined they'd believe me. It was like Danny had taken away my identity, and I needed to prove who I was.

Physically, however, I was making progress. Even though I was still being fed through a feeding tube, I had started managing to eat some cereal on my own, and Mum had started pushing me round the hospital in a wheelchair. My head bowed, I was too out of it to care what I looked like or who saw me, but I'd made it out of my bed at least.

Slowly, I became more lucid and coherent – but real life wasn't much better than my nightmares. 'I'm so scared, Mum,' I told her, over and over. 'Danny raped me! And that other boy threw acid on me. It was terrible!'

'I know, Kate. It's okay, you're okay now.'

I was also only just starting to understand how serious my injuries were: I was half-blind and the doctors weren't sure if my vision was going to get better or worse; I couldn't swallow properly so I was dribbling badly; I couldn't eat properly because my throat had been so badly damaged; and I was still so weak after the last operation and the induced coma, I couldn't go to the loo or even use a bed pan, so I had to wear nappies and soil myself like a baby. As for my face, well, I couldn't even think about that. Not yet.

Instead, I worried about going totally blind. Would I ever have a normal life? Even breathing hurt, and I was so afraid. All the time, and of absolutely everything.

'I'm so scared, Suzy,' I cried as my sister lovingly fed me slivers of ice.

'I know, Katie, but don't worry. We're all here now.'

'Why has this happened to me? What have I done to deserve it? I've never hurt anyone, or done anything evil. Why me?'

'Shush, Katie, it's okay.'

How could it be okay, though? How could it ever be okay again? My old life was gone forever: when Paul brought in my iPod because he thought it might cheer me up, the songs I used to listen to just filled me with grief.

'Please turn it off,' I cried, when Christina Milian's 'I'm A Believer' started playing. Memories of me dancing around my bedroom in my knickers and singing along to it haunted me. That girl had been so full of hope and ambition and determination, but she was now dead and gone. She'd been murdered on the high street that Monday in March.

'Turn it off now!' I shouted.

Danny still came to me every night in my dreams and I'd wake up, screaming, in a mess of my own excrement.

'You're in hospital, Katie,' I'd tell myself, trying to calm down. 'Danny isn't here. Look, there's the Tigger toy Paul gave you, sitting at the end of your bed.'

The poor night nurse would then have to come in to clean me up but, one night, she couldn't manage on her own and called for a male colleague to help her. As soon as he walked through the door, I freaked out. He was a man, and therefore he could hurt me like Danny did.

'Please go, please,' I sobbed.

'You don't have to be frightened of me. I'm a nurse,' he said gently, but I couldn't contain my panic. Why was this happening to me? Was I going to be attacked again?

'Please don't hurt me,' I screamed, hysterical.

I also had a specialist burns psychologist, called Lisa, assigned to me. If I was too out of it to talk she would spend a lot of time talking to my parents and helping them, or she'd sit next to my bed and speak to me softly, explaining what was happening to me.

Apart from Dad and Paul, the only man I could cope with being near was Mr Jawad. He came to see me every day, giving constant encouragement.

'You're making great progress, Katie. I'm so proud of you,' he'd say, his eyes twinkling with intelligence and warmth and compassion. 'You won't be like this forever, I promise. You're not on your own, and I'll be with you every step of the way.' But even though I trusted Mr Jawad, I couldn't believe what he was saying. Danny had taken everything from me. He'd destroyed my dignity and pride, he'd crushed my spirit; he'd ruined my body and left a ravaged shell behind. My career was over, my life in tatters. I felt so empty, filled with nothing but fear and shame. How could I ever get through this? It seemed impossible. Hopeless.

Then I met Alice. One of the many amazing nurses who treated me, she was a middle-aged Indian lady, and she started sitting with me after her rounds or during her breaks. With chocolate brown eyes, long silky dark hair and a warmth that reminded me of Mr Jawad, she sat by my bed and talked about her son, her job, her friends. It was all idle chitchat, but her presence soothed me so much. If I wanted to cry, she just let me cry, and if I couldn't sleep, she sang lovely Indian lullabies. I didn't understand any of the words, but they made me feel safe, regardless.

'Things in life happen for a reason,' she said one night, in her beautiful, lilting voice. 'Don't be afraid, Katie. God has great things in store for you. This is not the end of you, and I will pray for you.'

I'd never really thought much about God before. Mum and Dad weren't religious, and I'd never gone to church or read the Bible, but I tried to take some comfort in Alice's faith. For the first time in my life, I prayed to a God I'd never really believed in. '*Please help me. Please give me strength. Please show me a way to get through this.*'

One night, as I lay in the darkness listening to the hiss of the monitors and the beep of my morphine drip, I started drowning in my despair. It just overwhelmed me. Simply existing as I was was no good – I couldn't live like this. There were too many eyes on me here, but I decided that when I was discharged, I was going to kill myself.

'*I'll take an overdose or throw myself out of the car when we leave hospital,*' I thought. '*This is just too hard for me, and my family. It must be tearing at them, too. They'd be better off without me. I'd be better off dead.*'

There and then, my mind was made up. It would be my secret and, as I thought about it, I wept with silent relief. I could carry the burden of living until then, if I knew the end was in sight. I could take control back, and I could escape Danny on my own terms. Sure, Mum and Dad and Suzy and Paul would grieve, but they'd see it was for the best eventually. It was the only solution, and there was no alternative.

But then, all of a sudden, the weirdest feeling crept over me. It felt like a warm hug, and it enveloped every inch of me. It floated through my wasted hands, my scarred back, my broken heart, and I felt as though I was filled with light.

'*Everything's going to be okay,*' a voice in my head said. '*Your journey's just begun. You'll get through this.*'

For the very first time since Danny had ripped my life apart, I felt hope flutter inside me. He wouldn't beat me. I wouldn't let him. Suddenly I knew I was strong enough to survive this, to build a new life for myself. I didn't know where that feeling of inner strength had come from: my mind? Or was it God, reaching out to me because I was so close to giving up forever? Either way, it got me through that long, dark night.

Chapter Nine
Facing the World

I tried hard to cling to that feeling the next morning. I tried to tell myself I had the strength to get through this – but there were so many mountains to climb, and they were bigger than Everest. Choking on a mouthful of mashed carrots for lunch, I dissolved into sobs yet again. I couldn't even bloody eat; what kind of sorry excuse for a human being was I?

After lunch, one of the nurses announced I was to be moved from my single room into the main ward, and the all-too familiar terror suddenly swirled again. There would be men there, strange men. Didn't they know how dangerous that was?

'I don't want to go there, Mum,' I cried. 'I just want to stay here. *Please.*'

But the medical team insisted. It was a month after the attack, and I had to get used to being around people again.

I was taken into a ward with three other patients who'd also suffered burns. I was still too traumatised and weak to worry what they thought of me or how I must look, and I just kept my head bowed and avoided eye contact. Pretending to sleep, I listened as they complained about scars on their arms and legs.

'*I wish that was all I had to worry about,*' I thought sadly.

Over the next few days, I sank into a depressed torpor. I vomited any time I tried to eat – something that would remain a problem for a long time due to my throat's constriction from scar tissue – and wept constantly but quietly, so the other patients wouldn't hear me.

Mum was worried and tried to cajole me into more trips in the wheelchair again. She pushed me around the hospital: with a baseball cap on and my chin against my chest, I didn't look up once.

'How about we go outside? You haven't breathed fresh air since the attack,' Mum said gently, and I shrugged. I didn't care either way.

As soon as the automatic doors slid closed behind us, I started panicking. There were so many people, so many noises. Cars horns, buses whooshing past, pigeons swooping …

'I don't like it,' I whimpered. 'I want to go back inside.' The hospital was safe – it was a sanctuary. Bad things happened outside it.

But the next day, I managed to stand up and get dressed on my own. It took hours to convince my wobbly, wonky limbs to do what I wanted them too, but eventually I got my tracksuit on. It was a tiny triumph, and it only reminded me of how much I'd lost.

'Let's try going outside today again, love,' Mum said, and my belly flipped with dread.

'Okay,' I whispered.

'Do you think you can walk?'

'I'll try.'

I was as frail as an old lady and my legs were as ungainly as Bambi's, but I kept my head down and took one step, then another. Mum suggested we go into the Starbucks in the foyer, and I nodded reluctantly.

Sitting in the corner with my hat pulled down, I sipped on a high-calorie strawberry frappuccino to help build up my wasted body. I felt so strange. It all seemed so foreign to me – the rumble of the coffee grinder, the hiss of the hot milk. They were noises I'd heard a thousand times, but I felt like an alien who'd just crash-landed on Earth.

Back on the ward, I lay on my bed, worrying about my eyesight. My left eye had been completely doused in the acid and the cornea was irreparably damaged, while my right had been badly affected, too. My eyelids had burned off, so my eyes couldn't stay lubricated, and that was causing even more problems. The eye doctors were doing constant tests but they couldn't predict what would happen, and I was still in danger of losing what fuzzy vision I had left.

'*How will I ever manage if I go blind?*' I thought, as snapshots of the sky and the beach and flowers and people's faces flashed through my mind. '*I'll be totally helpless, trapped in darkness.*'

That afternoon, a young girl in her teens was admitted. Her face had been burned in a gas explosion, and even though she was going to be left with no lasting scars, she was extremely shaken and upset.

'Don't cry, you'll be okay,' I smiled over to her. 'Like the doc said, once the scabs heal and fall off, you'll be as good as new.'

I felt so bad for her – until she turned and looked fully at me, her tear-filled eyes widening with shock. 'I thought my injuries were bad,' she blurted, 'but when I look at you, I realise how lucky I am.'

I turned away to hide my shock. It was like getting punched in the stomach, and it took my breath away. Even though I knew the girl hadn't meant to hurt me, I burst into silent sobs.

'*Oh God, what do I look like?*' I wept. For the first time, I allowed myself to wonder. The burns unit deliberately had no mirrors, but the skin on my hand was bright purple – was my face that colour, too? When I tried to eat a yoghurt that lunchtime, I tried to examine my reflection in the metal spoon, but it was tarnished and all I could see was a misshapen, puce-coloured blob.

'Don't worry,' one of the other women patients said, when she noticed me doing it. 'You'll look much better once you've had your skin grafts.'

'I've already had them. My whole face is a skin graft,' I whispered, a lump in my throat.

'Oh no, I'm so sorry, I didn't realise.'

'It's okay,' I lied, reminding myself of Mr Jawad's constant encouragement. I was a work in progress; I was going to be fine.

A little while after the girl's shocked comment about me, one of the nurses came over with a bundle of printouts. She handed them to me with a sympathetic smile and told me I might find them helpful. When I looked at them, I wanted to rip them into tiny pieces.

'*HOW TO COPE WITH DISFIGUREMENT,*' the top one's title read. I shoved them into my locker in horror. Disfigured? I wasn't disfigured! I was Katie Piper, model and TV presenter. That word had nothing to do with me. Absolutely nothing.

Mum and Dad came to visit that afternoon, and I broke down. I knew the other patients hadn't meant to hurt my feelings and the nurse was just trying to be kind, but now all I could think about was my face. My beautiful face.

'Don't let it upset you, darling.' Mum tried to cheer me up.

'I want to know what I look like,' I insisted.

'Soon, love. You're getting better all the time.'

Was I really? It didn't seem like it. I still couldn't eat properly, and I even had trouble with baby food like spaghetti hoops, and custard. It felt like there was something permanently lodged in my throat, and I'd either choke or vomit any food I ate back up again.

Later that day, my best friend, Kay, came to visit. I was so embarrassed about how I must look, I could barely meet her gaze.

'It's so good to see you,' she said brightly, trying to disguise her shock. 'You're doing so well.'

'Thanks,' I said.

'I came by before, but I wasn't allowed into see you.'

'I know, Mum and Dad said. Thanks for the CD and CD player.'

While I was in the coma, Kay had left an audio book of *The Secret*, a self-help phenomenon about the power of positive thinking. I'd listened to it now and then in the hope that it would raise my spirits; that I could somehow convince my body to heal through sheer willpower and determination.

'I've brought you a little fan and another CD. It's got some of our favourite music on there, like 50 Cent!' she smiled, not realising how much I didn't want to listen to music like that any more. It just reminded me of dancing in clubs as guys tried to catch my eye.

I had half expected Kay, once she'd seen me, to make her excuses and rush out of the door, too scared to be near me, but she stayed for three hours and kept up a steady stream of chatter about work and going out. It was all so far removed from my new life, Kay might as well have been talking a different language, but it was so lovely to see her. She still wanted to be my friend, and suddenly I didn't feel so alone.

'Thanks so much for coming,' I whispered as she got up to leave.

'I'll see you soon,' she said, and I wondered what she must think of me. Did she pity me? We used to be so similar, but not any more.

*

A few days later, on 6 May 2008, Dad took me to a session with Lisa. As we shuffled through the hospital corridors, I wondered what it would involve. Was she going to let me see my face? My curiosity had been building, and I was getting desperate to know what I looked like.

'Hi, Katie,' Lisa said as we took a seat in her office. 'I think it's time to look at your reflection.' I nodded, suddenly afraid. 'Let's just do a little bit today. We'll start with your chest, and work our way up over the next few days,' she said, and I nodded again, even though I had no intention of taking it bit by bit. I had to know now – what was the point in pussy-footing around?

In my mind's eye, I could see my old face so clearly. My bright blue eyes underneath perfectly groomed brows, the small and pert nose, the golden complexion, the wide mouth and the strong jawline. I hadn't seen it for two months, but I knew every last millimetre of it. '*It can't be that bad*,' I thought as I lifted the mirror to my face.

It was worse than I ever could have imagined.

My face was red raw. I was a piece of rotting meat. I had known my eyelids were missing and that my head was shaved, but where was my tanned skin? Where was my neat nose? Why did my lips look like they'd been pulled inside-out? And my eyes, oh my eyes! The left was milky and blind and the other was empty, like it belonged to a corpse.

My old face was gone: there was not the smallest sign of it in the reflection that stared back at me. This was my new face – this was the ruin Danny had made. This was *me*.

I barely registered Dad leading me back to the ward. I was enveloped in a shock so great I could scarcely breathe. I couldn't see the other patients or the nurses scurrying around – just that *thing* that had stared back at me from the mirror. It was like another head had been transplanted onto my body, one that I didn't recognise in the slightest. How could someone look like that? How could *I* look like that? None of it made any sense.

One thing I did know, however, beyond a shadow of a doubt, was that no man would ever want me now. I would die alone.

Back in my bed, I sobbed in Dad's arms. 'I didn't know it was so bad,' I cried, so ashamed that people had seen me like that. Mum, Dad, Suzy, Paul, Kay, the hospital staff and the other people on my ward … I'd sat talking to them, with no idea that I barely looked human. They'd probably felt sick just looking at me. How well they'd hidden it; how kind they'd all been not to run away from me, screaming in horror and disgust.

As if I was watching a film, visions from the past flickered through my mind. Slathering Mum's lipstick on my mouth when I was little. My first boyfriend taking my face in his hands and kissing my cheeks. Getting ready for a night out in Basingstoke, plucking my eyebrows and applying mascara with surgical precision. Posing and preening in front of the camera. Men turning in the street and whistling as I walked past. Countless blokes complimenting me … their voices got louder and louder, ringing in my ears: 'You're so beautiful', 'You have such a gorgeous face', 'What a stunner!', 'You should be a model!'

The face that I'd built a career on was now hideous. The beauty I'd traded on was destroyed. I'd gone from one extreme to the other; if it wasn't so tragic, I might have laughed out loud. What bitter, cruel irony.

'I'm so ugly,' I whimpered to Dad.

'You're still the same Kate underneath,' he answered.

I wasn't, though. I might as well have been a different species from that fun, feisty, independent, invincible young woman. She was someone I used to know once; she had been my best friend, but now she was dead. I had to grieve for her, and I also knew that I had to try to forget her if I was ever to find any peace ever again.

The next day, while I was still reeling, I was fitted for a neck collar, chin strap and vest. The woman explained I had to wear them to help flatten the scars and aid with the healing, but they made me feel so claustrophobic. Then one of the physios mentioned that I'd have to wear a mask over my face, too.

'I'm sorry?' I asked in confusion. It was the first I'd heard of it.

'Yes, a clear plastic mask,' the physio continued. 'You'll have to keep it on for twenty-three hours a day, for eighteen months to two years. They'll probably sort it out in a few weeks,' she finished breezily.

I felt my heart sink. As if my face wasn't bad enough already, I'd have to wear some kind of Hannibal Lecter mask as well.

'I didn't know,' I stammered, trying not to cry.

I'd been in hospital for over five weeks, and I hadn't once thought about going home. The hospital had been my whole world for what seemed like an eternity; I just assumed I'd be there forever. I was accepted here, even if my injuries were worse than everyone else's. I was safe. Which was why when Mum said they were planning to discharge me soon, I totally crumbled.

'No way,' I shook my head. 'I'm just going to stay here, thanks.'

'But you have to come home at some point, Kate darling,' Mum replied.

'What am I going to do?' I begged later of one of the nurses, a lovely lady called Susie with freckles and strawberry-blonde curls. But what could she say? She just stroked my hair and let me get it all out.

The following afternoon, I was fitted for pressure gloves to help the scars on my hands, and then I went with Mum to the hospital café to meet Adam, the police liaison officer, and two detectives who were working on the case.

Now that I knew how horrendous I looked, I could barely meet their eyes. Did I disgust them, too? Did they come away from seeing me and say to each other: 'Did you see that? Have you ever seen anything like it?'

'Hi, Katie,' Adam smiled, and I mumbled a greeting. One of the detectives, Warren, explained they needed me to film some more video evidence, I started trembling. What if I did it, but Danny got off? He'd make me pay; he'd take his revenge. But I couldn't back out – I had to be strong.

'Are you feeling up to it?' Mum asked.

'Yes,' I replied, even though it was the last thing on earth I wanted to do.

For the next two and a half hours, I sat in a little room talking into a video camera. The last time I'd been in front of one was before the attack, when I'd worked on *Fame TV*, but those five weeks felt like five decades.

In a faltering voice, I described how I'd met Danny on Facebook, how he'd pursued me and we'd started dating. Remembering the early days of our romance made me feel nauseous. How could I have liked him? Kissed him? Missed him when we weren't together? But it was nothing compared to describing the rape. Retelling my story made me relive every torturous second in that hotel room, and I wept in shame. I told him how Danny had told me he'd attacked other girls before and my heart ached for them, too.

'You did really well, Katie,' Adam said afterwards. 'We'll need to do one more, about the acid attack itself. Maybe tomorrow?'

'Okay,' I agreed, reluctantly.

The next day, I was forced to relive Stefan throwing the contents of that cup at my face as well. I struggled to find the words to describe the pain, the terror; the moment my beauty was ravaged and my new face created.

'Look at what they did to me!' I broke down, pointing to my ruined face. 'Look!'

Still much too traumatised to think clearly, I assumed that was all I'd have to do. The police had my evidence, Danny and Stefan would plead guilty and that would be the end of it. I didn't think for one second it would ever go to trial. After all, their guilt was etched into my face.

After we had finished, Mum and Dad got my things together. I was being allowed home for a weekend's leave, to see how we all coped before I was properly discharged.

'Do I really have to?' I cowered on my bed. 'Can't I stay? I can rent a room or something.' Outside the hospital I still believed bad things happened. I could be attacked again. And people would see my face.

'Don't you want to see Barclay?' Mum cajoled. 'He's missed you loads.'

'He won't even recognise me,' I said sadly, picturing our Chihuahua-cross waiting for me at home. 'He'll probably start barking and be too scared to come near me.'

But no matter how much I complained or resisted, there was no getting out of it. I had to venture back into the outside world where I'd been raped and drenched in acid.

Flanked by Mum and Dad, I slowly made my way down in the lift to the underground car park.

'The car's over here,' Dad said, but I refused to look up in case there were any people around. With Mum leading me by the arm, I jumped into the back seat and slammed the door shut behind me.

'Everyone lock their doors,' I demanded. I tried to stop trembling as we left the cocoon of the car park and emerged into the bright light of day above.

Chapter Ten

Home Safe and Sound

I pulled my baseball cap down over my face as Dad drove out onto the street. It was rush-hour and the traffic was gridlocked, while crowds of people thronged the pavements. Kids in uniforms hurried home from school, office workers were popping out for an after-work pint … They were so close, just a few feet away on the other side of the door, and I crouched down to the foot well of the car.

'They're too near!' I shouted, pressing my face against my knees. 'They can see me!'

'They can't Kate, it's fine,' Mum said, soothingly.

But nothing could convince me to sit up on the seat again. During the three-hour journey home, I hunkered there like a frightened animal.

When we finally pulled up outside the house where I'd grown up, it was dark, but I was still too terrified to get out of the car. Someone could be waiting with another cup of acid, perhaps another one of Danny's friends he'd paid to punish me.

'No one's there,' Dad said, opening the front door. Panting with panic, I flew out of the car and ran inside as fast as my weak legs could carry me.

'See? Home safe and sound,' Mum smiled, putting down two plastic bags that were filled to the brim with all the medication I had to take. Then I noticed the banner Suzy had hung before she'd gone on holiday that morning. '*WELCOME HOME, KATIE!*' it said. She'd also left me some Alan Partridge box sets, while Paul had written me a letter decorated with pictures from all the cartoons we'd loved as kids, like *Galaxy High* and *He-Man*.

Sinking onto the sofa, I smiled as I read his funny reminiscences about games we used to play. Swimming our Action Man and Barbie in a pool we made from a red crate. Bathtime with *Star Wars* figures and a plastic doll we called Diver Dan.

> '*We wondered how we'd ever ride a bike without stabilisers,*' he wrote. '*But do you remember the day when the stabilisers came off, and suddenly you realised you were riding all by yourself? You were doing it, and what seemed impossible in previous years was now actually possible? What a feeling! I know you'll feel that way again in the future. Love you lots, McFly.*'

'McFly!' I giggled. That was from *Back to the Future*, one of our all-time favourite films.

'Thank you, Paul,' I whispered.

Just then Barclay came running into the lounge. My heart skipped a beat as I waited for him to start growling, for his hackles to rise. But he just looked at me for a moment, then ran straight over and jumped on my lap.

'Hello, Barclay,' I cried. 'You know it's me, don't you? Good boy!'

With Barclay at my heels, I wandered from room to room. Nothing had changed – except that all the old photos of me had been taken down. My old school picture on the mantelpiece, a snap of me with my grandma, one of my modelling shots on the pin board … all gone. Suzy had moved into my room when I left home, so I'd be staying in her old bedroom. But I quickly realised they'd taken the mirror in there away, too. They must have thought it would upset me too much.

The familiarity of home didn't make me feel any safer than being in the car, however, and I gave Mum and Dad a long list of demands.

'No one's allowed to answer the door, or the phone,' I ordered. 'All the windows have to be locked all the time, and I don't want any candles lit, either.'

I was petrified of fire, of getting burned again. Every time the phone rang, I jumped out of my skin as it reminded me of Danny constantly harassing me. I was also terrified of opening the door and seeing Stefan on the other side of it. I slumped in front of the DVDs Suzy had bought me and tried to concentrate on Steve Coogan as the inept radio host. It used to have me in stitches, but now the best I could manage was a ghost of a smile.

As though he could sense my distress, Barclay didn't let me out of his sight. If I went to the loo, he followed me, and if I started to cry, he nudged me with his furry little head.

I hadn't lived at home for so long that it was weird being back. But I knew there was no way I could return to my flat in Golders Green. Even seeing the familiar front door would have tipped me over the edge, and besides, all my flatmates had been told to move out for their own safety, in case Danny had any surprises in store for them.

That night, I climbed the stairs and got into Suzy's single bed in her green and purple room. A tiny part of me was glad to me home, but the fear was overriding it. It wasn't safe here – I wasn't safe. And when I eventually drifted off to sleep, Danny came to me in my dreams and raped me all over again.

'It's okay, Katie, it's just a dream,' Mum soothed me awake. My screams had brought her running to my side.

The next morning, I was still on edge. Every four hours, I trudged upstairs to Mum and Dad's room for them to massage my skin, but apart from that I barely moved off the sofa all weekend. When a local policeman knocked on the door, I almost had a panic attack. Had he come to warn us that Danny was out on the loose?

'It's okay, sweetheart. He's just here to talk to us about security for the house,' Mum said.

On Sunday evening, it was time to negotiate the journey back to the hospital. At least this time it was dark, so people couldn't see me. But lots of things could hide in the darkness, couldn't they?

'Doors locked, please!' I reminded Mum and Dad, putting my head down on my knees and counting the minutes until we got back to Chelsea and Westminster Hospital. Back on my ward, I sighed with relief. I was safe again.

The next day, I went into surgery for my ninth operation in the space of six weeks. A little patch of skin was taken from my buttock and grafted onto my ear. When I woke up, my bum was really sore.

'*Thank God Mr Jawad put me in that coma after the huge skin graft,*' I thought. Considering how much bigger that graft had been, I would have been in total agony. It had definitely been the right decision.

Soon afterwards, my photographer friend, Michael, who I'd gone to dinner with just before the attack, came to visit. I was mortified that he was seeing me this way, and when I met his eyes, they filled with such sadness.

'I can't believe they did this to you, babe.' He shook his head.

'Me neither.'

'If only I hadn't gone on holidays after we met up that night. If only I'd been there, I might've been able to protect you,' he said suddenly in a rush, his voice cracking with emotion.

'No, Michael, don't. They would've got me in the end. No one could've done anything to stop it,' I reassured him.

But that wasn't completely true, I realised. One person had had the power to stop it happening: me. If only I'd gone to the police after the rape. If only I'd got Danny arrested. If only I hadn't gone with him to the hotel in the first place. If only … Guilt and uncertainties gnawed at me, even though I tried to convince myself it wasn't my fault. Danny had put the fear of God in me; he'd convinced me that my family and friends would suffer if I told anyone about the rape. He'd bullied me into a corner and worn me down, until I didn't know which way to turn. Deep down, I knew I wasn't to blame, but it didn't stop me from hating myself and what he'd turned me into.

The next afternoon, Mr Jawad suggested I go to see a lady from a charity that specialised in camouflage make-up. She was visiting the hospital that day, so I reluctantly made my way to her little room. As if make-up could help me.

'Mr Jawad sent me down,' I mumbled, as her eyes widened in shock at my injuries.

'Hello, dear,' she stammered. 'Why don't you sit down and we'll see what we can do?'

I squirmed as she looked closely at my face. She said it was too soon to put any foundation on my skin as it hadn't healed enough yet, so she dabbed some on my scarred hand instead. As she rubbed it in, liquid oozed from my nose and dripped onto my legs, and she handed me some hankies.

'Thanks,' I muttered.

'You must be so bored hanging round the hospital. Maybe you could try to learn a new language or read some of the classics? That would keep you busy.'

'I can't read too well, because of my eyes. If I try to focus for too long, my vision gets blurry,' I said, looking away. I knew she was just trying to be kind, but I wanted to smack her.

'Have you heard of Braille?' she asked, and I burst into tears. Of course I knew what the system of raised dots that let blind people read was called. But how could she suggest that I might be blind myself someday soon? How could she be so insensitive?

Back on my ward, I couldn't pull myself together. I cried through my physio and a visit to the eye ward with Mum and Dad, and then I exploded with rage.

'I can't take any more,' I screamed, throwing my magazines and Tigger toy to the floor. 'Just leave me alone!'

Mum and Dad hovered helplessly, not knowing what to do.

'I said leave me alone! Go away! I want to be on my own.'

'Okay, love, if that's what you want,' Mum agreed, seeing it was for the best. 'Ring if you need us. We're always here.'

They went back to their room in the Patients' Hotel, and I cried till my fury subsided. Then I picked up the phone.

'I'm sorry, Mum,' I wept. 'I just can't cope with this. I don't know how. It's just one thing after another.'

'I know, I know. Shush, it's okay.'

The following morning, I was discharged for real, even though my treatment was far from over. I had countless check-ups and consultations and operations ahead, but it was time for me to leave the burns unit and start the next part of my journey towards recovery.

'You've made excellent progress, Katie,' Mr Jawad said. 'There's a long road ahead, but I'll be with you every step of the way. I'm only ever at the other end of a phone, and I'll ring you all the time to see how you're doing.'

'Thank you,' I hugged him hard and thought about how Mr Jawad was one of the most wonderful people I'd ever met. He'd shown me that not all men were evil; that they weren't all like Danny and Stefan. All the hospital staff had been amazing: my other surgeon, Isabelle, who looked just like Princess Di; nurse Susie with her smattering of freckles and soothing words; Alice, whose prayers had comforted me in the night; the no-nonsense ward sister, Gloria, who'd been so protective of me that she had refused to admit a policeman when he'd forgotten his ID one day. They worked, day in and day out, to help people like me. They didn't want fame or wealth or celebrity – their only motivation was kindness, and they were the antidote to the poison that flowed in Danny's veins. Like my family and friends, they were the light to his darkness. As I said goodbye to them, I knew I never would have made it this far without them.

The journey back home was just as traumatic as the last one had been. Once I was safely indoors, I took my place on the sofa again.

I was like a zombie, deeply inside myself, Barclay on my lap, only moving for my physio and massages every four hours. I didn't want to speak to anyone, I didn't want to see anyone, and I was too afraid to go near the computer. That was how I'd met Danny, and the harmless machine in the corner of the front room suddenly seemed like some kind of sinister, crouching monster, offering a way for him to reach into my life and touch me again.

The nightmares kept on coming: Stefan leaning over my bed with a vat of acid, Danny forcing himself on me … My fear during the day was rarely any better, and I became terrified of everyday things like drinking a cup of coffee. I didn't want hot liquid anywhere near me in case I got scalded, and refused to let Mum or Dad drink it, either. Simple things like taking a shower could be minefields, too. The water sprinkling on my face made me remember the acid, so I'd stand away from the spray and wash myself with a flannel cloth. But even that was a struggle. I hated touching myself; I loathed feeling my skin. I disgusted myself so much, I couldn't bear to look at my body.

I spent hours studying my face in the mirror. By now, it looked even worse than the first time I'd seen it in hospital. Bright red and lumpy, the burns were shrivelling and contracting as they healed. I couldn't look away. I spiralled deeper and deeper into misery. I didn't even look like anyone in my family any more. And if, by some miracle, I ever had children, I wouldn't look like them, either. I'd never know how I would have aged, how my face would have changed as I got older.

'It's all part of the healing process. Just take one day at a time,' Mum kept reminding me, but I couldn't believe it would ever get better.

Days dragged by, with only the regular trips back up to the burns unit and eye clinic to mark the passing of time. Travelling in the car never got any easier, and I flatly refused to go anywhere else.

Glimmers of hope appeared, though. One day, I noticed my eyelashes were starting to grow back. They were short and stumpy and wispy, but they were there. It was a tiny sign of improvement, and it filled me with happiness. Maybe things weren't so hopeless after all ... but then, during one of my appointments to the eye clinic, the optician said my eyelashes were growing back at the wrong angle and scratching the lens of my eye. She had to clamp my eyes open and pluck them out one by one. Compared to what I'd already been through, the pain didn't bother me too much, but what it represented cut me to the bone. I wasn't, in fact, getting better, and I never would. I had no control over my appearance; I *had* no appearance, and the sooner I accepted that, the better.

The next time I was at the burns unit, I got another reality check. The nurses were changing the dressing on my bum, where skin had been removed to graft onto my face, and were checking it hadn't become infected. As they peeled the tape away, I yelped in pain and looked down at my private parts for the first time since the rape.

'*Oh God, I'm so hairy,*' I thought in horror. '*And I used to be a Brazilian waxer, too!*' All of a sudden, I remembered a time when I had stood half-naked at a modelling shoot, a make-up artist dusting my body with glitter. In contrast, I was now surrounded by attentive nurses, disfigured, with an out-of-control lady garden and a bit of my bum sewed onto my face.

I started to giggle slightly hysterically, and I couldn't stop.

'Katie, are you okay?' one of the nurses asked. 'What's wrong?

'I'm okay,' I said as I gasped for air. 'It's just … it's totally ridiculous! How the hell did I get here?'

A few days later, I went to St George's Hospital in south London to get a mould of my face done, to make the first of the masks I'd have to wear constantly for up to two years, depending on my progress.

'Are they going to cover me in plaster of Paris and give me a straw to breathe through, Mum?' I fretted all the way there. 'You know I don't like anyone touching my face.'

I had worked myself up into a complete state by the time we got there, but the mask expert was a nice Scottish man called Iain, who put me at ease straight away.

'Don't worry, we're just going to put some blue putty on your face, then put some wet bandages on top. They'll set, and then we'll have an impression of your face so we can make the mask. It'll be like a massage!' he smiled brightly at me.

'Okay,' I agreed, sliding into a chair.

As Iain applied the putty, he didn't stop cracking jokes.

'How does that feel?'

'Really soothing! My face is always so hot, and it's cooling it down nicely.'

'Told ya!' he said in his lovely Scottish lilt.

But despite those rare moments of light-hearted relief, just living was still a constant battle. Any time I walked through the hospital to one of my million appointments, strangers turned to gawp at me in absolute astonishment, their mouths dangling open. In a perverse way, it was like the old days when I made heads turn in the street, only now I attracted horror instead of admiration or envy. People in the burns unit were used to my injuries, but anywhere else, I would see the shock spreading like a Mexican wave. Men, women and children pointed and stared and whispered, and if I got into the lift, I could tell people were nervous around me; as though my deformity was contagious, and they felt they'd end up disfigured, too, if they so much as brushed against me.

I wasn't angry with them, though. I felt bad for them, because they had to look at me. I was too repugnant for words – a hideous person who was good for nothing. '*I probably put them off their dinner*,' I thought. I was so appallingly ugly.

If I ever caught my reflection in a window or mirror, my own jaw fell open too. '*Where did I go?*' I'd think. '*What is that thing that's taken my place?*'

Chapter Eleven
Healing

Like desire and happiness and confidence and pride, my appetite was also just a distant memory. I felt permanently nauseous, and any time I did try to eat, I still couldn't swallow properly.

My doctors decided to investigate. They booked me in for an endoscopy, where they inserted a tiny camera down my throat, then announced that I had more internal damage than they'd realised.

'You must've swallowed the acid when you were shouting for help,' they explained. 'There's a great deal of scar tissue around your oesophagus, so we'll have to do a series of operations to try to correct it.'

'This is never going to end, is it?' I sniffed. How could one cup of liquid have destroyed so much?

The next day, just over eight weeks after the attack, my mask was ready. Mum drove me to St George's while I slumped in the back seat, covering my face with my hands so no one could see me.

'What's it going to be like, Mum?' I kept asking. 'It'll be rubbery, right? Like a fancy dress mask or something?'

We made our way to Iain's consultation room, and sat down with him.

'It's all ready!' Iain smiled, lifting the mask and holding it up to my head. Made of see-through hard Perspex, it covered my face, with a hole for my eyes and deformed lips to poke through, while two thick, blue straps went round the back of my head to hold it tight against my skin.

As Iain adjusted them, it felt so constricting. Claustrophobic, like a hand pushing down on my face.

'It has to be tight, so it smoothes out the joins in the skin grafts. I know it's uncomfortable, but it'll really help make your skin more supple and less lumpy,' Iain explained gently. 'We'll make new ones every few months, as your face changes.'

I nodded, tears welling. Until that moment, I hadn't let myself think about the reality of wearing the mask. But I couldn't avoid it any more. That piece of plastic was proof of what a freak I'd become. It set me apart; it was a barrier that dehumanised me even more. I touched the plastic with quivering hands and fought to stem the tears. How could I live with this? On top of everything else?

Then, deep in my gut, fierce defiance rose up: '*You might not be beautiful any more*,' I told myself, '*but you're still alive. You're still here. You're not blind, and you're not dead. Don't let Danny win, Katie. You have to keep on fighting him*.'

There and then, I realised the mask was actually going to help me get rid of the face Danny had made for me. It was going to help undo his evil, and if that's what it took, then that's what I had to do. I was going to live with it, and I was going to embrace it. It was going to be my salvation, this rigid piece of plastic.

'I look like the Phantom of the flippin' Opera,' I quipped, flashing a weak smile, and I saw the relief in Mum and Iain's eyes.

At home, I resolutely ignored the sadness and messed around with Suzy to keep my spirits up. 'Somebody *stop* me!' I exclaimed like Jim Carrey in *The Mask*, feeding sweeties through the mouth-hole.

'You're bonkers!' Suzy rolled round on the floor in hysterics. It didn't matter if our laughter was slightly manic; it blazed so brightly it outshone my misery, for a little while at least.

Even though I'd made my peace with the mask, it was hard getting used to it, particularly as I had to sleep in it. The constant, unrelenting pressure gave me pounding headaches, and the claustrophobia I felt in it just compounded my nightmares: I dreamed it was Danny, pushing down on my face, and woke up in pools of sweat.

The next few weeks passed in a blur of hospital appointments. They were at least one reason to get out of bed in the morning, and Mr Jawad was so enthusiastic, he always made me feel better.

'You are healing so well, Katie,' he always said. 'Look at the difference already!' But my emotions were still up and down like a seesaw; okay one minute and in tears the next. I was ugly, I was useless; I was a pathetic waste of space.

Each day rolled into the next. The number of massages I needed gradually decreased. But even so, every afternoon Mum had to massage me in her bedroom as *Loose Women* chattered out of the old portable TV in the corner. Denise Welch and the other presenters became like my friends, a lifeline into the outside world when I was starved of human contact, and I looked forward to it every day. When Mum's back was turned, I'd grab her mobile and sneakily enter the daily competition, even though if I won the holiday to America, or whatever the prize was, I wouldn't have been able to make myself go, anyway.

My throat still wasn't better. The doctors kept dilating it to clear the scar tissue that had healed over my oesophagus, but within a matter of days it would close over again. The only things keeping me alive were high-calorie protein shakes I forced myself to sip. Clothes hung off my emaciated frame and my periods stopped. The hair on my head was thinning and I was growing downy hair on the tops of my arms. I looked like a little boy instead of a woman, and even my feet shrank a size.

Constantly weak and woozy, I barely had the energy to sit upright, and I knew I had to start eating properly if my skin was ever going to recover. It needed vitamins and nutrients to heal, but I was getting seriously malnourished. I weighed just seven stone. When I forced myself to look at my body in the bathroom mirror, it just made me despise myself more. Spindly legs and a concave stomach. Ribs jutting out so prominently, I could count them. Arms and legs like twigs. Boobs so shrivelled, I could see the silicone implants under the paper-thin skin. And that face ... But part of me was glad, too. I didn't want to look feminine, I didn't want to look sexy: I didn't want to be someone a man would want to rape. I never wore anything remotely fashionable, just kid-size tracksuits and high-necked tops to hide the scars on my neck and chest. It was as if I'd lost the right to wear nice things. I was so ugly, it was laughable to even make an effort.

My weight wasn't the only cause for concern, as I was having lots of problems with my nose, too. My nostrils were closing up as they healed, so the doctors kept stuffing them with tubes and pipes to keep them open. I was constantly dripping snot, only able to breathe through my mouth. It felt like I'd been punched in the face, and my voice became weird and nasally.

'Danny's hurt every single part of me,' I cried to Mum. 'From my balding head right down to my shrivelled feet. He's maimed me, inside and out.'

As for my vision, the specialist had started suggesting things like cornea transplants and donor eyes, but I didn't want to risk losing the sight I had left.

In the middle of June, two and a half months after the attack, I had to go in for surgery to have skin taken from behind my ear and inside my mouth and grafted onto my eyelids. I was terrified it would leave me blind or even more deformed, so when I arrived at the hospital to be told I was going on a general ward rather than the burns unit, I was appalled.

'But people will see me,' I said in a tiny voice. 'They'll all stare at me.'

And of course, I was right. The other patients gawped and gaped, and even the nurses did double-takes.

'Who did this to you?' one asked, and I wanted to tell her to get lost.

'My boyfriend got someone to throw acid on me,' I muttered.

'That's terrible!' She shook her head in disgust while I prayed she'd leave me alone. Half an hour later, when they told me the surgery had been postponed, I couldn't get out of there fast enough. I knew the nurse hadn't meant any harm, but I just wasn't ready to talk to strangers yet about what had happened. It was still too raw, like the weeping flesh on my wretched face.

But I couldn't get out of regular appointments with Lisa, the burns psychologist.

'I don't see the point in these sessions,' I told her one afternoon in June. 'What's happened has happened, and no amount of talking is going to undo it. I just want to block it out, and never think about any of it again.'

'You have severe post-traumatic stress disorder, Katie,' she said. 'You have to talk about it. I know you're in a constant state of fear, but you can learn to build a bridge between the logical part of your brain and the emotional part.'

She was right about that – I was still terrified of absolutely everything. Someone was going to murder me, I was sure of it. Every time I was forced to leave the house or hospital, I was on tenterhooks, waiting for the moment it would happen. The gun shot or the knife or the acid that would finish off what Danny had started.

I point-blank refused to take any kind of anti-depressants. After my nightmarish hallucinations on the morphine, I didn't want anything that could distort reality; I wanted to recover on my own.

To help me cope, I found myself writing letters and poems to Danny. Adam, the police liaison officer, had told us he and Stefan had both pleaded not guilty and the case was likely to go to trial, but I refused to believe it would come to that. How could they do something so wicked and not feel enough remorse to own up to it?

'*Why did you do this to me?*' I scribbled furiously into a notebook. '*I don't understand how on the day of the hotel room attack, you were kind to me and seemed to care about me. Then that evening, you found it so easy to harm me in such an awful way. I don't understand. I didn't deserve it. I will never understand what was going through your head with the acid. Don't you think I'd suffered enough being raped and attacked by you? Danny, you know I'm a good person. Even after what you did, I wouldn't have caused you any trouble. I guess you wanted to ruin my looks to ruin my life, but you already ruined it when you raped me. Why acid? It's so cruel, to melt my face and blind me. You once looked at me and told me I was beautiful and perfect, but you decided to take that away from me forever. Why? Why me? I seriously want to know why you pursued me – then totally destroyed me. Why? Katie.*'

I never posted it. Of course I wanted him to face up to his actions and their awful consequences, but I couldn't bring myself to have any contact with him. Even contacting my friends was hard enough. They were still in London, and their lives were going on as normal. Castings, photoshoots, parties, dates. When they phoned, I didn't know what to say to them, but I didn't envy them. The thought of living in London again terrified me, and I didn't know how they did it. Getting night buses home at 2 a.m., running to the late-night off licence for a bottle of wine, wandering around Soho in the dark ...

'*I'll never do any of that again*,' I thought. '*It's far too dangerous. If I ever have to go anywhere, I'm going to order flame-proof protective clothing off the internet. And I'll never go on a date again. Never ever*.'

But what man would ever want me now, anyway? And, even if that wasn't true, how could I have sex with someone when the memory of the rape was so vivid? How could I be naked in front of him? What if we started having sex and it triggered some kind of flashback? What if I freaked out and tried to kill him?

'*I'll never get married, never have kids*,' I thought. This was my life now – surviving was the best I could hope for. Not happiness or love or a family of my own. Those dreams had died with the old me.

As the days went by, I became more and more desperate to talk to other people in my position and find out more information about acid attacks. I decided to conquer my fear of the computer.

'*It can't hurt you, Katie,*' I told myself as I sat down at the desk and flicked the monitor on. I didn't go near Facebook or my email – there was no way I could handle that – but I did start looking up other acid attack victims on Google. The vast majority were from Indian or Muslim areas, where acid was used to punish women for things as trivial as turning down marriage proposals. As the heartbreaking images flashed up on the screen, each one worse than the last, I wanted to weep for those poor women. They weren't fortunate enough to have people like Mr Jawad to treat them, and in the space of a few months, I'd already healed more than they had in years.

'*I've actually been so lucky,*' I thought, rubbing the mask over my face.

I also logged on to a few support groups for acid attack victims, but they were all based in America, and there was so much bitterness on the message boards, it was like a graveyard of hopelessness and despair. I knew I would find no comfort or solace there.

Hospital and home, hospital and home … As my face healed, and the skin got tighter, I wasn't able to show any emotion in my face, so I had regular physio to help loosen it up. I was fighting a losing battle, though.

'Okay, Katie, raise your eyebrows and smile,' the physio said during one session. So I'd tried, but nothing had happened.

'Why aren't you doing it?' Mum asked, bewildered.

'I'm trying!' I barked in frustration. 'I just can't!'

But even if I couldn't register any happiness, I was full of joy when the police arrived a few days later and announced they'd established links between Danny and Stefan. They had grown up on the same Hammersmith estate, and phone records showed they'd been in contact before the attack.

'Thank God,' I exhaled. I'd been worried that Danny might get away with it if the police couldn't prove he'd engineered the whole thing. Both Danny and Stefan were still claiming their innocence, but I couldn't even contemplate going to trial. They'd change their pleas before it got to that, I was sure of it.

But my happiness was always fleeting, no matter how much I tried to stay upbeat; no matter how much I listened to self-help CDs about positive thinking, or reminded myself of how lucky I was to be alive. Some days, I felt like crying constantly, or I'd snap at Mum when she tried to get me out of bed.

'Just leave me alone,' I moaned one afternoon, when she tried to cajole me into going downstairs. 'You have no idea what I'm going through.'

'You can't spend your whole life in bed.'

'I said leave me alone!'

'You won't be like this forever. Remember what Mr Jawad says – you are going to heal. No one knows the end result,' she said.

'I'm a freak, and I'll always be a freak. Now go away!'

'Okay, if that's what you want,' Mum said finally, tears rolling down her cheeks as she left the room.

I knew I was being horrible, but sometimes I just couldn't control the rage I felt that this had happened to me. Mum never once blamed me for it. She was always there for me, as was Suzy, who left Post-it notes hidden around the house, telling me how much she loved me. Or Dad, who gently helped me upstairs for my massages. And, Paul would give me DVDs or find computer games that we used to play as kids to keep me entertained.

One evening, as Dad rubbed my hands, he talked about how I'd been born blue: the umbilical cord had wrapped around my neck, cutting off my oxygen supply.

'We were terrified of losing you, but you were fine. You didn't cry like other babies, you just looked around, like you were taking everything in. Did we ever tell you what the nurse said? She said you were an old soul, and I think she was right.' Dad paused, and cleared his throat before he continued. 'You'll get through this, I know you will.'

'I hope so, Dad,' I sighed.

Even if sometimes I couldn't see it, I continued to make progress. Every day, I managed to stand in the back garden on my own, to feel the wind on my skin and look at the sky over my head. And, by the end of June, I even agreed to go for a walk by the river in a nearby town.

Although I knew the mask would attract plenty of attention, it actually made me feel safer. It was like a shield, and it would protect my face if someone else tried to throw acid on me. 'I don't want to go out in our village, though,' I insisted. 'I might see people who know me; old mates from school or old boyfriends.'

I pulled on a hat to cover my face, and we drove to the river. I took a deep breath and got out of the car. There was no one about as we wandered along the bank, but the swirl of the water made me agitated and anxious.

'I think I'd like to go home now, Mum,' I told her.

'Okay, Kate. You've done brilliantly. I'm so proud of you, you know.'

A few days after this, Suzy took me to a local hairdresser to get my hair done. It was an absolute mess. Stress and a lack of nutrients had made it weak and in parts it had even fallen out. The trip to the salon was meant to cheer me up. It didn't.

'Oh, have you had an accident?' the hairdresser cooed, and I saw Suzy glare at her. I just made a noncommittal noise, but still she went on: 'Oh, your hair is in a terrible state! In fact, I've never seen hair in worse condition.'

I glanced at Suzy, who looked like she was ready to erupt.

'You have to be really careful with the bleach,' I told the stylist quickly, anxious to move the conversation on. 'You can't get any on my skin, okay?'

As she applied it, I focused on my breathing. It was only hair dye; it wouldn't do me any harm. But the whole experience was horrible, and the skin on my neck was so tight, I couldn't even bend over the sink properly. Afterwards, my hair still looked rubbish, and I felt even more despondent than before.

Not long after that, I agreed to go to a local aviary, but as soon as we arrived, I knew it was a mistake to have come. The attraction was packed, and there were crowds of people there. I kept my hat pulled down and my eyes on the ground, but I could still feel the stares.

'*Please don't look at me,*' I thought. Kids who'd never seen anything like me, blokes who would have asked for my number before, young girls who looked like I had: they all stared. It was the girls' reactions that hurt the most, strangely. Pretty little things with blonde hair and blue eyes and trendy clothes, they reminded me of what I had lost, and the grief was so sharp it took my breath away.

'*I was just like you once!*' I wanted to run up to them and shake them. '*I was like you until Danny and Stefan did this to me. I couldn't stop them and now I'm trapped inside this burned shell. But I want to be me again; I want to be like you.*' But I didn't say a thing. What was the point?

'Let's go and watch the birds of prey show,' Mum suggested brightly, and I shook my head.

'There're too many people over there. I want to leave, right now. Please, Mum, I just want to go home.'

Chapter Twelve
One Step at a Time

Hope and despair, optimism and rage. I couldn't seem to climb off this emotional rollercoaster.

At the end of June, I started going to church with my friend Sam's mum, Rita, who lived nearby. The murmur of prayers soothed me and helped me remember the peace I'd found that night in hospital, but it was never a feeling that endured beyond the church's walls. Like the day the police phoned to tell us Danny had been shown photos of my injuries during an interview, but had refused to look at them. He'd pushed them away, they said.

I burst into tears of pure, red-hot rage. How dare he? This was the face he'd created, and even he wouldn't look at it. Didn't he owe me that, at least?

'Has he changed his plea yet?' I sobbed.

'No, he's still pleading not guilty,' Warren, the detective, replied. I sat completely silent, a deep pain slicing through me. Then once the police had gone I went to my room to be alone. 'Katie?' Dad knocked on the door. 'Can I come in?'

'Okay,' I sniffed, and he came in and sat beside me on the bed.

'Why has this upset you so much, love?'

'I just can't handle the thought of him seeing me like that, Dad. I must have looked horrific in those photos, barely human. How did it make him feel? Was he repulsed by me? Or glad that he'd hurt me so much?'

'He can't hurt you again, that's the main thing. He'll get what he deserves, I promise.'

But would he? Danny had boasted about getting away with so much in the past that he might wriggle out of this, too, and then what? I'd have to emigrate, and even then he'd probably hunt me down. Never stopping, like a twisted Terminator bent on revenge. He had to get what he deserved. He just had to.

The next day, Marty came to visit. It was the first time he'd seen me, but for once, I didn't feel cripplingly self-conscious. Slipping into a pretty floral tea-dress, I didn't agonise about how ugly I must look. Marty had been there with me in Mocha after the acid attack. His voice had cut through the fog of pain, and I knew there was a bond between us now that nothing could sever.

'You probably can't remember, but I came with you to hospital,' he said, his voice low with sadness as we sat in the back garden. 'You were screaming for something to take the pain away, and it broke my heart.'

'Thank you for being there. Thank you for helping me,' I smiled, thinking about the old days when we'd race down to the Chinese takeaway below our flat and stock up on mountains of spring rolls and fried rice. We'd stuff our faces and giggle about people we fancied. It seemed like a million years ago, but I was sure our friendship would survive it all.

With him and Mum by my side, I felt strong enough to go for another walk by the river, then we wandered into the nearby church.

'Take a picture of us, Mum,' I giggled, thrilled to be just acting like a normal person.

As the days went by, I kept on pushing myself. Little things, like managing to stand under the shower and wash my hair. The trickling water still made me anxious, but I gritted my teeth and forced myself to endure it. I also ventured outside with Suzy, who drove Sam and me to Southampton so I could get a wig. My own hair was still a mess and I wanted something to cover it up.

'Pretend it's for you,' I hissed to Sam as we walked up and down the aisles.

So she picked out a blonde Britney Spears-type mane and we hurried back into the car before anyone could get a proper look at me.

One night soon after, I looked at my legs and decided enough was enough. 'Suzy, can you help me with this? I look like a gorilla. An anorexic gorilla!' I smiled, pulling up my tracksuit bottoms to show her.

'Eek! No problem,' she exclaimed, following me into the bathroom.

'I don't think I can handle shaving,' I said with a shudder, remembering how Danny had threatened to slice my face with a razor blade. There was no way I was going near a razor.

'How about wax then?'

'But that could burn me!' I squeaked.

'We could use some hair-removal cream. I'm sure I've got a sachet somewhere.'

'Wouldn't that burn me, too?'

'We won't keep it on for long, and if it starts to sting, we can wash it straight off,' Suzy reasoned.

I reminded myself of what Lisa always said: I had to use my logical brain instead of my emotional one. 'Okay then, let's do it,' I nodded.

As Suzy slathered my legs in the white goo, I wrestled with the panic. '*Stay calm. Deep breaths. Just relax.*'

'Right, five minutes are up!' Suzy said, turning on the shower head and washing it all away with a flannel. 'See? Perfect, hair-free pins!' she grinned, and I mentally patted myself on the back. I'd done it!

'Thanks, sis,' I smiled, rubbing my legs dry with a towel. It was amazing – something as trivial as depilating my legs had become a minefield fraught with danger, but I'd got through it.

The experience seemed to release something inside me, as I started painting my toenails and fingernails religiously, too. They were one of the few parts of my body that had survived the attack unscathed, and I spent hours buffing and filing them, and carefully applying pretty shades of bubblegum pink, coral and pearl. It was one little way of reclaiming my body, of resurrecting the old Katie, and it made me feel a little bit less ugly.

One night, however, as I painted my pinkie nail, I caught a glimpse of something in the little vanity mirror of my manicure box, and gasped. It had puckered skin and dead eyes. Tufts of hair and a horrid, misshapen nose. A grisly mask, like the face of a character from a Hammer Horror movie.

'*What is that thing?*' I thought in alarm, swivelling round to see if there was something behind me. Then I remembered. That was me, and no amount of nail varnish was going to make it any less shocking. '*But you're getting better all the time,*' I reminded myself before the tears came, like they always did. '*Mr Jawad always says that!*'

I decided there and then to keep a photo diary charting my recovery. Mum could take my photo every week, and then I could look back and see how far I'd come, how much progress I'd made. Racing to the computer, I created a file called 'My Pictorial Journey to Recovery', and put some pictures Mum and the doctors had taken in hospital in there.

As I flicked through them, my belly lurched, but I couldn't look away. It was grisly and gripping in equal measures.

'*How the hell did I survive this?*' I thought, staring at an image of my bloated, disfigured face covered in skin from corpses. '*Thank you, God. Thank you, Mr Jawad.*'

But it was still one step forward, and ten steps back. The nightmares came without fail, I still couldn't eat, and I was still in and out of hospital constantly to have my throat and nostrils dilated, my eyes tested, my mask adjusted, and for physiotherapy sessions and appointments with Lisa. Sometimes the pain in my nose and throat and eyes was so great, I wondered how my malnourished body kept going. Was it going to give up under the strain? Would my heart just stop beating one day, when it had had enough? After everything, would I slip away on the operating table, unable to take any more?

Three months after the attack, I had an important visitor. Pam Warren was a lady who'd suffered severe burns in the Paddington rail disaster of 2000, which had left thirty-three people dead and more than 400 injured. Engulfed in a fireball, she'd suffered full-thickness burns to her face, hands and legs. After twenty-two skin grafts she had had to wear a mask like mine for eighteen months. Paul had contacted her by email, and now she was coming to see me with a friend.

Even though I knew Pam would understand what it felt like to be a burns victim, I was still so ashamed of my face. As we waited for her to arrive, anxiety lanced through me. What if she recoiled just like everyone else? I paced up and down in the lounge, jumping when the doorbell chimed. I still couldn't open the door myself – it was one of the phobias I couldn't seem to conquer – so Mum did it, and ushered the two women into the lounge.

'Hello,' I smiled shyly, looking from one to the other. Which one was Pam? They were both scar-free, and I couldn't tell.

'Hi, Katie, I'm Pam. It's lovely to meet you,' the brunette smiled, extending her hand. I couldn't believe it – she looked completely normal. Better than that, she actually looked *attractive*. Gobsmacked, I listened as Pam described her injuries and showed me photos taken in hospital just after the train crash. Her burns had been absolutely horrific, and I looked from the photos to her face in rapt astonishment.

'You've healed so well,' I stammered.

'Yes, but I never thought I'd look like this again.' Pam returned my gaze steadily. 'I plummeted to the depths of despair, but the hospital team who worked on me were amazing, and the mask really helped, too. I know what you're going through, but I'm living proof that this does get better.' She smiled encouragingly at me.

Pam explained that she still had bad days, but she'd managed to regain a normal life. She had a successful business and had moved on from the tragedy. I didn't want to be rude, but there was one thing I was dying to know. 'I hope you don't mind me asking, but do you have a boyfriend?' I said.

'Yes,' Pam nodded. 'And he thinks I'm beautiful.'

'You are.'

Pam told me to get in touch if I ever needed to talk, and they left. After they had gone, I sank back onto the sofa in a contented bubble. Pam had suffered appalling injuries, and she'd got better. Like she said, she was living proof that there was light at the end of the tunnel, hope at the end of the nightmare. Any time I felt low – and God, there was no shortage of those moments – I just had to think of Pam. I never believed I'd look as normal or pretty as her, or thought any man would want me. But maybe one day, in years to come, my scars would fade, leaving something less shocking in its place. Maybe, just maybe, I could have something like a normal life, too.

A few days after Pam's visit, I had another boost. My eye specialist revealed that although my left eye was useless, the right was finally in the clear. The constant drops and ointment I'd been applying had done their job, and it had almost perfect vision.

'So there's no danger of it deteriorating? I won't go totally blind?' I asked.

'No. You'll have to keep using drops to keep both your eyes lubricated, and we'll keep monitoring you for things like the ingrown eyelashes, but it should be fine,' he replied, and I squealed in happiness. I wasn't going to go blind – my biggest fear had been assuaged, and it seemed like yet another miracle.

A week later, Mum offered to take me for a consultation at Charles Fox, a beauty salon that specialised in camouflage and theatre make-up. Remembering the disastrous visit with the other make-up lady, I almost backed out, but I was desperate for something to improve my appearance. The skin on my face was now contracting so much that my eyes and mouth looked droopy, as though I'd had a stroke, and even though the mask was helping, the skin was still severely scarred.

We drove to their Covent Garden salon, and I sprinted inside before any of the shoppers or tourists could see me. A friendly make-up artist called Paul led us into a private room at the back, and he set to work with heavy-duty foundation and thick powder.

'My boyfriend did this,' I offered, sensing he was wondering what on Earth had happened to me. 'He got someone to throw acid on me.'

'They should bring back the death penalty,' he exclaimed. I said nothing, hoping that was the end of it. I knew he meant well. 'Don't worry, we'll make you look fab,' he went on, but I doubted it. Paul had probably never had to work with a canvas like this before.

An hour later, he was finished. He swivelled my chair round, and I looked into the mirror. My face was covered in a half-inch-thick layer of lumpy powder, and the eye make-up and lipstick just looked so strange on my wasted features. I knew he'd done his very best – but the old saying about not being able to make silk purses out of sows' ears came to mind.

'You look like Kylie!' Mum piped up when we got back in the car, but I just rolled my eyes scornfully.

'If only! I look more like a tranny,' I said, sliding down in the seat so no one could see me. It wasn't quite the transformation I was hoping for. But inside, I heard Mr. Jawad's voice urging me on. Just the fact I'd gone there in the first place was something to be proud of.

Going anywhere other than to church or the hospital still terrified me, something that was really highlighted for me one day – three or four months after the attack – outside Chelsea and Westminster Hospital.

I was standing outside the hospital getting some fresh air when a young guy in a hoody started hurrying towards me. I completely freaked out. '*Oh God, this is it*,' I thought, beads of sweat trickling down my forehead, my heart suddenly going at five times its normal speed. '*He must be another one of Danny's friends! He's going to murder me!*'

I turned on my heels and raced into the hospital, suffocating with panic, before I realised he was just a normal guy running for the bus. I knew it was irrational, I knew it didn't make any sense, but I just couldn't control the fear. It lay just beneath the surface of my consciousness, erupting to control me whenever it liked. It dictated every single thing I did: I was its puppet, just like I'd been Danny's.

But, as ever, help wasn't too far away. A constant support, Mr Jawad never stopped investigating new treatments that could help me. He was always researching, always trying to do more and more. During one of my consultations in August, he told me about a specialist rehabilitation clinic in the French village of Lamalou-les-Bains, near Montpellier.

'It's called Centre Ster, and they use cutting-edge rehabilitation methods that aren't available in the UK,' he explained. 'It would be so beneficial for you to go, Katie. Do you think you could handle the travelling?'

'*No!*' a voice screamed in my head – after all, I could barely even manage getting to the hospital. But then I thought about it. Mr Jawad seemed to think it would make a real difference. I didn't want him to be disappointed in me, and if he said this was important, then I had to put my faith in him.

'Yes, I can do it,' I smiled, and he beamed back at me.

'Good girl. Now, it is a specialist treatment, so we will need to apply for funding through your local Primary Care Trust. You'll also have to go there for an initial consultation, so they can assess you. Leave it with me, and I'll sort it all out.'

'Thank you, Mr Jawad,' I said, for the millionth time. No matter how often I said it, I could never thank him enough; this big teddy bear of a man, who'd worked for free in Pakistan to help victims of acid attacks. Who'd made it his mission to rebuild me, no matter what it took. I'd never really had a hero before this nightmare started, but now I had him.

I also had the police, who were toiling behind the scenes and fighting for justice. Adam and Warren came to see me a few days later, and we all sat down in the lounge.

'Is there any news?' I asked nervously.

'Stefan has pleaded guilty to grievous bodily harm. Danny has pleaded guilty to actual bodily harm for attacking you in the hotel room, but he's still claiming he's innocent of GBH and rape. If he's convicted of both, he could get a life sentence. But you have to prepare yourself for this going to court, Katie,' Warren said. 'I know you were hoping he'd own up to it, but it's not looking likely.'

'Okay,' I said, taking a deep breath to calm myself. 'But you have all my video testimony, right? I won't have to testify, will I?'

Adam and Warren exchanged glances, and the blood turned to ice in my veins.

'Your video evidence will be shown to the jury, but you will have to take the stand for questioning, too.'

'No! No way! I can't be in the same room as them,' I said, defiantly. 'What if he tries to attack me? I just can't. Please don't make me!' Terror swirled as I imagined having to see Danny again. Those black eyes, that cruel smirk, those meaty hands that had overpowered me. And he would see me, too: the ruined, ravaged face that was his evil handiwork.

'No!' I repeated, 'I can't.'

'They'll put a screen around the witness box so you can't see him and he can't see you,' Adam said soothingly.

'But he could jump over that and get me!'

'He won't be able to, I swear, Katie. You have to do this. Otherwise, they could both get away with it.'

'Maybe he'll change his mind and confess! He might plead guilty at the last minute, too, and we won't have to go to trial?' I looked at them with desperation shining in my eyes.

'There is a chance that'll happen, but you have to prepare yourself that it might not. You need to realise, too, that it will be reported in the press. You'll be granted anonymity so you won't be named, but Danny and Stefan will be.'

My head reeling, I tried to take it all in. I could hope and pray until kingdom come, but it wouldn't do any good. If justice was to be done, I would have to go to court. I would have to see him, the animal who'd done this to me.

I didn't have a clue how I'd get through it, but I was going to try my hardest.

Chapter Thirteen
Preparing for Battle

The prospect of the court case plagued me. The date had been set for 22 September, but I pushed it to the back of my mind. '*Danny will change his plea in the next few weeks,*' I kept telling myself. '*He has to. He can't make me go through that, too. Even he can't be that wicked.*' Any time the fear or bitterness rose up like a tidal wave, I started scribbling. It was only way I could vent my anger and, as I typed a poem to Stefan in response to some newpaper reports about him, I felt a tiny little bit of release:

So you've said it, admitted it was you,
You stupid fool; we knew it could only be you,
That day you ran away in the street, leaving me in a burned heap,
Now it's your turn to suffer at the mercy of God

My impending visit to the clinic in France for an assessment weighed on my mind, too, triggering yet more panic. Like dominos falling, it was one worry after another. How would I cope in the airport? How could I get on a plane? What if the plane crashed? French women were all so chic and glamorous – what would they think of me? But I couldn't let Mr Jawad down, and I couldn't let myself down, either.

On 23 August 2008, I packed my suitcase. I'd recently started making more of an effort with my appearance, and I carefully folded the pretty dresses and smart tops that had replaced the sloppy tracksuits I'd lived in for so long.

'*I just need to pretend I feel fabulous on the inside*,' I thought, throwing in some high-heeled shoes. '*Maybe I can trick my brain into believing it*.'

The next morning, Mum and I headed off to Gatwick Airport, where we'd arranged to meet Mr Jawad before the three of us flew to Montpellier.

'Have we got everything? Passport, tickets, medication?' Mum asked for the hundredth time as we headed for the motorway in a taxi.

'Yes, Mum,' I tutted, ignoring the tight ball of anxiety in my stomach.

I was beginning to feel so bad for Mum and Dad. Looking after me was impacting their lives in so many ways. It was like I was a child again. Dad wasn't working as often as he used to, to care for me, and as he was self-employed I worried about him losing money. Mum also had to take compassionate leave from work. I hated putting them through so much worry, too. I'd become emotionally reliant on them, clinging to them for comfort. But even so, they never did anything but shower me with love and affection.

When we arrived, I tried to steel myself for the crowds, the stares, the whispers. We got out of the taxi and made our way to check-in, but instead of keeping my head down like I normally did, I held it up high.

'*Sod it, I don't care what people think,*' I told myself. But, of course, I did. Every single horrified look was like a knife-wound to my heart, and it cut me to the quick. I wanted to run away, lock myself in the Ladies and demand that Mum take my straight home. But what good would that do? I had to be brave.

'*Maybe those blokes are staring because they fancy me,*' I thought when I clocked a gang of guys who looked like they were going on a stag do. It was daft, and I knew there was no way it was true, but it gave me the strength to keep walking to the check-in desk, where Mr Jawad was waiting.

'Katie and Diane, hello!' he boomed. As always, his happiness was contagious, but when we boarded the flight, I started shaking with panic. There could be something wrong with the engine; we might explode on the runway. Or a terrorist might be on board with a bomb hidden in his hand luggage. I had to read the safety instructions straight away. Where the hell were they? As if my life depended on it, I studied the laminated card detailing the emergency exits, and where the life jackets and oxygen masks were stored.

'Are you okay?' Mum squeezed my hand, and I tried to smile.

I couldn't relax for a second of the two-hour flight, and when we touched down I didn't feel much better. Just like back home, then people stared as we waited by the luggage carousel and went to catch a bus outside the terminal, but I wasn't surprised. A freak was a freak in any country, right?

As we drove through the picturesque countryside towards Lamalou, Mr Jawad kept up a running commentary: 'The entire village is built around the clinic.' Mr Jawad turned around in his seat and explained. 'Everyone who lives here is either a patient or a staff member, so it's perfectly safe.'

'So there are no criminals or dodgy people or anything?' I asked.

'None.'

That night, we stayed in a little hotel and went to bed early, and the next morning we headed to the clinic. Nestled on a mountain overlooking lakes and vineyards and rolling hills, it was a world away from grey, rain-soaked England.

'Welcome!' a lady said when we had arrived, and she whisked us off to show us round the state-of-the-art facilities. Everywhere I looked, there were people with burns or scars, patients in wheelchairs or on crutches. It was like being in the burns unit in Chelsea and Westminster – I'd be accepted here, surrounded by people who understood.

Meeting Dr Frasson, who ran the clinic, was also reassuring. He examined my injuries and talked about the treatments they offered, like intense massage and hydrotherapy.

'We can definitely help you, Katie,' he said. 'It would probably entail four or five visits, at a few weeks each.'

'That's great,' I said, and I meant it too.

'I'll try to get the funding organised, then,' Mr Jawad grinned. 'It might take a few months, but don't lose heart.'

We flew home that evening, as the next day I was due for another appointment in hospital for another round of operations on my nose and throat. Still struggling to swallow, I had shrunk to just over six stone, and now my doctors were starting to get seriously worried.

'You are severely malnourished, Katie, and it's putting a real strain on your organs,' one of them said. 'We need to get some food inside you, so we're going to insert a feeding tube up your nose and down your throat.'

It sounded simple enough, but manoeuvring the wires up my damaged nostrils was no mean feat. 'Swallow them down,' the nurse urged, and I started choking.

'I'm trying,' I gasped, fighting the manic urge to laugh. It was just another surreal day in the life of the new Katie Piper.

After an overnight stay in hospital, the next day, and feeling stronger than I had in ages, I shuffled down to the eye clinic with Mum for a check-up. The specialist examined me, and then said my blind eye had improved.

'I'm not sure how, but it has regained some vision,' he said, and Mum and I started crying.

'That's brilliant. I can't believe it!' I whispered, over and over. 'Thank you, thank you, *thank you*!'

I couldn't see clearly, just different light and dark shapes, but the improvement gave me so much hope. I was so happy with the news that I managed to spend that night in hospital on my own. Every single other time, Mum or Dad had been in a room nearby, so that all I had had to do was pick up the phone and they had come running.

'I'll be fine on my own,' I told Mum, who had an appointment with her boss the next morning. 'Honestly, you don't need to get someone else to come and stay with me, Mum.'

'Are you sure? I feel really bad leaving you here.'

'I'm positive. I'll be okay.' And I was. The nightmares still came, of course, but I got through it. It was another little victory, and I was so proud of myself.

But there was another setback just around the corner. My throat was starting to close over again and the nasal feeding tube stopped working. The only option left was to insert a feeding tube, called a PEG, directly into my stomach.

'But it'll be really visible,' I cried. 'I'll look like even more of a freak.'

'We have no choice,' the doctor said. 'You can't afford to lose any more weight.'

On 5 September, five months after the attack, they cut through the wasted muscle on my belly and inserted the tube. After the anaesthetic wore off, I was in agony, and every tiny movement sent ripples of pain through my whole body. I couldn't sit up or cough or go to the loo without crying out with pain. That was bad, but the fact that yet another part of me had been damaged was even worse. My belly had been one of the few scar-free bits of my body I had, and now its smooth skin was violated, too. I looked at the tube sticking out of me with hatred.

'When you're stronger, we'll teach you how to syringe food and water into the valve,' the nurse said. 'But for now, we'll keep it attached to this drip.'

'Whatever,' I groaned.

The pain was enormous, and I writhed around my bed, crying and whimpering. 'It's terrible, Mum,' I gasped as she mopped my sweaty brow. I wanted to rip the bloody thing out, but even in the depths of agony, I knew it was a necessary evil. Without it, I would die.

Five days after it was put in, I was strong enough to go home, but the PEG took some getting used to. Whenever I dreamed of Danny at night, I sometimes jumped out of bed in a panic, forgetting I was hooked up to a drip. The PEG would tug hard on my belly, and I would yelp in pain. Sometimes, too, when I went to the loo, the tube would fall down the toilet. I'd pee on it by mistake, and then have to pluck it out again.

But no matter how much I hated it, the PEG was helping. With each passing day, I was less weak, woozy and listless. My energy was returning, and it was just in the nick of time. The trial date was looming, and Danny still hadn't admitted to his guilt. I had to accept it was going to court, and I'd need every single ounce of strength to survive it.

The nearer the court date got, the more my panic welled. I longed to pull out; I wanted to pretend nothing had happened and just get on with my life. How could I be in the same room as him again? How could I sit just metres away from him? My body was still so fragile, and I was worried what the trauma would do to me.

'I don't want to do it,' I whispered to Mum. 'I don't think I can.'

'You can,' she said. 'This is so important. He can't get away with it, Kate.' I knew that, but it didn't quench the terror.

A week before the trial was due to start, the police said I could go and visit the court. It was supposed to put me at ease – as if anything could do that when Danny was going to be nearby – so Dad and Suzy took me to Wood Green Crown Court in north London.

As soon as we walked into the small, wood-panelled room, I froze. It was just like a set from some crime drama on TV, except that this was real life. In a matter of days, it would be packed with members of the public and the jurors, the judge, the legal teams. Me and Danny.

'You won't necessarily be in this room, but it'll give you an idea of the layout,' the man from the witness protection unit said. 'This is where you'll sit to give evidence.' He pointed to the stand. 'And that's the dock, where the defendant will sit beside his barrister.'

'But they're so close! And there's only a tiny rail to keep him in. Dad, I can't be that near to him!'

'Don't worry,' the WPU man went on. 'You'll be behind this, and only the judge and jury will be able to see you.' He grabbed a blue screen and ducked behind it. 'You can hear me, but you can't see me.' He popped his head around the side. 'Now you can see me again!'

I glanced at Suzy, who had started giggling to herself. Did this guy think that I was brain damaged? I was scarred, not stupid. I understood the principle of sitting behind a screen, but it simply wasn't enough. How could that protect me from Danny if he decided to attack? Maybe he could get a knife in prison. Maybe he could fashion some kind of weapon? All it would take would be one leap and I'd be in his clutches again.

'Can't they use a courtroom that has one of those bullet-proof glass boxes, Dad?' I asked. That would make me feel a whole lot better. Not safe exactly, but a little bit less vulnerable.

'We'll speak to Adam and Warren about it,' Dad promised.

Back at home, my trepidation mounted all the more. I shuffled restlessly about the house, and the trial was all I could think about. As far as I was concerned, my face was undeniable proof of the acid attack, but who knew what lies Danny had conjured up? He'd certainly told me plenty of them. He was a fantasist, a twisted maniac who'd deceived me at every turn. And the rape … Oh gosh, the rape. I hadn't reported it in time so there was no DNA evidence, and cases like that were notoriously difficult to prove. Would his defence go for the jugular, and make out that I was some silly idiot who somehow 'deserved' it? Would they parade my modelling past as proof that I supposedly had loose morals? Would they call me a liar? I'd have to explain every disgusting thing he did to me in that hotel room, then have it dissected and debated. I'd have to sit there as the jury looked at my mangled, mutilated face, and through it all, I'd know Danny was just metres away.

Unsurprisingly, Mum and Dad were at their wits' end, too. Tension hung in the air at home, and all our tempers were frayed with the stress of it all.

'No, I don't want to go out for a walk,' I screamed to Mum one afternoon. 'I don't want anyone to see me like this! I can't sleep because every time I close my eyes, I see Danny's face. I'm being fed through a tube in my stomach, I look terrible, and now I have to stand up in a courtroom and be called a liar.' After all I'd endured, after everything I'd been through, how could I do this, too? It wasn't right, it wasn't fair. I was going to be tortured and tormented all over again – this time in a court of law.

There was still one thing I had to do for the trial: write an impact statement for the judge, explaining how the attacks had affected me.

Late one night, I sat at the computer. I took a deep breath, flexed my fingers and I let it all come out.

'*I have lost my future, my career, my spirit, my body, my looks, my dignity – the list goes on,*' I typed furiously. '*All I am left with is an empty shell. A part of me has died and that will never return. This is worse than death. Being beaten, raped and mutilated by acid has left me like a living corpse.'*

I typed and typed, all the pain and anger flowing from my fingers onto the keyboard.

'*My life has changed. The defendants' lives have not. I am only twenty-four years old, and my youth has been destroyed. The acid mutilated me and maimed me, condemning me to lifelong isolation and emotional anguish. Such a vengeful act sentenced me to a plight worse than death. My scars are permanent, both physically and emotionally. The acts of the defendants have destroyed my life. I cannot forgive these acts, and any consolation, advice or help given to me will never be enough to get over this or compensate for it. Even if I smile occasionally on the outside, I am dying inside.*'

Finally, 22 September arrived. The Crown Prosecution Service said I wouldn't be needed for the trial for the first few days, but I had to be in London to wait for their phone call just in case.

Before we left, Paul handed me an envelope with a letter and a little angel carved from wood inside. 'I thought you might like this,' he said. I started to read.

> '*Keep this guardian angel in your pocket in court, and give it a squeeze whenever you want to feel like she's watching over you. Although we can't be there with you, we're all*

thinking of you every minute of the day and sending our love and strength. Hopefully this angel will pass it on, and you'll feel it through her.'

It was such a sweet thought. Mum wouldn't be able to sit in the gallery as she was giving evidence, too. And, I didn't want Dad or Paul there as I went into intimate details about the rape. It was too embarrassing.

'Thank you so much, Paul,' I said, clutching the angel in my hand.

The CPS had arranged for us all to stay in a Hilton Hotel in Watford, but as soon as I walked into our room, I burst into tears. Even though it was a different chain, it looked so similar to that one I'd been raped in. It had the same poky en suite bathroom, same nondescript decor, same desk and chair, same metal-armed hinge on the back of the door, like the one Danny had slung my belt over to make a noose …

'Shush, love, don't cry,' Dad said, slipping his arm around my shoulders.

'It's just that it reminds me of that night,' I whimpered, clinging to him until my tears dried.

Too anxious to eat much, that evening we picked at the food we ordered to our room and looked at the TV with unseeing eyes. The trial consumed my every thought.

The next day, we just killed time and waited for the phone to ring. Mum convinced me to take a walk around the shops in

Watford, but I was so distracted, as all I could think about was what must be unfolding in the courtroom.

That afternoon, Adam rang. I was needed in court the next day, they said. The court would see my video evidence, and then the prosecution and defence would question me.

It felt like I'd just been condemned to death.

'We should try to get some rest,' Mum sighed. I curled up beside her in one bed and Dad took the other, but it was a long time before sleep came to me. I lay there, listening to the sound of their gentle breathing, thinking about what I had to do.

'*Please, God, please help me*,' I prayed. '*I don't know if I'm strong enough to do this. You must be sick of me asking you for stuff by now, but I can't do this on my own. Please, give me the strength to cope*.' Eventually I drifted into a fitful sleep.

The second Dad's alarm sounded, I jumped out of bed. This was it. On autopilot, I washed and slipped into a smart beige top and tailored grey trousers. I was so skinny I had to fasten the waistband with a safety pin. I slipped a pink hair band over my head and looked at myself in the mirror.

It was six months since the attack, and even though I had improved, I was still severely disfigured. My lips were so swollen they looked like the worse case of trout pout in the world. My eyelids still sagged and my skin was still puckered and scarred. My nose was deformed, just like my left ear, and my eyes looked deeply haunted and afraid.

Trembling, I didn't say a word as we walked to the car, and we drove in silence to the court. As I opened the door and climbed out, I frantically looked around for another of Danny's friends armed with a cup of acid. Danny knew I was going to be here, and wouldn't that be the perfect revenge? There was no one there, and I scurried into the building where Danny was waiting.

Chapter Fourteen
Standing Alone

A clerk shepherded us into a little side room, and explained he would take me into the courtroom while it was empty. I'd take the stand, the blue screen would be put in place, and then everyone else would be brought in.

'Do you understand? Are you ready?' he asked, and I nodded. My mouth was so dry, I couldn't even speak. My palms were slick with sweat, my limbs felt like jelly, and my heart was beating so fast I thought I might pass out.

'Good luck, Katie.' Mum forced a smile.

'Just tell the truth, that's all you have to do,' Dad added.

Again I just nodded, then the clerk ushered me through a door and into the wooden-panelled courtroom. I sat down, and he hauled the screen around me. I could barely see over the rail, and he gave me cushions to sit on, then placed a bucket at my feet in case I felt sick. All I could hear was the thud of my heart. Any second now, Danny would be here. '*Danny is coming! I don't want to die. Please, don't let him attack me again.*'

'Calm down, Katie,' I told myself, as nausea washed over me.

I thought I might vomit or soil myself like I had in hospital. '*Logical brain, I need to listen to my logical brain.*' The police had agreed to put Danny in one of those glass boxes; he couldn't get me. He'd be locked inside.

As the seconds ticked by, I fought to regain control. I was so close to freaking out, a heartbeat away from running away. Then I heard the door open, and saw the jury shuffle in. I saw their shock and pity as they looked at me, and I desperately wanted to hide my face. I tried to guess which ones might be on my side. The middle-aged woman? Surely she would believe me. But what about the men? Would they take Danny's side? Maybe they had grudges against the police. Maybe someone they knew had been wrongly accused of rape, and they mistrusted all women.

I didn't know these twelve strangers at all, and they didn't know me, but my future was in their hands.

By now the judge had entered, and the court settled down. When he ordered someone to 'bring up the defendant', I wanted to scream with terror. My vision swam and the world seemed to tilt on its axis as I heard his footsteps crossing the courtroom.

'*Danny's here*,' I thought, gripping the guardian angel Paul had given me. '*He's here.*'

I shook violently, waiting for him to break free and rip the screen away. What would I do if he did that? I'd have to chuck my drip away, jump out of the stand and try to get to the door.

I heard the door of the glass box open and close. Danny was inside, and I whimpered in relief. '*Thank you, God.*'

The judge turned to me: 'We're going to watch the first part of your video evidence. If you need to take a break, just say so.'

Despite the screen, I had a clear view of the TV, and I gasped as the tape started to roll. It had been recorded only a week or so after the attack, and I was wrapped in bandages, wearing a nappy. It was me at my most vulnerable, my most pathetic. The jurors watched the tape in horror, and I noticed some of them were crying.

Then my voice came through the speakers, only it didn't sound like my voice at all. It was raspy and gravelly.

'*Is that thing really me?*' I thought, listening as that strange voice described meeting Danny. How he had pursued me on Facebook, how we'd gone to the Comedy Club on our first date and how things had progressed from there.

Then they played the second part of my video evidence. I couldn't tear my eyes away from my ravaged face. It was red raw, my hair was shaved, and my eyes were so *dead*.

'*I don't recognise that person*,' I thought, as my voice started recounting the disgusting details of the rape. As I sobbed on screen, tears rolled down my face in real life, too. They collected in the bottom of my mask, a little salty pool at my chin which stung a little, but which I couldn't get to wipe away.

This time, I couldn't look at the jurors. It was so humiliating, those strangers hearing what he'd done to me. I was stripped completely bare, without a single shred of dignity.

Next, it was the video of me describing the acid attack and, if anything, I looked even worse than before. The skin on my face was weeping and wet and I squeezed my eyes closed as my sobs rang out: 'They have destroyed my life.'

I don't know how I got through those hours.

Back at the hotel, I couldn't even talk to Mum and Dad about it. I had to keep my pain locked up tight. They tried to take my mind off it, with silly games like charades and pretending we were on *Big Brother*, but it was useless.

'Who would you evict from the *Big Brother* house, Kate?' Mum asked.

'Danny's defence lawyer.' I smiled weakly.

As bad as it had been watching my video evidence, I knew the questioning was going to be a hundred times worse. And it was.

Back in the stand the next day, knowing Danny was so close, I flinched at his lawyer's questions. They came at me like machine-gun fire, and I cried with frustration and bewilderment. He tried to make out I was the controlling one, whose obsessive behaviour had tipped Danny over the edge. Utter rubbish! Didn't the hundreds of texts and emails he'd sent me prove otherwise? The lawyer alleged I was a typical model, thoughtless and demanding, always late for our dates. He quoted emails I'd written Danny in the first flush of our romance, where I'd said I missed him and couldn't wait to see him again. That was true, but back then I had had no idea what Danny was capable of: his carefully constructed facade hadn't started to crumble yet. The lawyer also claimed there was a sex

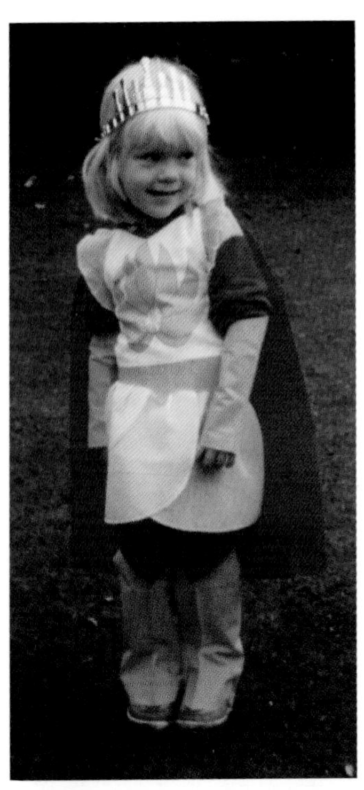

Left: Me, as She-Ra 'Princess of Power', aged three.

Above: I adored my older brother Paul and wanted to be just like him, hence my scout's uniform.

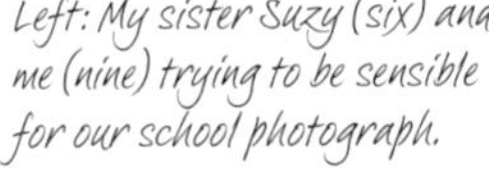

Left: My sister Suzy (six) and me (nine) trying to be sensible for our school photograph.

Right: My beloved Barclay and me, Christmas 2007.

Above: Yee-hah! Messing around on a photo shoot for a lads' mag.

Right: Back when I was a wannabe presenter on Fame TV.

Below: Taken in my flat in Golders Green, after eating too many blue M&Ms!

Below: Out in London's West End, with (L-R) flatmate Sofia and my friends from the Jewellery Channel, Nathan and Lisa.

POLICE APPEAL FOR ASSISTANCE

SERIOUS ASSAULT

On the **31st March 2008** at about **5pm** in **Golders Green Road** a **serious assault** occurred during which a 24 year old female received injuries when a **corrosive substance was thrown in her face**.

Did you see anything?
Did you hear anything?
Can you help?

Anyone with any information is asked to contact Barnet Police on:

or if you wish to remain **ANONYMOUS** phone Crimestoppers on:

0800 555 111

METROPOLITAN POLICE

Working together for a safer London

CRIMESTOPPERS 0800 555 111

Above: Getting ready for Cage Rage, where I met Danny.

Left: This is the appeal poster police put up after the attack. I was still unable to talk then.

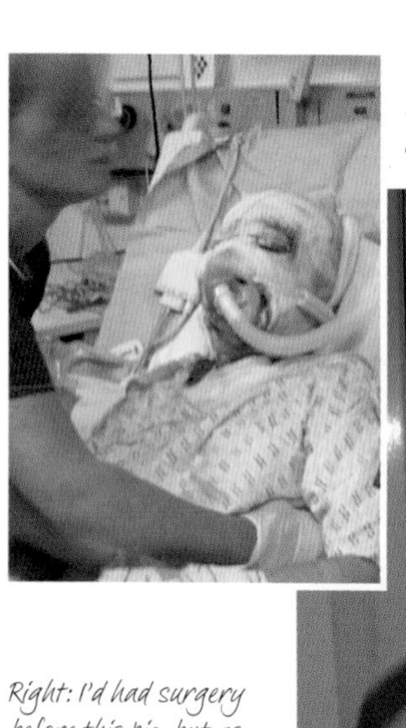

Left: I was still in a coma here, unaware of what had happened to me.

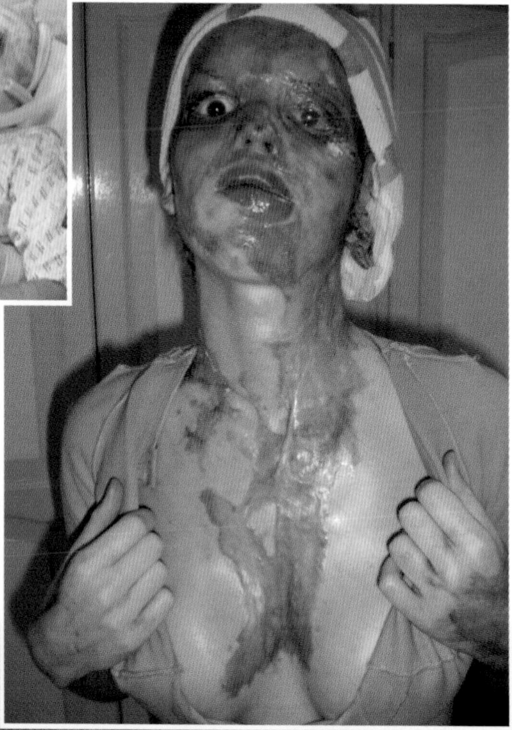

Right: I'd had surgery before this pic, but as you can see the damage was still bad.

Below: I couldn't bear Mum taking my photo any more.

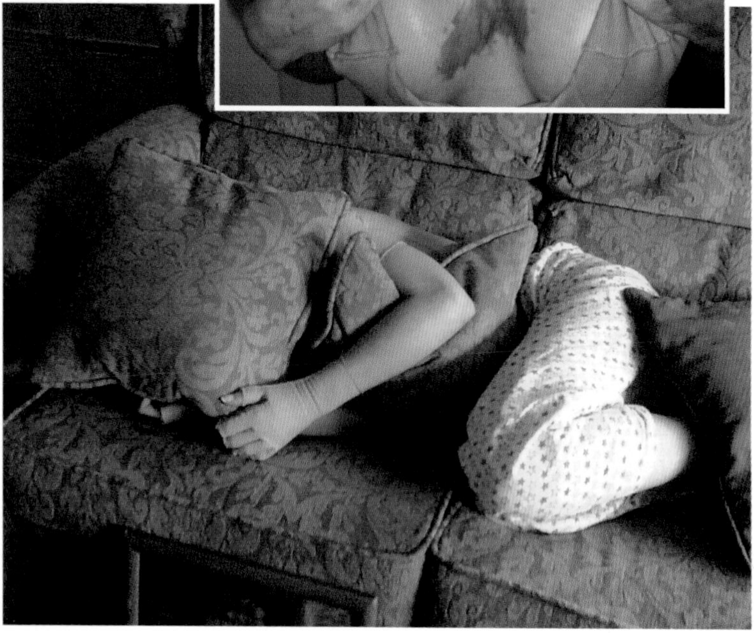

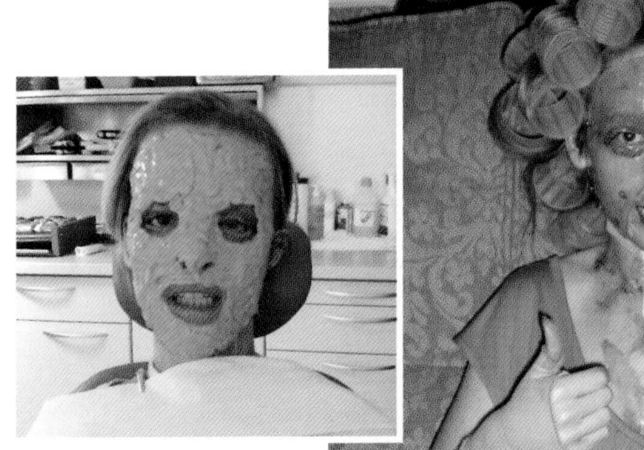

Above: The blue putty Iain put on my face while making a mould for my mask.

Above: The mask was uncomfortable, but I found ways to cheer myself up. A scampi 'n' lemon Nik Naks sandwich!

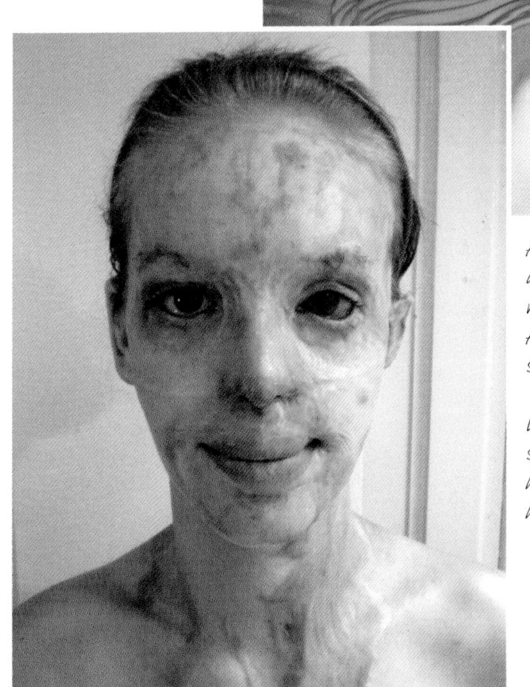

Left: Six months on and my skin is healing. The redness has gone down and I've got a hopeful smile.

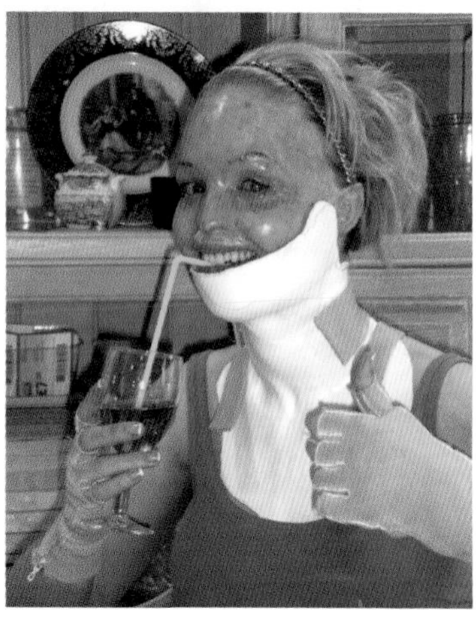

Above: Me, on my first trip to France, looking very skinny. Mr Jawad gave up his bank holiday to come with me.

Above: Back from another trip to France with a new contraption. I was happy to see Mum, so celebrated with a glass of wine.

Above: Smiles all round. With Paul, Mum, Suzy and Dad at the amazing post-trial party in London.

Right: My first appearance on This Morning. Phillip and Holly were so lovely to me and Mum fancied Phil!

Right: I was having one of my bad days here and being comforted by Dad.

Above: Me, proudly holding my Bravery Award, which was presented to me by Lorraine Kelly.

Right: With Simon Cowell at the launch of the Foundation. I'll never forget that night. It felt like a brand new start.

© PA PHOTOS

Above: The man who saved my life and soul, Mr Jawad, and me posing for a cheeky snap at Buckingham Palace.

Above: All dressed up and on the red carpet at the BAFTAs. The BAFTAs!

© SARAH DUNN

Right: On a shoot for the Foundation website and feeling happy to be alive. It's been a long journey, but each day gets a little bit easier.

tape of me and Danny, and that I'd freaked out because Danny had been going to release it in the public domain. Ridiculous – if one had existed, why didn't Danny produce it for the court?

Danny's defence also made the case that it was strange that I hadn't reported the rape to the police, but how could I have, when Danny had threatened to kill me, my family and my friends? It was all so stupid, so pointless, so cruel. How could anyone look at me, maimed and mangled, half-blind and clinging to a drip, and insinuate I was the villain?

'Do you have a daughter?' I wanted to ask the lawyer. 'How would you feel if Danny had done this to her? Would you still defend him then?'

I thought the questions would never end. Half the time I didn't understand their relevance and that just frightened me even more. What was he getting at? Where was this line of questioning leading? Were they never going to let me out of this room, and away from Danny?

Finally it was over, and I was dismissed. Outside the courtroom, however, Warren said there was a chance I might be called back to give more evidence. We travelled back home with no sense of relief.

Dad went to the court on his own over the following days as a spectator – I had no idea how he managed to be so near to Danny and not want to kill him. I knew from the strain on his face that it wasn't easy.

'Did you know Danny's thirty-two?' he asked one evening, when he came home.

'No! He told me he was twenty-eight,' I stammered. It was yet another lie. He must have thought I'd be more attracted to him if he was nearer to my own age. 'God, was anything he said to me true?' I demanded, thinking about how he'd created an illusion of my dream man. Successful and sporty, ambitious and intelligent, and just the right age, too.

'There's more,' Dad went on. 'Danny's been refusing to come up to court, pretending to be ill, not standing up or sitting down when he's supposed to. It's like he thinks he's above it all.'

That didn't surprise me one bit. His arrogance knew no bounds; to the point of stupidity if he was antagonising the judge. It was something I hoped would help show the sort of man he was.

A few days later, I went into hospital to have my throat and nostrils dilated again. When Mr Jawad removed the stitches in my nose, I fainted with the pain. They put me on a trolley and wheeled me into a high dependency room. As I woke up, however, I realised it was the same room I'd been in before, when my hallucinations had been raging; when I'd thought I was in a prison cell and Danny was in there with me, raping me and attacking me over and over. All of a sudden, I was back in that nightmare. The stress of the courtroom had got to me.

'No!' I screamed, in the grip of an instant, full-blown panic attack. 'Get me out of here!'

Mum heard my cries and raced in.

'Shush, it's okay.' She tried to calm me down.

'I can't stay here. Please!' I was hysterical and inconsolable until they wheeled me into an empty children's ward nearby. Lisa came in to talk to me and, gradually, my sobs subsided.

'It was a flashback,' she said. 'You know those hallucinations you used to have weren't real. They were caused by the morphine.'

'Yes, but they're like memories – as if these things actually took place,' I said, embarrassed by the fuss I'd caused. It was so difficult to explain. My brain knew those things hadn't happened to me, but the memories were so vivid. They were as real as memories of me dancing in Chinawhite or working in front of the cameras as a presenter.

Over the following week, my friends were all called to give evidence. I knew it would be traumatic for them, and I felt so guilty that they had to go through it because of me. Were they afraid of retribution, of Danny getting one of his friends to intimidate them into silence, too?

During that week, Warren rang to update us on the proceedings. Apparently, Danny's defence were claiming I was involved in some kind of crooked money laundering scheme. He'd alleged I had threatened him, and that's why he had arranged for Stefan to throw the acid on me.

'What? He's saying I'm a criminal?' I exclaimed, dumbfounded. 'That's a load of rubbish!' What was he going to come up with next? Did he lie in his cell, wildly thinking up claims to throw at me? How did he come up with this rubbish?

To prove my innocence, I had to hand over all my bank statements to the police. But even though I knew I'd done nothing wrong, my mind ran away with itself. Someone had lent me £30 once – what if the police thought that was evidence of my guilt? What if they locked me up, too? It would be just like my hallucinations come to life.

'*I'll die if I have to go to prison*,' I thought wildly. '*It'll be the end of me*.'

Thankfully, the police quickly saw through Danny's lies. They dismissed them immediately, but that didn't stop the defence from dragging me in for more questioning: I had to go back into that room with Danny, and back into the firing line. It just prolonged the torture.

'Are you okay?' Mum asked, as I waited to go in to court for the second time. I just looked at her, unable to speak. She tried to hug me, but I pushed her away. No one could help me now.

This time, the defence lawyer homed in on the fact that, after the rape, I'd gone for the morning-after pill. They'd seen it on my bank statement, and seemed to think this was proof that I hadn't been raped. I didn't understand their logic. Didn't it just prove it – that I didn't want to have a rapist's baby? Anyone with an ounce of intelligence could see that, but no matter how clearly I tried to explain it, the questions kept coming. Insinuating I was lying, implying I'd made the whole thing up. Trying to make me say certain things. I could see how tenuous their arguments were, but could the jury? Would they be swayed by these arguments? Would it plant a deadly seed of doubt in their minds?

When I was dismissed for the second time, I couldn't get out of there fast enough. But part of me wanted to stay, to sit there and beg and plead until I could see the jurors believed me. Instead, we went back home, all of us emotionally wrung out once again.

The next morning I turned twenty-five. Just twenty-five years old, but I felt about ninety.

'Happy birthday, big sis!' Suzy popped her head round the door and gave me my present. New brown Ugg boots, to replace the ones that had been ruined the day of the acid attack.

'They're gorgeous,' I grinned, tears pricking at my eyes. But I wasn't going to give into the sadness today – today I was going to celebrate the fact I was still alive.

Mum and Dad had planned a little party and invited some of my friends down from London, but as I got ready, I started to panic. Some of them hadn't seen me since the attack, and I knew what a shock my new face was. How would they react? I didn't want to see the revulsion in their eyes, too.

'*I have to make sure my hair is just right,*' I thought, frantically curling it with tongs. If my hair and nails and clothes were perfect, it might compensate for my face. I might shock people less.

'I don't want to make an entrance,' I babbled suddenly, when Mum came into my room. 'I have to be sitting downstairs when they arrive. I can't walk into a room if they're already in it.' I knew it was silly, but that seemed suddenly really important. I didn't want to walk through the door and see them swivel to look at me. I didn't want to feel all their eyes on my face, appraising the damage and comparing my new face with my old one.

'Okay.' Mum smiled. 'But you had better hurry up though, as they'll be arriving soon!' She disappeared back downstairs.

Ten minutes later, as I agonised over what shoes to wear, the doorbell chimed. Oh no. I heard muffled voices, the thump of my heart, then Mum padding up the stairs. She knocked on my door and walked in.

'They're here. Are you ready?'

'I can't do it, Mum!' I shook my head, on the verge of tears. 'You'll have to tell them to go away.'

'C'mon now, they've come all this way to see you.'

I sat on my bed, my head in my hands. 'I don't want to,' I insisted, but Mum took my hands and pulled me to my feet.

'It'll be fun, you'll see,' she encouraged, leading me out of the bedroom.

Even though every step was a struggle, I made it down the stairs. I arranged my broken face into as much of a smile as it could make, and I walked round the corner into the lounge.

It was just as I feared. Everyone stopped, their heads turning towards me. Marty and Michael and Tania and lots of others, they looked at me, and I swayed in my heels. But no one turned away in disgust. Instead, they all smiled and came running up to hug me.

'Happy birthday, Katie!' they sang.

'You look great, honey!'

'So good to see you!'

'Love the dress!'

Their love and concern were unmistakable. I smiled at Mum and mouthed: 'Thank you.' It was a wonderful afternoon, a few hours of precious release after the stress of the trial.

Mum and Dad had hired a magician who did cheesy tricks with scarves and balloons, and everyone tucked into my birthday cake cupcakes. I didn't eat much because of my throat, but I didn't mind.

'*This time last year, Michael took me out for dinner in a flash West End restaurant,*' I thought, but I refused to dwell on it as I ripped open my pile of presents. A watch, a handbag, a high-necked top because they knew I preferred to cover the scars on my chest … All of a sudden, I felt so lucky to be surrounded by these people. The family and friends who loved me, no matter what I looked like.

'Thanks so much everyone,' I exclaimed. I wished they could stay forever, but as it began to get late, they started to gather their coats and bags to get the train back to the capital.

'Take care. We'll see you soon!' They all kissed me goodbye. As Mum shut the door behind them all, I struggled to hold back tears.

'What's wrong?' Dad turned to me, concern written all over his face.

'I just … I didn't want them to leave.' They were going back to London, back to their lives, and how I wished I was going with them. I wished we could go for pizza then hang out at our place, but those days were gone. My mates had a new flat now. Their lives had moved on, while I was stuck here. What kind of existence did I have? It was like a miserable half-life, filled with nothing but hospital appointments and court appearances and suffering and tears. Sure, there were flashes of light. Like today, when I felt safe and happy to still be here. But they were few and far between, and it was no kind of existence for anyone, let alone a twenty-five-year-old girl.

Mum and Dad just didn't know what to say to make me feel better. I tried to put on a brave face for them, but inside I felt like I was falling apart.

The next morning, I didn't have time to sit around and piece myself back together. We had to go back to court – and wait on the verdict that would dictate all our futures.

Chapter Fifteen
Survivor

All day long in that little room we waited and waited. Every time the door opened, we looked up, on fire with expectation but – nothing. Why was it taking so long?

'It's a bad sign,' I said grimly as I paced up and down. 'If they believed me, they'd have found him guilty by now.'

'Not necessarily, Kate. These things take time. It just means they're being thorough,' Mum reasoned.

I picked up a magazine, flicked through the pages, then tossed it back down in frustration. What did I care about the latest celebrity break-up or the new must-have platform shoes? Those things that used to interest me seemed so trivial and inconsequential now.

I pictured Danny, sitting in his cell. Was he nervous? Was he frightened? '*I hope so*,' I thought bitterly. But I didn't really believe it. He was so cocky and arrogant, he probably thought he'd get off scot-free. He was probably planning what to do when he was let off. A roast dinner cooked by his mum, and a few celebratory drinks down the pub, where all his mates would clap him on the back and cheer. 'Well done!' they'd laugh, like he'd been a victim of a miscarriage of justice. 'That bitch didn't get the better of you. You showed her, Danny!'

Then what? He could go on to hurt some other girl like he'd hurt me, and next time, he might actually kill her. He'd think he was totally untouchable, above the law. I shuddered.

For eight long hours, we waited. Then, at 5 p.m., a clerk came in.

'Any news?' I demanded, springing to my feet, but he shook his head and said the jury was retiring. They still hadn't reached a verdict, so we'd have to come back tomorrow.

'Oh God,' I groaned, bursting into tears as Mum pulled me into her arms.

I didn't sleep a wink that night, and the next day was even worse. Wired on adrenaline, I could barely sit still. I walked up and down that little room a thousand times, freezing any time I heard footsteps. The verdict had to come today. Any second now, Warren and Dad would walk in with beaming smiles, and tell me he'd been found guilty. But the minutes dragged by, and no one came. I tapped my foot. I clenched my clammy hands. He was going to get off, I *knew* it. I'd have to leave the country immediately – race home, grab some clothes and jump on a plane to some far-flung country where he'd never find me. I'd spend the rest of my life looking over my shoulder, waiting for Danny to come.

'What's taking them so long?' I asked every five minutes, but no one had an answer for me. When 5 p.m. rolled around again, déjà-vu washed over me. The jury was retiring, the clerk said apologetically. We had to come back the following day.

'C'mon, let's go and get something to eat.' Mum took my hand and led me to the car. But I couldn't eat. I could barely breathe. Why couldn't the jury agree? Did some of them think I was lying? How could they have looked me in the face, and doubted Danny's guilt? Didn't they know how important this was to me?

The next morning, we were back in that room. By now, it felt like *my* prison cell, and I wondered how much longer this could go on. My phone kept ringing. Was there any news yet? Was I okay?

'I'm hanging in there,' I would lie to the caller, though I was on the brink of cracking.

When Dad and Warren finally walked in, I could only stare at their faces. They were smiling. Did that mean everything was okay?

'Well,' Warren began, and I wanted to shake him and scream: 'Hurry up! Just tell me!'

'They couldn't reach a verdict on the rape. It was a hung jury,' he said. I collapsed back down into my seat like I'd been shot. '*No, please no.*'

'But he was found guilty of GBH with intent,' Warren went on, beaming at me. My head dropped to my hands, I couldn't feel any relief, only crushing disappointment and sadness. The jurors thought I was a liar; they didn't believe me.

'But he raped me! He raped me!' I cried.

'We know, love,' Mum whispered, her eyes filling with tears.

'I fought for my life in that hotel room. I had to talk Danny out of killing me. I had to find the words to stop him murdering me. And for what? I feel like I've been raped all over again,' I raged, staring up at their concerned faces.

'But it's good he was convicted of the GBH,' Dad reasoned. 'The police worked so hard to establish a link between him and Stefan. That wasn't easy, and we should be grateful for that.'

I was grateful, but I wanted to run into the courtroom and grab the jurors and howl at them: 'Do you want this to happen to another woman? Do you want this to happen to your daughter? How can you believe him? How can you doubt what he did to me in that hotel room?'

I was skewered by despair. The rape had degraded me so much. It was my dirty secret, and it had been torturous to sit in the witness box and relive every disgusting moment of it. I'd done it and they hadn't believed me anyway. Now I wanted to disappear. I wanted to die.

'It's okay, Katie,' Suzy whispered, taking my hand and squeezing it.

'What happens now?' I heard Mum ask, her voice low with worry.

'Well, that's up to Katie. If she is willing to continue and if the CPS agrees to a retrial, it'll go to court again.'

I'd have to go through it all again? I'd have to face Danny again? Have to be interrogated again? Have to be doubted again?

But I had no alternative. I'd come so far that I couldn't run away now. I couldn't let him win.

'You've been through enough, Kate,' Dad said, gently drawing me into a hug. I can't bear to think of you going through it again.' 'No. I'm going to stick to my guns,' I said, haltingly. 'I have to. I'll do it. I can't let him get away with it.'

Back at home, I went through the motions of living. I was walking, I was breathing, I was talking. But inside, I was hollow. We still had to wait for Danny to be sentenced for the GBH conviction. And, what if the CPS decided not to do a retrial, after all? That would be even worse than returning to court. Danny would definitely get away with it then and I would have no chance to prove I was telling the truth.

For two days, I could think of nothing else, then Warren came to see us. 'There will be a retrial, although it probably won't be for four or five months,' he said, and I wavered between relief and anger. Four or five months? I had to wait that long for this nightmare to end? What kind of society let a psycho like Danny have that kind of control over his victim? What kind of legal system made someone suffer this way in the aftermath? It wasn't fair, any of it.

After that, I spent hours online, pouring over the news stories about the trial. Protected by my anonymity, I wasn't named in any of them. I was just a twenty-five-year-old model, a victim without a name or a face – in more ways than one.

As I scrolled through the pages, I realised that if I'd read the stories before my attack, I would have thought: '*Poor thing. I'd rather die if that happened to me.*' The prospect of losing my looks like that would have filled me with horror. But it had happened to me, and somehow I had accepted it.

Clicking the mouse, I read through pages and pages of online column inches about the story. There was Danny's mugshot, his dark eyes staring belligerently into the camera as if to say: 'You'll never pin it on me.' There was Stefan, his cheeks scarred by the splattering acid.

Both of them looked so menacing, I felt a rush of hatred. 'How could you have done this to me?' I wanted to scream at the screen. 'Don't you have hearts? Don't you care?'

Life didn't stop just because the court case was in limbo. Over the next few weeks, I was in and out of hospital to have my nostrils and throat dilated again, and my mask refitted.

I also started thinking about telling my story somehow, to help other burns victims. However, it would mean I'd have to waive my anonymity: the whole world would see my face; they'd know what had happened to me. The rape, the shame, the pain ... I couldn't even take being stared at in the street, so how would I handle exposure on that scale? Plus there was also the risk of my story attracting unhappy or unstable people and their reaction to it: would going public put me in danger? But on the other hand, my treatment had been so pioneering, I was sure my story would give hope to other victims, and going public would also help people understand what had happened to me, too. They wouldn't ask me the unending questions, because they'd already know the answers. And maybe, just maybe, I wouldn't feel so ashamed any more.

During one of my visits to Mr Jawad, I told him of what I was thinking of doing. He offered to help put me in touch with a friend of his who knew some journalists, and I agreed to set up a meeting straight away.

A few weeks later, Mum and I went off to meet them at a restaurant in Chelsea, south London. When the day arrived I put on a smart pencil skirt, high heels and a gold sparkly jumper especially … and my mask, of course. As I examined my reflection, I felt the familiar grief and longing for the old me. Those reporters would probably be mortified to be seen with me, just like everyone else. But I held my head high as we walked in, and I smiled at their warm greetings.

They said they'd been putting out some feelers, to see if there was any interest in making a documentary about my story. I couldn't quite believe there would be. Why would anyone care? Why would anyone want to know about a freak like me?

A few days later, the retrial date was set for 4 March 2009. It was only four months away but it seemed like a speck on the horizon. I knew I had to push it to the back of my mind in the meantime, or the panic I felt about it would crush me.

Luckily, I had France to keep me occupied. My Primary Care Trust had agreed to fund the treatment there and a charity called

Dan's Fund for Burns were kindly covering my flights so, on 23 November 2008, I flew out to Montpellier with Mum and Dad for my first round of treatment.

The flight was as stressful as the previous one had been, but as soon as we arrived at the clinic in Lamalou, I breathed a sigh of relief. I was safe at the centre, much safer than at home. Danny couldn't touch me here.

A nurse showed us to my private room with a view of the mountains and my own en suite, then we met Dr Frasson again, who gave me a timetable of the treatments I'd be receiving. They sounded so good, I was sure they would help, so when Mum and Dad hugged me goodbye to head back to the UK, I wasn't *too* anxious.

'Are you sure you don't want us to stay?' Mum asked, but I shook my head.

'I'm sure, thanks. Like I said, I want to do this on my own,' I smiled, even though the prospect of travelling back alone was stomach-churning.

'We'll see you in four days then,' Dad said. 'I'm so proud of you.'

Not many people there could speak English, but I didn't feel so foreign – not when there were lots of other burns victims around.

On my first morning, I bumped into a guy around my age, with injuries almost identical to mine. He looked at me, pointed to my mask and smiled.

'I wear this, too,' he said in a thick French accent. For a split second, I freaked out. He might follow me back to my room and attack me. But I shook my head to snap myself out of it. It was just an irrational fear, I told myself. Nothing bad was going to happen.

One of the nurses then called me away to photograph all my injuries. As the camera snapped, I felt a wave of nostalgia for my old life. People used to photograph me because I was beautiful, someone to be admired. But now I was deformed, a burned thing to be pitied or reviled.

'*Don't think that way, Katie*,' I scolded myself. '*Take it on the chin. Or on what's left of it, anyway!*'

After that, my treatment started. They used an endermologie machine on me; as they moved it across my skin, it broke down the scar tissue and improved the texture, mobility and colour of my face. They also used ultrasonic technology on me, which looked like a hairdryer, to smooth the contours of my face and body. I had deep massages on my hands, chest and face, and group facial exercise classes to help improve my facial expressions. They also gave me hydrotherapy, where they used high pressure water jets to break scar tissue down.

While I was having these therapies done, I thought about how lucky I was to have been able to travel to France. If only there was a similar rehabilitation centre in the UK, other victims could benefit from it, too.

In a bid to improve my overall fitness, I was also able to go back into a gym for the first time since the attack. I wasn't nearly as emaciated as I had been before the feeding PEG was inserted, but I was still seriously out of shape.

As I climbed onto the cross-trainer, I remembered the old days, when I'd warm up for half-an-hour on one without even breaking a sweat. But after just four minutes, my whole body felt like lead and I was huffing and puffing like someone who weighed fifty stone. As I admitted defeat and climbed back down, I started to weep. I was only twenty-five, but I had the body of a decrepit old lady. I was as fragile as a sparrow, and I wasn't going to spring back into shape overnight.

All the treatments were amazing, but one of them frightened the life out of me. As I lay on a bed in my underwear, one of the therapists came in holding what looked like a can of hairspray. Then she started squirting my hands, my neck, my chest and my face.

'You must not move for four minutes,' she said, before disappearing out of the cubicle.

I lay absolutely still, rigid with fear, as the liquid dribbled down my body – just as the acid had, that day in Golders Green. All of a sudden, I was back there, slumped in the coffee shop with the acid dripping onto my chest and running down my thighs. I started crying silent tears and fought the urge to scream. In my mind, I heard Lisa's calm voice: '*Don't panic, assess the situation.*' I was in the clinic in France. I was safe. This woman was only trying to help me. The liquid kept on slithering over my flesh, and I fought and fought to keep control. Slowly, the panic subsided and I felt a sudden rush of elation.

'*I've got to keep it together*,' I thought. '*I have to accept I'll have little lapses like this, and keep reminding myself that I'll get through this.*' I was a survivor, not a victim, and I couldn't ever forget that.

By the time the four days were up, even I could see an improvement in my face. Underneath my mask, the scars weren't as red and horrific as they had been, and a rubber mouthpiece they'd given me to wear had really stretched and improved my smile. As I looked in the mirror, I felt a lump in my throat, but it wasn't the usual sadness. It was happiness, because at last I could see a tiny trace of the old me in that maimed face. The wide grin that had beamed back at me from countless photos wasn't back completely, but I could see a shadow of it, and it filled my heart with joy. The happiness carried me through the flight home, to where Mum, Dad and Suzy met me at the airport.

Suzy hugged me. 'You look great, and you've only been for four days!' she exclaimed. 'Imagine how amazing you'll look when the treatment's finished!'

'I know! I can't wait to go back next week,' I smiled.

But, a few days later and after another throat dilation, I started to feel really weird. My head was tingly and felt like it was full of air, and when Mum took me upstairs for my massage, she noticed my skin was puffy and swollen.

'It's making a strange, crackling noise when I touch it,' she frowned. As the hours went by, pain started building and building, so Mum phoned the hospital. They told us to come in straight away.

As we sped down the road in our car, the doctor phoned back to ask Mum if we were in an ambulance.

'No, we're driving,' she answered. 'Should we be in an ambulance?'

'Just get here as fast as you can,' he said, and I saw the fear on Mum's face.

As soon as we arrived at A&E, I was immediately hooked up to a heart monitor, and the doctor revealed I was suffering from surgical emphysema. There was a tear in my throat, and it was leaking air into the surrounding tissue, putting pressure on my organs.

'Mum, it really hurts,' I groaned, as they moved me into a ward with four other beds. One of them contained a man who kept calling out and making strange noises. I was in too much pain to be able to think rationally. Was he going to hurt me?

'I'm frightened,' I sobbed, panic choking me.

Mum took my head. 'It's okay, he won't hurt you,' she said.

Eventually, I was moved into my own room, but it didn't help the terror abate. I was so weak, it was like those awful months just after the attack.

The next day, I was whisked in for x-rays and CT scans, but I was hardly aware of anything.

'We're hoping the tear will heal itself and the body will absorb the trapped air.' The doctor's voice seemed so far away. Lying in my bed crying, I barely had the energy to speak. Why was this happening, after everything I'd already been through? How much more could I be expected to take? I couldn't die now, could I?

Chapter Sixteen
Independence

I don't know how it did it, but my battered body fought the emphysema. My poor organs, which had been through so much already, didn't fail under the strain, and within a few days I was out of the woods.

As the doctors discharged me, I almost cried with relief. A week later, I was well enough to go back to France for my next round of treatment. Just like before, Mum travelled out with me, then headed back to the UK after I was settled.

I couldn't wait to see what magic they'd work on me this time.

'You must try to eat some normal food,' Dr Frasson said, explaining I would just wear my PEG feeding tube at night rather than all day.

So, on my first evening, I made my way to the dining hall. I shyly sat down at a table as everyone chattered around me, feeling as nervous as someone on their first day at a new school.

A guy around my age came and sat with me. In broken English, he said his name was Alain, and he'd been injured in a motorbike crash. 'I have a metal plate under the right side of my face,' he said, and I peered at him closely. I couldn't see a single scar, and it filled me with confidence.

As I picked at my boiled carrot purée, Alain kept up a steady stream of conversation about how he'd been to Manchester through his work. He was so friendly and warm, but any time I tried to answer him, food would invariably shoot out of my mouth, or my nose dripped onto my top lip.

It was mortifying but, as I made my way back to my room, I couldn't stop smiling. It was the first time I'd ever eaten in front of strangers – and I'd managed to chat to a young guy without freaking out. This was progress!

As the days went by, I hung out with Alain all the time. We watched DVDs or played pool, and he saved me cans of Coke from lunch and also translated the menu.

'Today, we are having crab for dinner,' he'd grin.

'Crab?' I'd splutter. 'Are you sure you've translated that right?'

Alain was attractive and sweet, but I didn't fancy him. My brain just wasn't working that way any more: I couldn't think about sex or romance, or even imagine that someone might fancy me back. It was enough that Alain didn't run away from me screaming. It was enough that I was able to sit with him and not think he was going to attack me, too.

Ten days later, it was time to go back home. 'We must keep in touch,' Alain smiled, and we exchanged email addresses. I couldn't believe it – after everything that had happened, I'd made a new friend. And not only that, he was a man, too. The clinic wasn't just helping me physically – my scars were looking a lot better and I was regaining much more mobility in my face – it was helping me emotionally, too.

'*I wonder what Mum and Dad will think. Will they notice much difference?*' I thought as a taxi took me to Montpellier airport. I suddenly felt desperate to make them proud and happy. They'd been through so much for me. They hadn't left my side in the hospital, and they'd even offered their own eyes, and their own skin, to help me. They'd selflessly given up their whole lives to look after me, sacrificing everything from their favourite TV shows to cups of tea to nights down the pub with their friends. Mum had been given a leave of absence from her job, and Dad took as much time off as he could. They'd done it all without question, without a single word of complaint, and I didn't want them to feel disappointed in me, or the treatment.

As I boarded the plane and sat down, I clutched my cross that somebody from my church had given me as a present. It was my lucky talisman, and as long as I had it, we weren't going to crash or blow up. It was going to be fine. As other passengers boarded, I saw them glance at the empty seats beside me then at my face – and walk on. No one wanted to sit next to me, and I wished I was invisible. Was I so horrific that they couldn't cope being near me? I refused to dwell on the situation and laughed to myself at how great it would be to have so much space.

More and more passengers boarded, and only when the plane was full did someone finally sit beside me. She was an American girl, but I just stared out of the window and ignored her: if she was staring at me in disgust, I didn't want to know.

Two hours later, we touched down, and I met Mum and Dad at the arrivals gate. Anxiety gurgled in my tummy. Would they notice any difference at all?

'Kate! You look wonderful,' Mum smiled, and we hugged each other close.

I knew I didn't look wonderful, but I did look a bit better. And that was good enough for me.

Christmas arrived. We all went through the motions, jumping out of bed early and running downstairs, but the ghost of Christmas past haunted us all. I had been so different the year before – beautiful and brimming with self-confidence, I had had the world at my feet. I had been so excited about working on the Jewellery Channel, so sure that 2008 was my year. I had had dreams of my career taking off, of meeting my perfect man; and now look at me.

As we opened our presents, I knew everyone was thinking the same thing. How innocent we'd been back then, with no idea of what was around the corner. No idea of the pain and heartache that was in store.

Every year, I'd always received a mountain of make-up and toiletries for Christmas, but this time around no one had known what to buy me. What good was posh lipstick for the likes of me?

So they gave me things like socks and nice hairclips, and I kept a smile plastered on my face.

As Mum, Dad, Suzy and Paul sipped bubbly or wine, I stuck to lemonade. Not a drop of alcohol had passed my lips since the attack – I was too afraid of losing control. Thankfully, my throat was well enough for me to eat and I managed some stuffing and mushy vegetables before we played charades in the lounge.

As I looked round the room, decorated in silver with thousands of twinkling fairy lights, I thanked God for my family, for Mr Jawad, and for the fact that I was still alive.

'*Next Christmas will be even better,*' I vowed. '*The retrial will be finished, and Danny and Stefan will be behind bars, where they belong.*'

In the New Year, it was back to France for more treatment. This time, I managed to travel over on my own, too, and Mum and Dad waved me off from Gatwick.

'We're so proud of you. We're only at the other end of the phone, so just ring if you want us to come over there,' Mum said.

'I'll be fine,' I said, kissing them both. 'Love you.'

The journey was a little easier than before, and when I arrived, I felt my worries slip away. Even though Alain was gone, I was glad to be back, and everyone was friendly and welcoming. When I accidentally flooded my room having a shower, the nurses rushed in and tried to mop the water up with bed-sheets. We ended up collapsing in hysterical giggles. And when I went into the dining hall, a group of two middle-aged women and a man beckoned me over to sit with them. Even though they barely spoke any English, I felt at ease with them. They all had their own problems, their own pain. They knew what it was like to lose everything you took for granted in one fell swoop, and no one asked me any awkward questions. Even when I choked on a fish bone, I succeeded in seeing the funny side of it.

'*They probably think I'm some crazy, suicidal English girl*,' I thought, as one of the kitchen staff slapped me on the back.

As the days went by, I started doing more and more. I went swimming in the pool, even though it meant men would see me in my bikini. I didn't flinch when the therapist sprayed my face with water. And I decided to take a walk around the village on my own.

Slipping my feet into my flip-flops and putting on some sunglasses, I marched out of my accommodation block and headed down to the shops before I could change my mind. In the village, there were, of course, lots of other people going about their daily business, but any time the fear reared its head, I reminded myself they were patients or staff. They wouldn't do anything to hurt me.

'You can do it, Katie,' I murmured under my breath. Ignoring the urge to run back to the safety of my room, I walked on, elated. '*I'm really doing it! I'm outside on my own!*' I thought – just as I stepped in a steaming pile of dog poo.

'Ewww, that's gross. I'm such a klutz!' I wailed, spinning on my heel and heading back to wash off my flip-flops. But even that wasn't enough to deter me.

Like a baby, I was learning to be independent. I was living a bit more all the time and, a few days later, I managed to go down to the chemist to buy an eyebrow pencil. As I browsed the different shades available, again I congratulated myself.

Even though the other patients always invited me to watch TV or play dominos with them, I preferred spending time on my own. Before the attack, I had hated my own company. I was a social animal, forever on Facebook or chatting to my flatmates. After the attack, I couldn't bear to be left alone. There always had to be someone home with me, someone to look after me. But now, now I enjoyed having time to think. I liked a quiet room where I could relax.

'*How weird*,' I thought with a smile. '*It's like I'm more at ease with myself than I was before*.'

The treatment continued. The intense physio, the hydrotherapy, the ultrasonic machine. I took photos of myself every day and emailed them to Mum, Dad and Mr Jawad, so they could see my progress. By any stretch of the imagination, I was still disfigured but, little by little, my injuries were improving. Shame and embarrassment still plagued me, but I clung to positivity and hope like a drowning person clings to a lifejacket. 'You're a survivor, not a victim,' became my mantra. I repeated it over and over, like some kind of self-hypnosis. Ever so slowly, I was learning to come to terms with what had happened. My beauty might be gone, but so what? Who said burns couldn't be beautiful anyway? I almost convinced myself. Almost.

*

Being away from home made it easier to forget about the upcoming retrial, but as soon as I got back from France in early February, the thought of it hit me like a truck. The next time I went back to France I realised, the trial would be over. One way or another, it would be done.

I started counting down the days till Danny and I would meet again. Plucked out of the safety of the clinic, it would have been so easy to slip back into my old ways. To hide away in my bedroom and refuse to leave the house. But I'd made so much progress in France I couldn't let it go to waste.

I had to keep pushing myself so, instead of letting the terror consume me again, I set myself little challenges to conquer. Like shaving my legs with a razor, even though my hand was trembling so much I could barely grip the handle. Like mucking around with Suzy, pretending to put make-up on over my mask. Having my feeding PEG removed after wearing it for eight months helped. It meant I could drink high-calorie shakes by myself, helping me to feel a little more normal. And, Dad was always trying to persuade me to try a new challenge, like going for a drive on my own.

'But what if someone tries to jump in?' I dithered, not sure I was ready for it.

Dad smiled sadly. 'Kate, this isn't London! You'll be fine,' he urged.

I locked every single door and drove off at the speed of a tortoise. After a while, though, I started to smile. I realised I felt safe in the car, and I cruised around the countryside savouring that little taste of freedom. I also forced myself to go shopping with Mum, even though I always wore a wide-brimmed hat, sunglasses and a scarf to hide behind.

One day, we went into a pound shop in a neighbouring town. Mum had wandered off down one of the aisles, and I stood in one spot, looking at something on the shelves. As I stood there, one of the workers walked up to me and suddenly pulled my hat off. He peered at me, at my mask and my scars, then screwed up his face in disgust. 'Get out!' he shouted. I burst into tears. In that second, I didn't want to exist any more. I just wanted to disappear. Mum came racing over and grabbed my arm.

'What's wrong?' she demanded.

'I said get out!' the man shouted again, and Mum and I dashed out into the street. Both of us in tears, Mum enveloped me in a hug.

'I'm so sorry. I should have been paying more attention. It's my fault,' she gulped.

'How are you to blame, Mum?' I sniffed, trying to pull myself together. 'It's that man's fault, not yours.' From my internet research, I already knew acid-attack women were outcasts in Asian society. They were ostracised, branded sinners or adulteresses. Did he think I'd done something to deserve it? How could he be so heartless?

His wasn't the only cruel reaction I received around then. Other people ran a mile if I walked near them in a shop, while one woman followed Mum and me around Debenhams one time, trying to get a closer look at my face. She trailed us down the aisles, blatantly staring at me as I flicked through the rails.

'Why won't she leave me alone?' I whispered tearfully to Mum. It was horrible; I didn't understand why people felt they had the right to stare or comment on my disfigurement. Why did it make me public property? If I had severe acne or a missing limb, it wouldn't cause such a stir, but this was different in a way I couldn't fathom.

'*Maybe if I make that documentary, then they'll understand*,' I thought. '*Maybe they'll see I'm a normal girl underneath, with feelings like everyone else*.'

The documentary was looking more and more likely. Mum and I had met more journalists, and a film-maker called Krish said he was interested in making it. He asked if he could film a taster DVD to show to production companies, and I agreed.

It was weird to be in front of a camera again, and as he filmed me cleaning and then rubbing ointment onto my face, I couldn't help remembering the old days. The old me, dishing out dating advise on telly. How long ago that seemed.

'Right, that's enough for now,' Krish said soothingly, putting down his camera. 'I'm going to send the footage around, and see if anyone's interested. I have a good feeling about this!' Sure enough, one production company was keen. But it would mean a TV crew would stay with us and film me going about my everyday life.

'Are you sure you're ready for this, Kate?' Mum asked, her brow creased with concern. 'They'll be at home, at the hospital, even in France with you. After the stress of the trial, could you cope with all that, too?'

I thought about it. I did find it difficult to trust strangers, to talk about what had happened to me, but this was so important. If by doing it I managed to only help one other person with burns, then surely it was worth it? I thought that if I asked for a female crew, and if I felt comfortable around them, then I could do it.

'I'm sure,' I smiled, popping some blackberries into my mouth. All of a sudden, blue liquid started spurting out of my feeding tube. I mustn't have closed it properly, and it gushed onto the carpet like a stream of pee. Laughing uncontrollably, I tried to shut it off while Mum raced into the kitchen for a cloth to mop up the mess.

'I can't get it closed,' I gasped, tears of mirth rolling down my mask.

'Let me try,' Mum chuckled.

We laughed until our sides ached. It was the best way to cope.

I was permanently aware of the impending retrial, and it wasn't long before all the old worries came back to me: the terror of being in a room with Danny again; the risk of him attacking me; the shame of remembering the rape; the trauma of having everything I said called into question; the risk of him getting away with it. But this time round, there was one big difference. I was a hell of a lot stronger. I wasn't as brittle and broken as I had been, and I'd come a long way since those dark days when every little thing was a source of fear, a trigger for panic. This time around, I was determined Danny would pay. He was the weak one – not me – and I wouldn't let his lawyer walk all over me. I would be feisty and fearless and brave, like when I was a little girl. I had the truth on my side and, as we travelled to the hotel in Brent Cross, north London, the day before I was due to appear in court, I prepared myself for battle.

'Talk about déjà-vu,' I sighed to Mum as I unpacked in my room. She and Dad were in an adjoining room next door, but I knew I'd end up sleeping in there with them.

That evening, my friends Donatella, Sam and Daisy met us in the hotel restaurant for dinner. We talked about anything and everything except the trial.

'*We're just a group of mates out for a bite to eat,*' I tried to convince myself. But we weren't. I was disfigured, and I was hours away from being in the same room as the maniac who'd done it to me.

Back upstairs in our room, Mum sat me down on the bed. 'I know you're stronger, and I know this is still going to be a huge ordeal for you,' she stroked my hand. 'But you'll get through it. In just a few weeks, it'll all be over. You'll have the closure you need, Kate.'

I nodded, not trusting myself to speak. Then I hung up the grey trousers and shirt I was planning to wear the following day, and crawled into bed beside Mum. All night long, I tossed and turned, sweated and panicked and prayed.

When morning came, we travelled back to Wood Green Crown Court for round two. And this time, I wasn't going down without a fight.

Chapter Seventeen
Round Two

Stepping back into the empty wood-panelled courtroom was like stepping back in time, like walking into an old nightmare. The screen was once more placed round me, and the jury filed in, then the judge, then Danny. At the sound of his footsteps, fear snaked around me again, squeezing and squeezing until I almost passed out.

'*Think logically*,' I urged my brain. '*He didn't try to attack me last time, and he's not going to try this time either*.'

'*But the stakes are higher now*,' another voice inside my mind shrieked. '*He might decide to get rid of me once and for all*.'

'*He won't, he can't*,' I reasoned again. '*Calm down*.'

Blood whooshing to my head, I took a deep breath and looked at the jury. Just like last time, it was a mixture of men and women. Some of them stared at me with that look of horror and pity that I'd come to know so well, but others wouldn't meet my eyes. One of those people was a pretty young woman, blonde like me, and I felt a stab of pain. That still hurt the most: seeing a girl who looked like I used to. Before Danny gave me this new face.

'Don't believe his lies!' I wanted to yell.

I focused on my breathing. '*Inhale, exhale. Don't let the panic win.*' As we watched my video evidence again, I barely took my eyes off the jurors. Their range of reactions was extreme, and I found this oddly fascinating. Some were crying, some were staring impassively at the screen. One man even looked like he was about to nod off. I wondered what was going through Danny's mind, on the other side of the screen. Did he think he was going to get away with it? Was he sitting there flashing that cocky smile I knew so well?

Then the questioning began. Just like before, the ridiculous allegations that I was obsessed with Danny rather than the other way round, that we'd only had a tussle in the hotel room and that I'd slammed my head accidentally, that we'd had consensual sex.

'No, that's not true. What woman, after she's been knocked unconscious by a man, would wake up and want to have sex with him?' I demanded. On and on the random questioning went. It was all a load of rubbish and again I wondered how this lawyer could live with himself. He may have only been doing his job, but what a job it was. An animal like Danny didn't deserve any defence.

The questions were deliberately designed to confuse me and trip me up, but this time round, I was ready for him. I didn't sit there snivelling and whimpering. I answered everything clearly and concisely. I knew when he was trying to trick me into saying what he wanted, so I chose every single word with care, and I didn't hold back: 'This guy is dangerous,' I insisted. Did they want to live next door to him? Did they want someone they loved to be his next victim?

After three days in court, battling to keep calm and not let the lawyer bamboozle me, I was done. Part of me was so relieved, but I couldn't relax, not until it was all over.

'Now we just have to sit and wait,' Mum sighed as we checked out of the hotel. We drove home silently, lost in our own thoughts.

I wandered restlessly around the house. The trial was continuing, and I imagined Danny taking to the stand. What would he say? Would he cry about his supposed steroid addiction in a pathetic attempt to win the jurors' sympathy? Would he play the wronged man, targeted by some *Fatal Attraction*-type crazy woman? But how could he, when they could see my acid-scarred face?

'He has to be found guilty, Mum,' I cried, every ten minutes. If I was ever going to accept what had happened, I needed people to believe me about the rape. If they didn't, if Danny was cleared, then I'd never be able to shed the shame. He would win, and I would forever be his victim. I'd always belong to him.

Five days later, I was given permission to travel to France for the next part of my treatment, even though the trial was continuing. I couldn't wait to get away, and Mum and Dad promised to ring the second there was any news.

At the airport, I suddenly realised I didn't have my lucky cross. 'I can't get on the plane without it,' I said, on the verge of tears. Dad raced to Claire's Accessories nearby, and came back with a replacement one on a gold chain.

'This will keep you safe in the meantime,' he said, fastening it around my neck.

'Thanks, Dad,' I sniffed, rubbing it with shaking fingers.

For once, the clinic didn't bring any comfort. I was on a knife-edge, waiting for the phone to ring and dissolving into tears at the slightest provocation.

'How are you doing?' Mr Jawad asked gently when he phoned to see how I was.

I stifled a sob. 'The waiting is so hard,' I whispered. If Danny wasn't found guilty of the rape, then justice wouldn't be done. He was a rapist, and he needed to be held accountable. He needed to be put on the sex offenders' register, so other women could be protected from him in the future.

Two days after I had arrived in France, Mum phoned to say the jury had been sent out to consider their verdict. Right at that second, they were deliberating. I imagined someone – one of the women maybe – insisting he was guilty. 'But what about this …' one of the men would counter, and they'd argue over my testimony.

'*Please God, help them make the right decision*,' I prayed.

But by the next afternoon, the jury still hadn't reached a unanimous verdict.

'The judge has said he'll accept a majority verdict instead. It shouldn't be too much longer. Your dad's in court and he'll let us know straight away,' Mum told me over the phone.

'This is driving me crazy!' I cried, my voice catching on the last word. Would the verdict come today? Or would I be forced to endure another sleepless night?

An hour or so later, my mobile rang. It was Dad. My heart was beating so fast my whole body quivered.

'Hello,' I whispered, holding my breath. It had arrived, the moment I'd dreaded and longed for at the same time.

'Guilty!' Dad exclaimed, and I gasped in relief. Pure, exquisite joy washed over me.

I gasped. 'Are you sure?' I demanded.

'Yes! It was an eleven to one verdict.'

'It's over, it's really over!' I exclaimed, bursting into tears. They believed me, they actually believed me, and all the shame faded away. I wasn't dirty or disgusting – I was free, I was unfettered. The chains binding me to Danny were gone, flung from me at last. It was confirmation that it wasn't my fault, that I was wrong to have ever blamed myself for Danny's despicable actions. He was the criminal, and now he was going to get his punishment.

For the next few hours, I was barely off my mobile. I used up £60 of credit phoning Mum, Mr Jawad, Suzy, Paul, Marty and all my friends, and each time I said the words, I almost had to pinch myself to prove it was real.

'Danny was found guilty!' I sang, laughing through my tears.

For a fleeting second, I wondered how he must be feeling. I wondered if he was frightened about how long his jail sentence would be. He had to wait just over a month before sentencing, and I hoped that every minute would be torture for him. Let *him* know what it was like to wait powerlessly, at the mercy of someone else. Let *him* know what it was like to suffer. Then I banished him from my mind and danced round my room.

For the next ten days in France, I woke up every morning and smiled as I remembered. '*It's over*,' I kept thinking, and for the first time since the attacks, I felt truly happy. Wandering around the village, I took photos of the trees in blossom, the majestic mountains and the clear blue sky. I emailed them to Mr Jawad and my psychologist, Lisa, and told them how glad I was to be alive.

Back home, and with the anniversary of the acid attack approaching, I was in two minds. In a way, I didn't want to do anything to mark it, but I couldn't just ignore it and pretend it was just a normal day, either. After all, it was the day the old Katie had died. Should I do something to honour her? Or would that be too painful?

'Maybe we could go to the cinema and out for some dinner?' Mum suggested. 'That might take your mind off it.'

'Good thinking,' I agreed. Anything was worth a shot.

But as soon as I woke up, it was all I could think about. '*This time last year, I was sitting in our flat, packing to go on* Candy Crib,' I thought. '*Danny was texting and ringing me constantly.*' I remembered how desperate I'd been to get away from him, how I assumed he'd lose interest and leave me alone. If I'd known

what he was planning, I probably would hav[illegible]
and then. The old Katie never could have contemp[illegible]
her beauty. She was so vain, so self-obsessed, and her looks [illegible]
been her life.

'*I was getting sucked into that dog-eat-dog world,*' I thought sadly. '*It was so superficial. I hardly saw Mum and Dad at all, and I took them totally for granted.*' I hadn't spared a second thought for people like Mr Jawad and the dozens of doctors and nurses who'd saved me. They worked tirelessly to help others, but that kind of selflessness hadn't even been on my radar.

In the last twelve months, I'd seen humanity at its worst, and its best, too. Had it made me a better person, deep down, underneath the scars? Had it made me more 'beautiful', in a way I'd never even imagined?

'*Wow, I've never thought about it like that before,*' I thought with a jolt.

'So what do you fancy seeing in the cinema?' Mum asked, and I snapped out of my reverie. I scanned the listings and decided on *Lesbian Vampire Killers*, as it was a British comedy and starred James Corden and Mat Horne from *Gavin and Stacey*.

I had assumed it would be a bit of light-hearted relief, but I hadn't banked on there being quite so much blood or quite so many scares. Any time one of the vampires jumped out, I almost leapt out of my seat, and the whole thing made me anxious and uneasy. I knew it was just silly rubbish, but I couldn't seem to relax.

…m, annoyed at myself. Dinner …t much better. The vegetable pasta …de me sick, and I felt pretty low as we …e.

…e *last year, I would've been in hospital,*' I thought, …bering that unbearable agony. How I'd thought I was dead a…d that the nurses' voices belonged to other lost souls. But then I steeled myself: look at how far I'd come in twelve months. My body was so much stronger and my face so much more supple. The scars were fading, and even though I was far from regaining the self-confidence I once had, I'd managed to stop hating myself. The fear was still ever-present, but I was learning to control it.

'*Imagine where you'll be this time next year,*' I thought, trying to be more positive. But when I tried to envisage the future, it was a blank. I didn't think I'd ever be strong enough to live in London on my own or have a career again. Modelling and presenting and beauty therapy were the only things I'd ever known, but they were completely out of reach now. Would I have to stay with Mum and Dad forever? Would I be a female Peter Pan, never able to grow up?

Over the next few weeks, I had my usual appointments with Lisa, my nose and throat doctors; and, of course, Mr Jawad. We were still constantly in touch, and his regular emails and phone calls always made me smile.

As the days went by, I visited Rita and went to church. It still gave me strength and comfort, just like when I'd first got out of hospital. The documentary crew also started filming me then, starting with me just pottering around the house with Suzy. It felt weird being in front of a camera like that again. Sometimes when I caught my reflection in the lens, it still took me a moment to realise that the face staring back was me. Even after all this time, my new face still had the power to shock me.

The days were ticking down to Danny and Stefan's sentencing. It wasn't as terrifying a prospect as the trial had been, but I was still worried. If the judge was lenient, they could be out in no time. You often heard about murderers being handed ridiculously short jail terms. If that happened, I knew that it would crush me. It was the final hurdle, I thought. I just needed to survive this, and then I'd have closure. Then I could truly move on.

A week before the sentencing, Warren came to see us. He had with him the CCTV tapes they'd shown in court as evidence, and he asked if I wanted to see them. I nodded, thinking it might be cathartic, but when the grainy images appeared on screen, I felt sick. There was me and Danny, walking into the hotel the night of the rape. We were smiling and talking and holding hands, and we looked like any other normal young couple. I looked at the old me, so trusting and so naive. So beautiful. She was walking towards hell, and she had no idea. Then the footage cut to us leaving the hotel the next morning. With my trilby hat pulled down over my bloody head, I was racing to the lift with Danny behind me. We were tense and unsmiling – so different from the night before.

'Now we've got the CCTV footage from the high street, the day of the acid attack,' Warren said hesitantly. 'Are you sure you want to watch it?'

'Yes,' I whispered, and there it was on our telly. Stefan lurking for hours as Danny tried to lure me outside. He bought a chocolate bar, he nonchalantly read the paper, he talked on the phone. For hours, he waited for the chance to destroy me. In all that time, he could have changed his mind, but he didn't. He just waited and waited as Danny laid the trap. Anger gathered in my gut. Before this moment, Danny had been the focus for the full force of my wrath, because I'd thought that maybe he had bullied and intimidated Stefan into compliance. Now I knew that wasn't true. Stefan didn't think twice about what he was about to do, and that made me despise him, too. I just couldn't understand why he had done it and he never offered any explanation either.

Then we watched as I came out the front door of my flat, dressed in the sloppy tracksuit and Ugg boots I'd thrown on, uncaring after the rape. I watched as Stefan marched across the road towards me, that cup clasped in his hands. I watched as I rooted in my bag for my purse, then – *whoosh!* He threw the acid in my face, and I ran away, screaming. Even though there was no sound, I could hear my screams in my mind. Those awful, blood-curdling, inhuman screams.

Suddenly, the film cut to the security camera in the coffee shop. I watched as I sprinted inside, still wailing. I watched as I dashed behind the counter and tried to plunge my head into a bucket of ice. It was like watching my own death.

The next CCTV footage showed Stefan walking into A&E at Chelsea and Westminster Hospital, a few hours after he'd thrown the acid at me and burned his own face in the process. He was accompanied by two girls, and the three of them were laughing. *Laughing*, while I was blind and screaming in agony. What had he told those girls, I wondered. Did they know what he'd done? If so, how could they do that?

'Are you okay?' Warren asked softly.

'Yeah,' I mumbled, wiping away the tears I hadn't even realised were falling.

On 1 May 2009, we all headed back to Wood Green Crown Court for the sentencing. Mum, Dad, Suzy and me.

We were tense and preoccupied as we drove across London. Nauseous and sweaty, I stared out of the window without taking anything in. When we pulled up outside, I suddenly realised I didn't want to see Danny or Stefan – I'd never even considered I would on this day – so Dad went into court while the rest of us waited in a room nearby. Jittery with adrenaline, I tried to concentrate on painting Suzy's nails to pass the time. I tapped my feet. I stared at the clock and prayed.

An hour later, I heard the door open. It was Dad, accompanied by Warren and Adam.

'Danny got two life sentences. He must serve a minimum of

sixteen years before he's eligible for parole. Stefan got life too, with a minimum of six years,' Dad said, and I tried to let it sink in. Stefan's sentence didn't seem very long. Just six years for throwing acid in my face. Danny's was better. Sixteen years was a long time – but somehow, it didn't seem long enough.

I waited for a wave of jubilation, but none came. I didn't feel any of the joy I'd felt when Danny was found guilty of rape. It was a victory, but now it all just seemed so empty. All of a sudden, I realised their sentences hadn't miraculously undone the damage they'd inflicted on me. I was still almost blind in one eye, I was still disfigured, and I was still carrying the mental scars and having to wear the mask. I was the one with the real life sentence.

'It was the maximum sentence they could get under British law, which is great, isn't it? How do you feel?' Dad smiled, giving me a hug. I groped for the right words.

'I'm pleased. I'm so relieved it's over,' I said. And I was, even if deep down it did feel like an anticlimax.

Ever since the attack, I'd been geared for this moment. This result. But now that I'd got it, I realised it wasn't some kind of magic wand. I still had to live the rest of my life. Where the hell did I go from here?

Chapter Eighteen
Celebrations

The champagne cork popped across our lounge, and cheers rang out. It was the night of the sentencing, and I sipped my first taste of alcohol since the attack. The cold bubbles tasted metallic in my mouth, but a warm glow soon spread through my drained limbs, even if I did wince as I swallowed.

Even though it was all over, even though we were celebrating the best result we could have hoped for, I still couldn't exorcise Danny from my mind.

The next morning, I turned on the computer and started looking through all the news websites to see if the story had broken. It had. '**Two get life for acid attack**' one headline screamed. '**Life term for acid attack rapist**' shouted another. They called Danny things like a 'steroid-addicted thug', and I read them compulsively, hungrily, desperately, as though they held some hidden meaning that would tell me why he had done it.

Because I hadn't been in court to hear it, Warren sent us a typed transcript of the judge's sentencing remarks, which had also been quoted in all the news stories: '[The victim] had a face of pure beauty. You, Danny Lynch and Stefan Sylvestre, represent the face of pure evil.' That past tense made my heart constrict with anguish. I *had* a face of pure beauty. But not any more.

'The facts of this case are chilling and shocking. You planned and then executed an act of pure, calculated and deliberate evil. You decided to wreck the victim's life by thrusting a full container of sulphuric acid straight into her face from point blank range.' Tears ran down my face as I read on. 'Her psychological injuries are severe. There is a significant risk of clinical depression with a degree of change of personality and self-harm. However, her tremendous courage is not in doubt, and I feel sure her fight back to life will start soon. Her desire for justice and her unwavering truthfulness in the face of the most appalling adversity were the clearest examples of the bravery of the human spirit. She impressed both my colleagues and myself enormously. By sharp contrast, you, Danny Lynch, have shown not a hint of remorse, even less of regret.'

That was the one thing I couldn't understand. How could Danny have done this to me, and not feel even a tiny bit sorry? How could he hurt me so much, damage me so badly, and not even care? Had he no conscience? No soul?

Hardest of all, though, was reading the full extent of his criminal history. The police weren't allowed to tell us about it before, but here it was, in all its horror. He had a string of previous convictions, and in 1997 had been sentenced to four and a half years in prison for throwing boiling water in a man's face.

How terrifyingly similar: except he'd obviously decided boiling water was too good for me.

'*Why, Danny?*' I thought. '*Why acid? If you just wanted to ruin my looks, boiling water would've done that. But you blinded me, and you destroyed my insides, too.*'

And there was more. In 2007, he had broken into a woman's house and assaulted her as well. So he hadn't been lying in the hotel room, when he bragged about his past exploits. There was at least one other woman out there who knew what it was like to be at Danny's mercy. The judge was right – he was capable of acts of pure evil. Stefan, too, had a previous conviction for violence.

I felt so weary all of a sudden. I would never understand how the minds of people like that worked. How their souls had become such cesspits of hatred. How hurting someone beyond repair could be such a casual act.

I closed the computer down, and resolved never to look at those stories again. It was like picking at a scab, and I had to leave it alone or it would never heal.

A few days later, Dad stuck his head into my bedroom. 'Fancy a drink down the pub?' he asked. I looked at him like he'd gone mad.

'I don't think so,' I tutted, but he wasn't giving up that easily.

'Why not?'

'People will stare at me,' I muttered. What a ridiculous question. Wasn't it obvious?

'So what if they do? That's their problem. C'mon, Kate, it'll be good for you. You'll never get over this, otherwise.'

Good for me? France was good for me; no one took any notice of me there. But in my hometown, I was, '… that Piper girl. You know, the one who used to be beautiful before she was raped and mutilated by her ex-boyfriend? Poor girl.'

Going out there definitely didn't fall into the 'good for me' category.

'You have every right to be there,' Dad persisted. I sighed. I *was* so bloody bored of sitting at home, watching the same box sets over and over again. If I watched Alan Partridge one more time, I might scream. My feeding PEG had been removed, and I was a lot stronger, physically. Maybe Dad was right; maybe I should just face everyone.

'Let's do it.' I sighed with resignation. Pulling on my huge, Joan Collins-in-*Dynasty* sunhat and scarf, I made my way downstairs to where Mum and Dad were waiting.

'If I don't like it, we're going straight home,' I insisted as we went down the hill. Every time a car passed, I imagined the people making sympathetic clucking noises. 'There's that acid girl! Such a shame. She was so pretty, and look at her now.'

When we reached the pub, anxiety sucked like a leech.

'You two to go in first and find a seat. I don't want to walk in and have to stand there while we look, with everyone staring at me.'

So they did, and then I scurried in and they beckoned me over. Dad got a round of drinks in, and I sipped on a vodka, lime and soda and tried to pretend I was just a normal girl out for a normal Friday night tipple with her parents. Of course I still hated anyone looking at me, but I knew I just had to get used to it. It wasn't going to change.

Maybe because everyone knew about me, no one bothered us. As we meandered back up the hill afterwards, I was glad I'd done it. Which was why, when my friend Kay suggested a little party in London to celebrate the end of the trial, I didn't dismiss the idea out of hand.

'I'm not really sure,' I wavered. 'It's a lovely idea, but London's … well, I don't feel very safe there.'

'I know, but we could have it in a nice area. One that doesn't have any memories for you. There's a nice little pub near where I live in south London. It has a private area upstairs, which you can hire for parties. It would be perfect!'

I mulled it over. Going to the pub in my hometown was one thing, but this was something else entirely. Danny and Stefan were from London; their family and friends still lived there. It was where I was raped and attacked. The city was enormous and dangerous and totally unpredictable. Still, it would be wonderful to see everyone together. I could invite Mr Jawad, people who had helped me, and all my old mates. I could thank everyone who'd helped me get this far. Sure, it would probably scare me senseless, but I had to keep pushing and pushing to rebuild some kind of life for myself. So I gratefully agreed, and Kay said she'd start sorting it out.

Just as for my birthday party, I wanted to look as good as I possibly could, so Suzy offered to take me on a dress-finding expedition. I hadn't really done anything like that since the attack – any previous trips to the shops with Mum were purely an excuse to get me out of the house, and I almost always said no. But I dug deep and found a sliver of courage, a shred of determination, and I agreed. I even managed to ditch my usual hat and scarf, and we drove to a big shopping centre with the film crew, who were still filming me for the documentary.

Without my disguise, I attracted plenty of attention as Suzy and I wandered around the shops. Other shoppers did double-takes when they saw my face, my mask, my scars. A group of guys nudged each other, then one gestured to his face. 'Did you see that girl?' he mouthed, incredulous. It was horrible.

'I hate seeing young blokes like that,' I muttered under my breath to Suzy.

'Pretend they're not there,' Suzy whispered, and I felt a rush of gratitude towards her. She was my baby sister and I'd always looked out for her – but those roles were now reversed. She was the adult now, taking care of me.

'Shall we go in there?' she suggested, pointing to Karen Millen.

We flicked through the rails, *ooh*-ing and *aah*-ing at the gorgeous dresses, and I thought about what I wanted. Something stylish, but not sexy. Something flattering, but not too tight. I wanted to feel attractive, I wanted everyone to look at me and smile in approval – but I didn't want to look like someone a man might want to rape. Nor did I want to look ridiculous: a disfigured freak in an uber-fashionable frock. It was a minefield of conflicting desires.

Then I spotted a stunning black and white dress and squealed in excitement. 'This is amazing! I've got to try it on,' I grinned, rushing into the changing room.

'Perfect!' Suzy said when I came out and gave her a twirl. Glamorous and sophisticated, with capped sleeves and a scooped neck, it was just right.

As we paid, I turned to Suzy. 'I can't believe I've come out in my mask and no hat,' I giggled. I hugged her to me with gratitude.

Our next stop was to a nearby department store for some nail varnish but, all of a sudden, my courage deserted me completely. How could I walk up to one of those chic cosmetic counters and deal with the perfectly groomed sales assistants there? They didn't have a hair out of place, while I was probably unlike anything they'd ever seen before.

'I can't do it, Suzy.' My voice trembled, and I knew I was close to losing my composure.

'You're allowed to wear make-up!' she said.

But I was certain that they'd take one look at me and think, '*Why is she even bothering? She'll need more than this to fix her face.*'

So I waited at one side while Suzy bought what we needed. I felt so embarrassed at my weakness, so disappointed at my wobble.

'Don't be daft. You've done really well!' Suzy insisted, and I realised I had. I'd faced the outside world in my mask and I'd gone into three shops.

We arrived back home completely elated. It was another milestone, and I couldn't stop smiling as I modelled the dress for Mum.

'Beautiful.' She nodded her approval and I smiled. I'd never have thought anyone would use that word in relation to me again.

Five days later, we all went up to London for the party. So we didn't have to travel back home afterwards, we checked into a hotel. As we walked into our room, I felt a flutter. But this time, it was excitement rather than fear.

'I'll leave you girls to it. I'm going down to the bar,' Dad said, looking dapper in his smart blue shirt.

'Who wants a drink?' Suzy laughed, opening a bottle of wine. Giggling and chatting, we started to get ready, and it was just like old times. My hair in rollers, I carefully applied my camouflage make-up. I'd decided to have a night off from my mask, so I rubbed on the heavy foundation and powder that evened out my skin tone and disguised the scars. Then I put on fake eyelashes and drew on some eyebrows. Next, a flick of lipstick and a spritz of perfume, even though I still couldn't smell very well through my shrunken nostrils. Holding my breath in concentration, I tousled my hair so it fell in loose curls around my face, then I slipped into that gorgeous dress and looked in the mirror at the end result.

'*Well, you've made the best of what you've been left with,*' I thought, trying not to focus on my blind eye, my disfigured ear, or the scars on my chest. I remembered the pictures of other acid attack victims I'd seen – they barely had faces at all. I was so lucky to have received all that pioneering treatment, and I'd come a very long way from that earth-shattering day when I'd seen my new face for the first time. Besides which, Mr Jawad, my family and friends, Alain and all the other people I'd met in France – my appearance was irrelevant to them. They loved me for me, and I was learning how to do that, too.

'I feel a little bit like before!' I laughed in delight, and Suzy and I went downstairs to where Mum and Dad were waiting.

'Wow!' Mum gasped as I did a little twirl.

As we travelled by cab to the bar where the party was, I went over in my mind about what could happen. There might be a fight; I could get glassed. Someone might drop a cigarette and there could be a fire. What about some kind of shooting? I might get mugged, assaulted or raped.

'*None of that will happen,*' I scolded myself. '*Don't let the fear hold you back.*'

When the cab pulled up, I got out, but flinched when I saw two big torches on either side of the door. They spewed orange and crimson flames into the air, and I almost burst into tears.

'I can't walk past them!' I yelped. 'What if they fall on top of me? Or a little spark flies off and sets me on fire? My dress will go up like a match!'

'They won't!' Mum smiled understandingly. 'C'mon now.'

I inhaled, and started walking towards the entrance. Towards the fire that could undo all of Mr Jawad's work to fix me. The nearer I got, the more my heart thumped. I inched my way forward. I could hear the whoosh of the flames. '*Please don't burn me.*' I took another few steps and I could feel the heat on my bare arms, my face, but I didn't turn back. Almost there ...

'You did it,' Suzy cheered, and I realised I was inside the bar.

'So I did!' I laughed as we climbed a spiral staircase to the area Kay had reserved.

Marty and some of my friends were already there, and their faces lit up when they saw me. 'You look amazing. So glamorous!' they all exclaimed. Mr Jawad and his wife; my flatmates; my cousins ... Everyone was in high spirits, and even the tea-light candles fluttering on the table tops didn't unsettle me too much, although I did furtively blow a few of them out when I thought no one was looking.

Mr Jawad insisted on buying champagne for everyone, and then I made a speech I'd prepared.

'I have a truly amazing family who is so precious to me. My parents are my best friends, and Suzy had to be a big sister to me. But not any more, because I'm coming back now! I want to express my gratitude to the Metropolitan Police Service, who got me the justice I deserve. They've made it so I can move on and feel safe again. And I want to praise someone who's radically improved my future. During my trial, they called him a medical genius.' My voice faltered as I turned to my hero. 'Thank you, Mr Jawad.' He'd always had so much faith in me, and he'd shown me how to believe in myself, too.

'To Katie!' everyone chorused, and I realised how incredible this moment was. A year earlier, I had wanted to kill myself. I had fantasised about flinging myself out of the car on the way home from the hospital, and in the months that followed, I often hadn't seen a way forward, couldn't see how my life would ever be worth living. Yet here I was, laughing and chatting, surrounded by people who loved me, and whom I loved in return.

The rest of the evening passed in a lovely blur: Mr Jawad taking my photo on his camera phone to show my amazing progress to the other surgeons who'd worked on me; posing for a snap with all my old flatmates; Mum crying as she told me what a wonderful daughter I was.

It was all over much too quickly, and we were high on adrenaline as we made our way back to the hotel. We stopped for chips – the fact that I couldn't eat them didn't matter a bit – and when we got into our room, Suzy and I lay chattering for hours. It was a perfect night, and I knew it marked a new beginning. I was ready to move forward. To move onwards and upwards. It wouldn't be easy, but I was ready for it at last.

Chapter Nineteen

First Date

I picked half-heartedly at a chocolate cupcake and sighed deeply. 'What's the matter, love?' Rita asked kindly as we sat at her kitchen table. I shrugged.

'I just worry sometimes … that no man will ever fancy me again,' I mumbled, feeling stupid. Rita was my friend's mum, but it was easier to talk to her about these things than someone my own age.

'Don't be daft!' Rita scoffed. 'You're a wonderful person, and if a man can't see that, then he's not worth having.'

'I'd date a guy with burns. I understand it's what's underneath that counts. But I don't know if blokes think that way,' I told her mournfully.

It was a few weeks after the party, and I was trying to figure out how to be a normal girl again. Now that the trial was over, that unrelenting, unbearable weight was gone. I still jumped every time the doorbell rang and woke up screaming as Danny still haunted my dreams. I still freaked out if a young guy marched towards me in the street, and I still hadn't managed to walk outside on my own yet. But I was so hungry for normality.

'It'll happen, Katie,' Rita smiled.

I longed to believe her. Apart from my never-ending hospital appointments and the odd trip to the pub with Mum and Dad, my days were pretty repetitive and boring; even the filming for the documentary had ended. I wanted a relationship, even though I didn't know if I was ready for one, and doubted any man would want me, anyway. I wanted a job, even though I hadn't a clue what I could do. I wanted a *life*.

'I just don't know where to go from here,' I said to Mum one day, when I was at the hospital to have my throat dilated once again.

'What about a course in something? You could go back to college,' Mum suggested, but what could I study? I'd never been particularly academic, and a packed college campus teeming with strange blokes would scare the hell out of me.

As the weeks went by, I thought about my options. My old dreams seemed so trivial now; I wanted to do something worthwhile. I wanted to help people like Mr Jawad did. But how? I'd recently had eyebrows tattooed on my face, and I wondered if maybe I could train to be a permanent make-up artist. But then part of me worried about how unsteady my hands were and how my partial sight would mean I couldn't see what I was doing properly. Instead, I thought about helping women who'd lost their hair through cancer or alopecia, or maybe I could do some kind of charity work for burns victims.

But first things first. I couldn't run before I could walk, and I still had a lot of hurdles to cross: like going outside on my own. 'You do it in France,' I gave myself a pep talk. 'You can do it here, too!'

One afternoon, I decided enough was enough. I had to just go for it. 'I'm taking Barclay for a walk to the shop,' I announced to Mum, sounding much braver and more blasé than I felt.

'Really? That's great,' she smiled, handing me his lead.

Anxiety, panic, terror – they all swarmed round me as I opened the front door and stepped outside. Mum waved me off, her eyes shining with a mixture of pride and worry. Gingerly, I walked out of our front garden and down the street.

'*Please don't let anyone talk to me*,' I prayed as Barclay stopped for a pee. '*Please don't let anyone abduct me or assault me or hurt me. Please, please, please God.*' My body was rigid and tense, and my mouth as dry and coarse as sandpaper. I kept glancing over my shoulder to make sure I wasn't being followed.

It was only a five-minute walk to the shop, but it seemed to take forever, and when it finally came into view, I whispered a prayer of thanks. Tethering Barclay to a rail outside, I raced in and bought some magazines, then bolted back out. Next, to home and safety …

And then: 'Excuse me,' a man's voice said. My heart thudded hard inside my trembling body. What did he want? Was he going to do something to me? '*Leave me alone!*' I wailed inside.

'Can you give me directions to the train station?' he asked, but I just kept my head down and marched back up the hill. Typical! Just when I desperately wanted to be left alone, someone had to speak to me. Talk about a baptism of fire. But the nearer I got to home, the more I started to relax. I'd done it!

'Well done!' Mum beamed, greeting me at the door. We grinned at each other as Barclay yapped at our feet.

Buoyed by my success, a few days later Mum asked if I'd mind her going back to work two days a week. It meant I'd be on my own in the house for a few hours in the morning, before Dad came home from his barber shop at lunchtime, but I was ready for it.

'Are you sure?' she said. 'Because if you want, I can give up work. I can stay here with you every day.'

'Thank you, Mum. But I don't get up until lunchtime anyway, so I probably won't even notice,' I reassured her. And I didn't. I was absolutely fine and, after that, I started going out with my friends Sam, Nikkie and Daisy. We'd just pop to the local coffee shop or have a quick drink in the pub, but it was enough to make me hope that one day I'd succeed in putting my life back together. Like a jigsaw, bit by bit, it was coming together.

One Friday night at the end of June, we all headed out for a drink. Dressed in wet-look leggings and a pretty green top, I had my mask off and a full face of camouflage make-up on. I still felt achingly self-conscious when I noticed anyone looking at me, but the dim lights in the pub helped diffuse my embarrassment. And so did a few stiff drinks.

'I'm a bit tipsy!' I hiccupped to Sam, and we burst out laughing.

Half an hour later, a guy turned to me while I waited at the bar. 'Hi, how are you?' he smiled. 'Are you having a good night?'

'Yes, thanks!' I grinned, taking in his warm brown eyes and handsome face. But then I remembered how I must look. He was probably just being polite, or talking to me out of pity.

'My name's Jonathan,' he offered his hand. 'Do you live around here?'

'I'm Katie,' I replied. 'Yeah, I'm staying with my parents nearby.'

Over the next half-hour, we chatted like we'd known each other for ages. Jonathan said he was from a neighbouring village and told me he was a recruitment consultant. I deflected any questions about what I did or why I was living back at home. I didn't for a single second think he fancied me until, at the end of the night, he suddenly leaned in and started kissing me.

'*Oh my God!*' I thought as his lips moved against mine. It was the first time I'd been kissed since the rape. Since my face was disfigured and my life destroyed. I waited for a flashback of Danny to pounce, but nothing came. Just the soft pressure of Jonathan's lips against me. His warm hand against my arm.

'*I'm actually kissing someone! And he's fit, too!*' I thought incredulously. When we broke apart, I smiled dreamily.

'Can I have your number? I'd really like to see you again,' he asked, and I recited it as he punched it into his phone. Then he was gone.

'I can't believe it!' I murmured to Sam on the way home.

'It's great! He was lovely,' she exclaimed, but I shrugged. Part of me was so glad it had happened. I'd truly thought no man would ever want to kiss me, and the more time that passed, the harder that would have been. But another bit of me dismissed the whole thing. It was dark, he was drunk. He probably had no idea what I truly looked like and if he did, chances are he would have run a mile. As a survival strategy, I wouldn't get my hopes up.

'*I shouldn't have given him my number,*' I thought, suddenly angry with myself. '*He could be a murderer for all I know!*' Sure, Jonathan had seemed nice, but Danny had played that part to perfection, too. I should just put him out of my head completely. Be glad it had happened, but accept it for what it really was. Like so many things in my new life, this wasn't black or white. It was a murky grey, clouded by my fears and desires.

The next afternoon when I was round at Rita's again, my mobile pinged. '*Hey Katie! It's Jonathan here. It was lovely to meet you. Fancy a drink by the river today?*' I stared at the text message, then suddenly started crying.

'What on earth's the matter?' Rita exclaimed.

'I met this guy, and I really like him. He's just asked me out.'

'But that's great! He's obviously keen!'

'No it's not, trust me. He probably doesn't remember I'm burned. If he sees me in daylight, he'll go off me straight away. What am I going to do?'

'Just go out with him! If he doesn't like you, it's his loss.'

It sounded so simple, but I couldn't.

'*I'd love to Jonathan, but I've got a family lunch,*' I fibbed.

But he didn't give up that easily as he rang me a week later. When I saw his name flash up on my mobile, I legged it upstairs to my room like a teenager, then had to frantically calm down and catch my breath. I pressed the receive button and then chirped: 'Hello?'

'Hi, Katie! What have you been up to?' he asked, and my mind went blank. I hadn't been up to anything, except the usual hospital appointments, but I couldn't tell him that. Nor could I say: 'Well, Jonathan, I am overcoming my agoraphobia, but most days I just sit indoors while my parents massage the skin my psycho ex burned with acid not long after he raped me.'

As if.

'Oh, you know. This and that!' I breezed. 'How about you?'

After that, we talked every few days. Just idle chitchat about his job, the weather, the latest news but Jonathan was so warm and funny, he always had me in stitches. 'We should meet up sometime,' he kept saying and I kept agreeing, even though the prospect made my tummy lurch. Maybe it was better to keep him at arm's length. But he'd lose interest – he didn't want a penpal, did he? And besides, I really did want to see him again, too.

'Argh! What am I going to do?' I screamed in frustration. After a few weeks, I finally caved and agreed to meet Jonathan for a drink. Too embarrassed to tell Mum and Dad in case it all went wrong, and because, after feeling like a child for so long, I wanted to have something just for me, I went to Rita's to get ready with Sam and the girls.

'Can you come to the pub with me?' I begged as I pulled on the black and white dress I'd worn to my party in London.

'We can't gatecrash your date!' Sam exclaimed.

'I can't meet him on my own. You can go into the bar first, just to make sure he's there. We'll pretend we don't know each other, and I can text you if it gets weird. Please? I'll feel so much better if I know you're nearby.'

'Okay, then,' Sam agreed. I removed my mask and started applying my camouflage make-up. It was a bit like another mask, I thought a little sadly. It was all about hiding the scars, still. '*At least it'll be dark in there*,' I reminded myself.

We all travelled to the bar together, then the girls went in. I took a deep breath, counted to ten, then followed them in. I didn't look in their direction in case I got a fit of nervous giggles, but marched down to the basement area where Jonathan was waiting.

'Hi, Katie, you look great!' He smiled as he spoke, and I slid onto a stool opposite him. 'Can I get you a drink?'

'Vodka, lime and soda, please,' I grinned, willing myself to calm down. I'd done this so many times before; it was just a date. Only a date. It was fine.

Jonathan reappeared with my drink just as my phone pinged. It was a text message from Sam asking: '*What's he like?*'

'*Nice!*' I typed back, as discreetly as possible, when I noticed Sam and the girls coming down the stairs to sit nearer to us. What were they doing? Oh God, if they so much as looked at me, I was going to start laughing. '*Pull yourself together, Katie!*' I thought determinedly.

'I have something to confess. All my friends are here,' I smiled sheepishly at my date.

'I thought I recognised them,' Jonathan laughed, and I felt some of my nerves melt away. Thankfully, he didn't ask why I'd felt the need to bring them, and we chatted about our college days. Then, without a moment's premeditation, I suddenly turned to him.

'There's something else I want to tell you. My ex-boyfriend got someone to throw acid in my face,' I blurted. He blinked in shock. There was a moment of charged silence. Then he shook his head.

'That's horrendous. I'm so sorry,' he said gently.

'I hadn't been going out with him for very long. He also … he … he raped me.'

What was I saying? '*Shut up, Katie!*' my mind was yelling at me. Jonathan didn't want to hear this on our first date. But I was powerless to stop it. Like a tap that had just been unblocked, it spewed out of me: 'Then he got a guy to throw the acid at me in the street. It happened almost eighteen months ago, so I'm still recovering, really. I'm getting treatment here and in France.'

'Wow … I don't know what to say,' Jonathan stammered. 'I'm so sorry to hear about that. It's just terrible, Katie.'

'It's okay. I just thought I should tell you,' I finished awkwardly, taking a slug of my drink and cursing myself. Any minute now, he'd probably make his excuses. Get up and walk out, never to be seen again. What man would want to deal with all that?

But Jonathan didn't get up. He smiled at me with admiration, then asked if I wanted another drink. I looked at my empty glass and nodded. I hadn't driven him away, and I felt so relieved I'd told him. He still didn't know about the mask, of course, but I'd cross that bridge if and when I came to it. For the moment, I could relax.

A few hours later, I looked at my watch and said I'd better get back. Sam and the girls were waiting to go home with me, and Jonathan and I hugged goodbye. This time there was no kiss, but I didn't mind. I could tell by the way he looked at me that he liked me, and my bombshell hadn't deterred him.

'Maybe we could meet up again soon?' he asked.

'I'd like that a lot,' I smiled at him in delight. 'I'm going to France soon for treatment, but how about when I get back?'

'It's a date!'

That night in bed, I didn't worry about telling Jonathan about the mask. I didn't panic about being intimate with him. I didn't freak out about what might happen. I just smiled as I dozed off, thinking how nice it was to feel like a normal girl, who was liked by a normal boy. Jonathan didn't just want me to possess me because I was a model and I'd look good on his arm. He had no wicked plans to maim me. Jonathan wasn't Danny, simple as that.

A few days later, I arrived in the clinic in Lamalou where I carried on with my intense physiotherapy, the usual deep massage and water jets, but this time I also baked apple pies to overcome my fear of cooking. The heat from the oven gave me heart palpitations and my pie wasn't quite Jamie Oliver-quality, but triumph made it taste all the sweeter. One night, however, in the common room, I noticed some of the other patients throwing hoops at each other. One flew towards me, and I jumped out of the way like it was a grenade. It was yet another legacy of the attack – I couldn't handle anything being thrown in my direction. Another night, I developed severe pain in my nostrils. The doctor arranged for me to go into a local hospital in the nearby town to have the stents removed under general anaesthetic, and I had to travel in a taxi on my own. When we arrived, no one knew who I was or why I was there, and I didn't know enough French to tell them. 'My name is Katie,' I cried, agitated and upset, until finally they got their act together and whisked me into surgery. Mum, Dad and Mr Jawad had been waiting by the phones back in the UK, desperately worried, but I texted to put their minds at ease.

Apart from those setbacks, I was doing great. Being around the other burns victims was a constant reminder of how lucky I'd been. They hadn't had their faces rebuilt by Mr Jawad or had the use of the cutting-edge Matriderm and, as I looked around, I felt so fortunate – and guilty.

'*Everyone should have access to this kind of treatment*,' I thought as I sat on a bench outside the clinic. Everybody with burns deserved special support to help them get back into society. Leaves rustled overhead, and I closed my eyes as I listened to the larks sing. The sun felt warm on my face, and I inhaled the fragrance of freshly cut grass and summer flowers.

Lounging there underneath a willow tree, I savoured every sensation. Before the attack, I never would have pressed pause on my hectic existence – never would have stopped to smell the roses. And afterwards, every single thing was a potential threat.

I'd hidden away from the world for so long, and it felt so good to be back in it again.

Chapter Twenty
Feeling Loved

Jonathan had texted and phoned religiously while I was in France, and after I got back we arranged to go out for dinner.

I still gagged and choked and vomited a lot when I tried to eat, but that wasn't the only potential problem. I knew the restaurant would be much brighter than the dimly lit pub we had been to, and I knew I'd have to make an extra effort. Then a make-up artist I knew told me about a new mineral powder. It was lighter than the thick, heavy foundation I normally wore, so I thought it might make me feel less self-conscious.

'I need to get some,' I said to Mum. 'It will help me feel more confident.' By now, I'd told her and Dad about Jonathan. They'd smiled and said all the right things, but I knew they were worried. I'd seen the concern in their eyes, the fear that it would go wrong and that I wouldn't be strong enough to cope with it. I was worried about that, too, but I wasn't about to let it stop me.

'Don't worry. We'll go out and get some then,' Mum suggested, so off we went to raid every chemist within a twenty-mile radius until we found it.

However, a few hours before he was due to pick me up, Jonathan texted to say he'd been caught up with meetings at work. '*Can we reschedule?*' he asked. I started crying. He didn't like me after all, I knew it! He'd had second thoughts; he'd met someone who looked normal. He'd decided I was too hard work.

'Or he could just be telling the truth,' Mum reasoned, but I instinctively thought the worst. I was still fragile, and everything was magnified out of all proportion. A make-up hunt was of the utmost importance. A cancelled date was the end of the world.

In the end, though, Mum was right. I got myself into a state over nothing, and the following night Jonathan and I met in the restaurant. Wearing a flowery maxi-dress, with my hair curled and my mineral foundation in place, I willed myself to stay calm. I ignored the butterflies in my tummy and tried not to panic under the harsh overhead lights. I tried to smile and chat casually and not be mortified as I gagged on my fish and had to run to the bathroom to vomit. I tried to stop my hands from shaking, and to believe Jonathan when he said I looked beautiful.

After that, we saw each other a few times a week. We went to the races with my old friend, Tamie; I met Jonathan's mother; and he came to our house to be vetted by Mum and Dad.

'What a lovely young man,' Mum smiled afterwards. 'Intelligent, sociable and relaxed. How he's not married at thirty, I'll never know!'

I rolled my eyes, but secretly I was chuffed they approved.

I began to worry about my mask, however. I took it off every time Jonathan and I had a date, even though I wasn't supposed to, and I knew I was sabotaging my recovery. Still, I couldn't bring myself to tell him about it. I'd dumped so much on him already. Having a girlfriend with a wonky face and scars that make-up could *almost* conceal was one thing – but having a girlfriend who looked like Hannibal Lecter was something else entirely. 'You'll have to tell him eventually, Katie,' Mum said, and I nodded. I would. Just not yet.

A few weeks later, I got a nasty shock of my own. For some reason, I felt the urge to check out Danny's MySpace page. He had no access to the internet in prison so I knew he wouldn't have updated it, but I wondered if anyone had posted anything about me on there.

As soon as I clicked on it, my hands started to tremble. There was a picture of me, in the *Daily Star* bikini I'd worn for a promotions job, and beneath it Danny had recently written: '*My beautiful princess. Sorry. I miss you, babe.*'

I screamed like he'd whispered the words in my ear. Like he'd reached out of the computer and touched me. How had he done that?

'Mum!' I shrieked, and she came running from the kitchen. 'Look! You have to ring the police right away!' I pointed at the poisonous words.

It took Mum a long time to calm me down.

Afterwards, I felt anger. He missed me, did he? Well, I missed me, too. But that pretty blonde in the bikini didn't exist anymore – he'd killed her. But he still wouldn't leave me alone.

The police discovered that Danny had posted the message from his cell with a mobile phone. Mobiles were banned, so his gym privileges were revoked.

'How the hell did he get his hands on a phone?' I cried. He could have been using it to find a hit-man to murder me. He could have been plotting to do away with me forever, or getting another friend to attack me.

'We're looking into it. There's nothing to worry about, Katie,' the police said.

And as if that wasn't bad enough, Danny had had the cheek, the despicable arrogance, to complain to the Ministry of Justice about his punishment of being refused permission to use the prison gym. The story was in the paper – even though I still wasn't identified – under the headline: '**Telly girl's evil rapist bleats for jail "rights".**'

Anger coursed through my veins, and I wanted to scream at the injustice of it all. Did Danny think he was hard done by? He had a roof over his head, he had food in his stomach. His body was whole, not ravaged like mine. He was lucky.

'Just because he can't go to the gym, he thinks he's got problems. What a laugh,' I cried. It was disgusting, but I wasn't all that surprised. Apparently, he was even trying to appeal his rape conviction, too. Why couldn't he just accept what he'd done to me?

*

My treatment still rumbled on. In August 2009, Mr Jawad decided I needed surgery to loosen my jawline and explained he would take skin from my groin and graft it on. It would give me more mobility in my face, but it felt like another step back. More operations, more recovery, more pain.

'You know best.' I gave him a strained smile.

When Mum and I went down for a session with Lisa, I told her how frightened I was of telling Jonathan about my mask.

'You can't stop wearing it, Katie,' she said. 'If you do, your face will deteriorate. You've come so far, you can't let that happen.'

'I know. But how do I tell him?'

'Maybe your mum could broach the matter with him? I'm sure he'll understand.'

I looked at Mum, who nodded in agreement. Was it pathetic of me to depend on my mother to tell my new boyfriend for me? I didn't want to be weak, but I didn't know what else to do.

After that, I had an appointment with the orthodontist. The pressure from my mask had been pushing my teeth out of shape, and I wanted a brace to correct it. There was so much I couldn't control about my body any more, but this was one thing I could, and my heart was set on it.

'It's too soon.' The orthodontist shook her head. 'It's not a good idea to do it while you're still wearing the mask. Let's wait for a while.'

It was the last straw in a rubbish day. I broke down. Mum tried to comfort me with the usual soothing words and platitudes, but I shrugged her off.

'For God's sake, stop patronising me!' I barked, and she turned away, hurt. Poor Mum – she was always first in the firing line. She got the brunt of all my anger and frustration, but I couldn't help it. Sometimes it just overwhelmed me, exploding out with a force that left me ashamed afterwards. We drove home in silence.

Half an hour later, Jonathan arrived at the door. I dashed to my bedroom to fix myself up while Mum showed him in. When I reappeared, I could tell from the look on their faces that she'd told him about the mask. Mum mumbled some excuse and left us alone, and then Jonathan turned to me.

'You shouldn't have worried about it,' he said as he smiled reassuringly. 'I understand why you have to wear the mask, and I don't want to hinder your recovery in any way. I have nothing but admiration for your strength and courage, Katie Piper. I think you're amazing.'

'Thanks,' I managed, flushed with pride and pleasure and relief. 'And you're not so bad yourself!'

The following week, when I went into hospital for the skin graft and jawline treatment, Jonathan came in to visit me. I must've looked a right state, with no make-up on under the unforgiving fluorescent lights, but he didn't bat an eyelid. He just held my hand, and sat with me for hours.

After that, our relationship got even stronger. Nights down the pub with our friends, sitting in with a DVD and a mountain of crisps and then a mini-break to Rome.

Jonathan and I became a proper couple, in every sense. It wasn't easy being intimate with him, at first. I was so squeamish about my private parts I hadn't even used a tampon since the rape, but I wanted to have a normal relationship again so badly. To be an adult woman again, after feeling like a helpless child for so long.

I trusted Jonathan implicitly – he was gentle and understanding, and any time a flashback of the rape struck, I just pushed those horrible images away. I still didn't feel sexy again, but I felt safe and loved. Jonathan was always telling me I was beautiful, even when I had my mask or no make-up on. He accepted me completely, and even though I didn't realise it at the time, I started accepting myself, too. I even bought a huge mirror for my bedroom, and stopped baulking at my reflection.

'He's actually the best boyfriend I've ever had,' I told Mum. 'How ironic that I should meet him now, when I look like this.'

But even though I loved Jonathan and he loved me, I still found it hard to let him in completely. Our love didn't magically fix me, it didn't repair the scars on my soul, and sometimes I held him at arm's length. I blew hot and cold as I worried that Danny would find out about him and try to hurt him somehow.

But I didn't have too much time to dwell on our problems. By October 2009, the documentary – which they'd called *Katie: My Beautiful Face* – was finished and ready to be aired.

I travelled with Mum and Dad to London for a preview screening at Channel 4's offices. Mr Jawad was there, too, along with his wife and children, and all the crew.

I cringed as my scarred face flashed up on the big screen. It was such an intimate thing, exposing myself like that, but my initial embarrassment faded as the footage rolled and I was soon absorbed. In a way it was quite therapeutic to watch all the things I'd been through back and see the progress I'd made.

'Well done, Katie. I'm *so* proud of you,' Mr Jawad exclaimed afterwards, as he took us to an Indian restaurant for dinner.

The next day, I anxiously played the preview DVD for Jonathan. I watched his face more than the screen, and I saw his fury towards Danny building.

'I just want to kill him for doing this to you,' he said afterwards, pulling me into his arms. 'I'm never going to let anyone hurt you ever again.'

A few weeks later, Mags – a lovely lady who did the PR for the production company – asked if I'd be happy doing some publicity for the documentary before it aired. I could do as much or as little as I wanted, she explained. It was all up to me.

'I'll do it,' I agreed. But I had no idea so many people would be interested: I did interview after interview with newspapers and TV programmes like *BBC Breakfast* and *This Morning*. Mum came with me, and she turned to mush when Phillip Schofield came over to say hello. She'd had a crush on him since his *Joseph and his Technicolour Dreamcoat* days, and giggled like a teenager as she asked if she could get a photo with him.

'Stop papping him, Mum,' I nudged her. 'You're embarrassing me!'

Talking to him and Holly Willoughby about how I'd met Danny, and the agony of the acid attack, I realised I hadn't let my attacker bully me into silence and submission. I was sitting on Britain's most famous sofa, speaking out to raise awareness, and I was proud of myself.

When the documentary aired, I was still caught up in all its pre-publicity, and I hadn't had time to really consider the reality of it being beamed into every home across the UK.

'*Bet no one will watch it anyway*,' I thought, as Jonathan and I drove to Tamie's house. We'd arranged to watch it there with some other mates. As Tamie laid out plates of food, fear started to stab at me. I'd already shown Jonathan a preview copy, so I wasn't worried about his reaction. But what about everyone else who saw it? Would they laugh at me? Would they think I was a freak and a fool who should do the world a favour and hide herself away? What if another evil man out there saw it and wanted to hurt me like Danny had?

As the documentary played, I dared to look round the room. Everyone was crying silent tears, and Jonathan squeezed my hand. After it had finished, everyone started speaking at once, with choice and colourful words to describe Danny, mostly.

'You're still beautiful,' Tamie cried. 'I hope he rots in hell.'

Later that night, Jessie, the documentary's director, texted me to say: '*3.8 million!*' I didn't understand. Surely that many people hadn't watched it? Were there 3.8 million complaints? Was my face just too much for TV? '*3.8 million viewers!*' Jessie confirmed, and I gasped. But that was crazy! Surely so many people couldn't be interested in my story? It had to be a mistake.

The next morning, when Suzy and I went shopping in Basingstoke, I knew it wasn't. As we browsed in Accessorize for a thank-you present for Jessie, a lady approached me hesitantly.

'I'm so sorry to bother you,' she smiled. 'But aren't you the girl from the documentary last night?'

'Yes,' I answered nervously.

'It was amazing. I laughed and cried, and I felt for you so much. You're still beautiful, Katie.'

'Wow. Thank you so much,' I stuttered, scarcely able to believe it. For so long, I'd been terrified of strangers, but now, one had walked right up to me and said the kindest, loveliest thing in the world. The lady walked away, and I turned to Suzy.

'High five!' she exclaimed, and I started laughing in shock and delight.

That was just the tip of the iceberg. With every day that went by, I realised just how big the documentary had been. 'Hi, Katie!' people said to me in the street. They stopped me in Paperchase: 'You're brilliant, Katie!' and, 'I hope that animal never gets out,' they called in Primark. It was actually quite overwhelming and for a second, the old fear growled and threatened to pounce. Everyone knew who I was – did that make me more open to attack? It might, but it also made me feel like I didn't have to hide away any more.

'*It's so weird*,' I thought. '*Before all this, I was a wannabe chasing fame. Now I've got what I wanted, but it's not fame I'm after this time. It's acceptance*.'

After the documentary aired, letters started pouring in, too. Addressed to, '*Katie, the girl off Channel 4*', they flowed through our letter box by the dozen, from people of all ages, men and women from all over the country. Other burns victims, women who'd endured domestic violence, girls who had been raped, blokes injured in bike crashes or car accidents, teenagers bullied because of acne or their weight. People who just wanted to send their love:

'When you walk down the street, I want you to hold your head high 'cause you, my darling, are one in a billion.'

'Be proud of your beautiful new face, Katie. It lets through the glorious shining sun of your beautiful soul.'

'Please accept the best wishes for the future from a stranger who was astounded by your courage and who thinks you are still so beautiful.'

'I am the father of two sons who are around the same age as you and would like to let you know that if either of them walked through my front door with you on their arm, I would be proud and delighted they had found such a lovely person.'

'Katie, you are beautiful. The brilliance of your courage outshines the sun. Never give in. Your dreams will come true.'

'Dear Katie, I'm eleven and you are my hero.'

'You are a rare and shining star. Never let your light go out.'

It was breathtaking, and I read them all with tears rolling down my face. These strangers cared about me. They'd taken the time to put pen to paper and write to me, and it meant the world. I replied to each and every one; personal, handwritten responses that could never convey the depth of the gratitude I felt. I tried to advise other burns victims about creams and treatments, and exchanged stories with them. Gifts were flooding in, too. Topshop sent me a whole box filled to the brim with jewellery; Karen Millen sent me a gorgeous red patent bag; and the cricketer Kevin Pietersen and his wife Jessica Taylor, who used to be in Liberty X, sent me a hundred different nail varnishes. With a smile, I remembered those men who used to send me perfume and porridge when I had started out presenting. In a way, I'd come full circle – but how different things were now. How different *I* was now.

'Why would they do this for me?' I cried to Jonathan, so touched by their generosity.

'Because they admire you, Katie,' he grinned.

The outpouring of support was unbelievable. I'd never anticipated anything like it, never dreamed so many people would care. As I sat surrounded by letters and presents, I felt any last vestiges of shame melt away. The internet was abuzz with people discussing my story, and someone had even set up a fan site. But, inevitably, it wasn't all positive. Some people left vile and sickening posts suggesting I deserved it because I was a model, or because I'd dated someone who was mixed-race.

'*That's what she gets for mixing with non-whites,*' one idiot had written. How could anything like this – anything at all in fact –

be to do with skin colour? Danny was wicked to the core and Stefan was his despicable sidekick, and their evil had nothing to do with their race. For crying out loud, Mr Jawad was an Asian Muslim and he was the kindest person I'd ever met. I didn't want my story to be fodder for crazy racists, used to fuel their disgusting white power delusions. For a minute I was tempted to post a message myself, explaining just what I thought of them, but then I thought better of it. They weren't worth my time.

Instead, I focused on the positive comments and for the first time in long time, I felt something warm spreading through. It was self-belief. I was going to get through this.

Chapter Twenty-One
No More Hiding

After the mobile debacle, the police reassured us there was nothing to worry about, but how could they be sure? Who knew what Danny had done with that mobile phone? Or who he had contacted? My brain went into overdrive as I imagined his bloody, brutal revenge. More acid? Or maybe fire this time. Would I be the target, or would it be someone I loved instead?

In November 2009, Warren phoned with some news that seemed incredible. Danny had actually been given the mobile by a female prison guard, with whom he'd been having an affair. Over four weeks the previous February, they'd exchanged 210 texts, twenty-three hours of calls – and who knew what else. My stomach flipped with revulsion. That woman was in a position of trust. She would have known what he was in prison for, she knew that he'd been convicted of the acid attack and was waiting for the retrial on the rape. And yet she'd had an affair with him, and not only that, given him a phone: a line to the outside world, with no thought for how he could use it to harm me or my family. What a stupid, selfish idiot. Was she deluded?

Or desperate? Or just plain evil, like him? While he had been canoodling in his cell, I had been on tenterhooks, terrified of going back to court. I remembered how I'd imagined him, alone and scared in his bunk. What a kick in the teeth. What a cruel joke.

The woman admitted misconduct in a public office and was due to be sentenced in a few months' time, so now I had that to think about, too. It just felt like every time I was moving forward, Danny dragged me back down. Would this never end?

A few days later, my phone rang again.

'Katie, are you sitting down? I've got some news.' It was Mags, the publicity lady for the production company, who was now acting as my agent.

'Has Danny escaped from prison? Is he on the loose?' I babbled down the phone, struck by a bolt of terror. It surged through my body, and I peered out of the window, expecting to see his evil face on the other side of the glass. He could be here any second.

'No, no, it's good news,' Mags said, and I sank to the sofa, shaky with relief. 'Simon Cowell just rang me. He saw the documentary, and he wants to speak to you.'

'He what? Are you sure it was really him?'

'Yes, babe! Can I give him your number?'

'Okay. Great!' I replied, certain it must be a wind-up. Simon Cowell was one of the most influential men in media-savvy Britain – why would he want to speak to me?

Five minutes later, my mobile started to ring. Private number. '*Oh my God!*'

'Hi, Katie. Simon Cowell here,' that famous voice said. There was no mistaking it. It really was him!

'Oh, hello,' I stammered, trying to sound nonchalant when really I wanted to giggle and scream with excitement.

'I watched the documentary, and I really felt for you. What do you want to do with your life?'

'Well, erm, I'm not really sure,' I managed, my heart thumping and my hands damp with sweat.

'We should meet up. Why don't you come to my office? I'll text you my number and we can sort something out.'

'Brilliant. Okay, thanks. Bye, Simon!' I hung up and jumped round my bedroom. A moment later, my phone pinged and I laughed as I saved his number into my contacts list. Since the attack, I'd only had nine people on my phone – and now Simon-bloody-Cowell was number ten!

The next week Mags came with me to meet Simon in Sony's swanky Kensington HQ. Dressed in a pretty ra-ra skirt, black jumper and suede boots, I was too excited to feel embarrassed as we walked into his office. It was like a posh Mayfair penthouse, with lilies floating in a bowl and expensive candles dotted around.

'You look great!' Simon smiled, shaking my hand. 'How are you doing? Are you okay being out of the house?'

'I'm good! The documentary finished a while ago, so I've come on a bit since then.'

'I was so impressed by you, Katie,' he went on, his manner so warm and caring that I felt like I'd just won *The X Factor*. 'Are you still interested in presenting? If so, I could help you find a job.'

Wow. The old me would have sold her soul for an offer like that. This was the big time, the major league, the golden ticket – a job offer from the biggest TV mogul in the whole country.

But I wasn't tempted for a second. I was so different now, and those ambitions had died a long time ago.

'Thank you so much, Simon,' I smiled shyly. 'But I want to do something to help people. Something that really matters to me.'

'That's marvellous! Just let me know if there's anything I can do,' he smiled. 'Want to come and watch *The X Factor* in a few weeks? You can bring your family if you like.'

'I'd love to. Thank you so much!'

All the way home, I thought how kind Simon had been, how amazing his job offer was. And yet I'd turned it down. I didn't want fame for fame's sake any more – I couldn't walk away from what had happened to me. I wanted to help people. But what could I possibly do? I was still afraid of so many things. I was living on benefits, and I had zero computer or administration skills.

'You can do whatever you set your mind to,' Mags said. 'Just have a think about what that is.'

A few weeks later, she asked if I wanted to go to the Cultural Diversity Network Awards, a fancy ceremony celebrating diversity on TV. It was the first time I'd ever been invited to anything like that, and I decided to go for it.

Like any girl, I agonised about what to wear – until Mags announced Victoria Beckham wanted to lend me one of her dresses. I couldn't believe it, until I opened the box, when I gasped. It was the same dress I'd seen a picture of Drew Barrymore wearing – deep purple with a pencil skirt and sexy strapless top.

'It's beautiful,' I squealed, stroking the fabric.

The day of the bash, Mags took me to the hairdressers to get my locks put in a sophisticated chignon that covered my scarred ear. I had also decided I didn't want to wear my camouflage make-up.

'I'm not going to hide my face,' I insisted, but there was more to it than that. Even though I had that stunning gown, a part of me still felt like there was no point in even trying to make my face look better. I wondered if my make-up made me look even worse – like I was trying to hide something that was painfully, pathetically obvious.

I arrived with my scars on show, and tried not to feel embarrassed as Mags and I took our seats. Nearby was a gorgeous Asian woman. Her features were doll-like, her make-up immaculate. Bright red lipstick on a Cupid's bow mouth, and liquid eyeliner flicked over her eyelids. I couldn't tear my eyes away from her.

'*She's like a work of art,*' I thought. Before the attack, I'd looked like that. I had been invited to parties because I looked good. I had been an ornament, a pretty little decoration. And now

I was invited – why? I didn't really know. As I stared at that Asian beauty, I didn't feel envy exactly. I didn't feel any grief that I'd never look like that again; I just wasn't sure if I belonged there.

Two weeks later, Dad, Mum, Paul, Suzy and I took Simon Cowell up on his offer to go to one of the *The X Factor* live shows. We drove to London, and clapped and cheered as the hopefuls sang their hearts out, after which Rihanna showed them how it was done.

As it was wrapping up, Simon texted and invited us backstage. We all made our way to his dressing room. The door flung open, and we found him inside with Sinitta and Rihanna herself.

'Lovely to meet you,' she smiled, leaning forward and kissing my mask. She kissed my mask. Rihanna kissed my mask!

Simon made me laugh by showing me his bathroom and sharing a secret: 'I like to lie in the bath and watch cartoons on my plasma TV. Helps me relax.' Who'd have thought it!

Just like before, he was so nice, asking Mum about her teaching job and Dad about his barber shop. I was on cloud nine as we travelled home again. This influential, important man accepted me. He cared about me, just like all those lovely people who were still sending me letters and their best wishes. Just like Jonathan, and my family and friends. Simon Cowell wasn't embarrassed to be seen with me.

As I drifted off to sleep, I thought maybe – just maybe – it was okay to be me after all.

*

I couldn't stop thinking about what Mags had said. In my heart, I knew what I wanted to do. I wanted to set up a charity for burns victims in the UK, to help them get the treatment I'd received in France. I visualised a sparkling new centre, where burns victims could feel safe, where they could have access to the intense rehabilitation that had helped me heal physically and emotionally, and totally changed my life.

'Katie, that's a brilliant idea! You have to do it,' Mags exclaimed when I told her.

But I was so frightened of failure. I was frightened that I wouldn't be able to do it, that I'd crumble under the stress and let everybody down.

'But I don't know the first place to start,' I said. I couldn't even use a photocopier, for crying out loud.

'I'll help you with all the paperwork. You can do it!'

Like Mr Jawad, Mags believed in me and, with their unwavering support, we got the ball rolling. In December 2009, after filling in a million forms, the Katie Piper Foundation was registered. Mr Jawad and Mags' friend Ros agreed to be trustees and, even though my charity was just me and my ancient laptop, it was the beginning of something.

'I have every confidence in you, Katie,' Mr Jawad smiled. 'From little things, big things grow.'

The next few weeks were a whirlwind of activity. Mum, Suzy and I travelled to Rome for me to appear on a talk-show there, then Dad and I did an interview with the *Sunday Times*. An

American film crew came over to film me, and Channel 4 wanted to do a follow-up documentary. They also asked if I'd like to do their alternative Christmas message. Previous speakers had included Ali G, Marge Simpson and Sharon Osbourne, and I couldn't believe they wanted me.

'There was such an amazing response to your documentary,' they explained, and I agreed like a shot. What an honour.

With all that was happening, it was perhaps to be expected that something had to give. My relationship with Jonathan had started to suffer. I had started spending more and more time at his, but with my days now chock-a-block with activity, I wasn't sitting round waiting for him to come home from work any more. As well as my hospital appointments, I was venturing out into the world once more. I was preoccupied with the charity and regaining my independence, and I knew he felt neglected. Not in a cruel, mean-spirited, jealous way – he was much too kind for that. He just missed the way things used to be when it was just the two of us.

Nor did it help matters that I didn't mention him in any interviews.

'Why are you denying my existence?' he'd demand, and I'd try to explain. I was trying to protect him from Danny, for one thing. Who knew how he'd react if he found out I had a new boyfriend? I couldn't risk putting Jonathan in danger like that. And I didn't want my private life to be public property, either. So much of what I'd been through had been exposed; I wanted to keep something back. Something just for me. But no matter how much I tried to make Jonathan understand, it was still driving a wedge between us. But we muddled on and by the time Christmas Day arrived, I had pushed my worries to the back of my mind. We'd be okay – we had to be.

On Christmas morning, I thought back to the previous year. I remembered how lost I'd felt, still reeling from the first court case and sick with nerves about the upcoming retrial. I'd accomplished so much in the twelve months since; overcome so many hurdles. I hadn't finished yet, but I was definitely on the right path.

Breaking me from my reverie, Paul handed me a present, and looked on expectantly as I ripped off the shiny wrapping paper. It was a calendar, with a different picture of Mr Jawad for every single month of the year – brilliant!

'I love it!' I managed in between guffaws. It was hilarious, but Paul knew Mr Jawad really was my hero. I didn't idolise a pop star or a Hollywood actor; I idolised the doctor who'd worked so hard to rebuild my face.

After our traditional turkey lunch, we all went into the lounge to watch the Christmas message I'd recorded a few weeks earlier.

'Who needs the Queen when our Kate's on telly?' Dad smiled proudly. As I watched my face appear on the screen, I only felt a little hint of the old embarrassment. Then I listened to my words:

'My life before [the attack] was very self-absorbed, self-obsessed, and it took a tragedy for me to reassess my life and how I felt and what I thought was important. Don't wait until there is tragedy in your life. Don't wait until you lose somebody. Don't wait until it's too late. Appreciate the beautiful things and the beautiful people that you have in your life now ... My Christmas message would be to tell people that I used to hide away and be ashamed of how I looked, frightened of people's reactions. If people are doing that or feel that way now, I would urge them not to, because they don't have to feel like that. You can become accepted, you can regain the confidence. And for the people that need to do the accepting, who maybe freak out when they see somebody who's different, you absolutely don't have to.

'Even when you think things can never move forward and you feel so low, there's always a way out. I never thought that I'd be sitting here saying this. Never.'

After it had finished, there was a moment of silence as we sat there, just remembering.

'Hear, hear!' Dad said quietly, and we all clinked glasses.

Mr Jawad was still constantly researching new treatments for me, and suggested I go to see a specialist in Turkey called Professor Erol, who used stem and fat cells to help burned skin. The treatment would even be funded by the Professor's own trust that he'd set up for people like me. He thought I was a perfect candidate, so in early 2010 we flew to Istanbul with Mum and Mr Jawad to have the procedure done.

As soon as we stepped out of the taxi in the business district, the looks started. They were even more blatant than at home, and I realised that some of the men must think I was an adulteress or sinner, marked for life as punishment for some crime. Their cold glares frightened me, and we hurried through the wind and sleet into the sanctuary of our hotel.

The next day, we went to meet Professor Erol, who had trained Mr Jawad and also treated a Turkish actress who'd been acid attacked by her boyfriend. 'I'll remove fat from your legs and bottom, and inject it into your face,' he explained. 'The stem cells will regenerate, building up the tissue and contours of your face.'

After it was done, I wouldn't be putting my mask back on. This fact, strangely, gave me mixed emotions. Sure, the eighteen months of wearing the mask as much as possible would be over. But, after everything, I felt anxious at the thought of losing it. Even though I'd loathed it in the beginning, even though I'd agonised over how to tell Jonathan about it, the mask was still my security blanket, my protective shield, in case anyone tried to hurt me.

The morning of the operation, I took it off for the last time and held it in my hands. It was my eighth mask, and my final one. I traced my fingers over the cold, hard plastic. It was like a piece of me, as much a part of my body as a lock of my hair. How strange to be losing it now. It had started off as my worst enemy and had become my best friend. It had helped me heal, physically and mentally, but I knew I couldn't wear it forever. I couldn't stop making progress, however difficult it might be. Wrapping it up in a cardigan, I packed it away in my bag.

When I awoke from the surgery a few hours later, my face looked like I'd gone ten rounds with Mohammed Ali. Battered and bruised, my lips were so swollen I could barely speak. Still, Mr Jawad and the specialist were confident it had gone well, and I was discharged back to our hotel to rest with an ice-pack over my face.

The next day, we flew back home. I recuperated at Jonathan's, and tried not to feel naked and vulnerable without my mask. A prop from my convalescence, I really did have to look the world directly in the eye now.

The following afternoon, Jonathan and I drove back to Mum and Dad's. There, we found a massive bunch of carnations sitting on the doorstep with a card that read: '*To Katie, I love you so much.*' There was no name, so I assumed he was another well-wisher who'd seen the documentary. Even two months after it had aired, letters and presents like flowers and CDs were still arriving by the bagful, from even as far away as America and Australia.

Carrying the bouquet indoors, I put them in water and didn't think much more about it until the next night, when Dad phoned as I was round at Jonathan's.

'Katie, I think it's best if you don't come home,' Dad said in a tight, anxious voice.

'Why? What's wrong?'

'There was a man hanging round the village, asking where we live. Apparently he was sitting in a car outside the pub for ages, with a cup on the dashboard.'

A cup. Those two little words were enough to make me freeze with pure fear. Was there acid in there? Was it meant for me? I didn't have my mask any more; there was nothing to protect my face. Or was it meant for Mum and Dad? Or Suzy? She looked like me from behind. What if he got her by mistake? Was he sent by Danny? '*Oh God, please don't let anything bad happen. Not now, not after everything.*'

'Don't panic,' Dad went on. 'Just stay there. I'll let you know as soon as I find out more.'

The man – a taxi driver, who was from London and totally unrelated to Danny – was the same one who had left the flowers. The police arrested him, and he told them he'd seen me on TV and he was in love with me. The cup on his dashboard didn't contain anything harmful and he was warned not to try contacting me again, but that didn't reassure me much. He knew where we lived, so he could come back at any time.

'He won't try anything else, Katie,' Jonathan reassured me. But no one knew better than I did how much damage one determined man could wreak.

The next day, a big parcel arrived addressed to me. I opened it up gingerly, as if there might be a bomb inside. I peered in. There was a tiger teddy, a bracelet, more flowers, photocopies of bank statements and a passport – all presumably designed to put me at ease. And a note: '*Please don't tell the police about this. I love you. I looked at the moon on New Year's Eve and I saw our faces together in it. I haven't kissed a girl in ages, but I want to kiss you.*'

I threw the note to the floor and burst into tears. Why me? Why me? *Why me?*

Chapter Twenty-Two
Funny Old World

The police re-arrested the man and charged him with harassment, and I made my feelings known in no uncertain terms. 'Tell that guy I do not want him contacting me in any way at all. He has intimidated and frightened me. I don't know him, and I don't want to know him,' I told the officer who rang to keep me updated.

But behind those strong words, I was a mess. My safety had been compromised, my home had been violated, and I didn't know if I was strong enough to cope. He was released on bail and barred from coming anywhere near our town, but Danny hadn't been particularly worried about breaking the law, had he?

'He's just a nutter,' Jonathan tried to rationalise it. 'He's probably harmless.'

Sure, he didn't seem violent or aggressive. But even if that man was harmless, he knew what I'd been through. He must have known how much his actions would scare me. Did he actually think we were destined to be together? That a relationship could grow from this terror?

To put my mind at ease, Dad installed floodlights in our front garden, but I was realising all over again just how dangerous the world could be. It was like a wake-up call. It was the dark side to waiving my anonymity for the documentary, and every time I left the house, I looked over my shoulder constantly. I felt myself slipping back as the fear took hold of me once again. But I knew I couldn't start hiding away again.

It was hard, though, especially when the news of Danny's affair was suddenly splashed all over the papers for a second time. The prison warden's defence claimed she was naive and immature, and Danny had bullied and threatened her. They maintained she had no idea he was accused of rape, but the judge at Blackfriars Crown Court sentenced her to twenty-one months in prison anyway. Good. When I read excerpts from their texts, I wanted to vomit. Danny had called her his '*princess*', just like he used to call me. And she'd written: '*I miss you, can't wait to see you and hold you. Sweet dreams.*' What a travesty. It was truly sickening.

What with that and my stalker, I was almost ready to call it quits and retreat from the world all over again. But I couldn't let myself. '*The good things outweigh the bad,*' I told myself. '*Don't give up, Katie.*' Besides, I had responsibilities now – I had the Foundation to think about.

At the beginning of February 2010, I started using an office in a secure business park in a nice part of London. A business man called Andrew Birks had generously offered it to me rent-free and, as I unpacked my meagre stationery supplies with Jonathan, I was brimming with excitement.

'You'll have to show me how to load the stapler,' I giggled. 'I haven't a clue!'

Thankfully, I was never there alone – one of the Channel 4 camera crew was normally filming me, and if they weren't there then one of my friends came over. But I was driving there all by myself. I was walking through the foyer, past suited business-men and women. I was able to get in the lift with strange blokes, even if it did make my heart pound to be trapped in an enclosed space with them. And I was even drinking coffee I made with my own two hands in the communal kitchen area. Sipping the hot liquid as I flicked through the charity's inbox, which was crashing under the weight of incoming emails, I sighed with contentment.

Meanwhile, my stalker pleaded guilty to harassment at Basingstoke Magistrates Court. The judge issued a restraining order, and I tried to put the whole thing behind me. To not think about what other men might be out there trying to find me, or fantasising that we should be together.

Gradually, I learned how to print documents and make spreadsheets. I set up a bank account and PayPal account, I bought cute little tweed jackets to wear to work. I also started going to meetings with other charities. Someone always came with me, but I was learning how to walk into a room full of strangers without an anxiety attack. To feel all their eyes on my face and not want to run away and cry. I was a woman on a mission, hell-bent on getting the charity up and running.

We couldn't afford to employ anyone so I had to spend lots of late nights in the office. Jonathan wasn't best pleased. He wanted to settle down, but I didn't, not yet. I didn't want to relinquish the little bit of independence I'd regained. I didn't want to rely on a man – even one as lovely as he. My independence was too precious to me, and so was the charity.

'We want different things,' I cried, during one of our many arguments.

Jonathan had been like an emotions defibrillator. He'd breathed life into my heart when I thought it was dead. He'd made me feel safe when I needed it most. He'd seen past the scars and shown me that I deserved to be loved, just like any other girl. He'd thought I was beautiful, and he'd made me feel sexy and desirable again. It was just what I had needed at that time to bring me back to life. But I wasn't that victim any more. I was stronger, I was more self-sufficient, and I had goals I was determined to reach. Even though Jonathan was happy for me, it meant we couldn't be together any more.

'Look after yourself.' We kissed one last time, and then it was over.

From the worried look in Mum and Dad's eyes when I told them, I could tell they expected me to crack under the strain. But I didn't. The knowledge that I'd had a boyfriend looking the way I did carried me through, and so did the fact that I was single by choice. I could have stayed with Jonathan, perhaps worked harder to mend the cracks. But I had had to go my own way in the end. I knew I'd always be so thankful for him.

Of course, I got lonely – I missed the affection and the intimacy we had had, but my days were so busy. Between check-ups, getting my brace finally fitted to straighten my teeth and visiting hospitals for the charity, I hadn't any time to mope. Mr Jawad was constantly checking in on me, and fun things took my mind off the break-up, too – like having a style day at Topshop with Suzy. With the help of a style adviser, we tried on a hundred different outfits, and I knew from the way Suzy beamed that she was happy to have her big sister back. Fashion had been such a big part of my old life, and reclaiming my love of clothes felt empowering and liberating somehow.

Mags also took me to the Television and Radio Awards in the Dorchester Hotel in London, and I managed to relax and enjoy myself even though I was conscious of being the only burned person there. Mingling with the likes of Laurence Llewellyn-Bowen, Eamonn Holmes, Ruth Langsford and Chris Evans didn't give me the same buzz that it would have in the old days, before the attack, but it was nice to be surrounded by people who accepted me; to take my place in a world I thought would have cast me out. Representing the Acid Survivors Trust International at the Asian Music Awards; going to Downing Street for International Women's Week – I had to pinch myself each time. I was in the same room as the then Prime Minister Gordon Brown. Me – Katie Piper!

Anyone who could have seen me there, wearing a smart black Karen Millen dress and chatting to Mr Jawad and Annie Lennox, probably would have thought I had completely recovered. But I hadn't. I might be driving to places on my own, but I never walked the streets of London by myself, ever. After all, I'd told the world how scared I was, and thanks to my stalker, I'd realised how vulnerable that made me. Even in the safety of my car, I sometimes had panic attacks if I spotted a man in a hoody, weaving his way towards me. Any kind of aggression or violence – in real-life or even on telly – made me burst into tears, like when I saw a cyclist and a motorist get into a fight as I waited at a red light. Electrical equipment made me uneasy, and I'd annoyed my family on more than one occasion by sneakily throwing out old hairdryers and fan heaters. People coming up to me in the street terrified me too, like the girl who had shouted, 'Katie!' and grabbed my arm from behind. She had just wanted to say she'd seen me in the documentary, but the shock almost made me faint. As for the gawping from strangers, I'd grown used to it. It still had the power to make me feel embarrassed, but I wasn't ashamed any more. Sometimes I ignored them, and other times I met their gaze and stared back at them defiantly.

'What's wrong with your face?' a lady in the newsagents gasped one afternoon. Instead of telling her, I feigned surprise.

'What do you mean? Am I bleeding?' I gasped.

'No,' she stammered.

Point made, I left.

When I looked in the mirror now, I didn't wish for my old face any more. What was the point? I was never going to get it back. No matter how much treatment I received, it would never fully recover. It was like getting over a bereavement or a bad break-up: I'd worked through the stages of grief, from denial to anger to acceptance. I reminded myself there were others much worse off than me. But that didn't stop me missing it. On my bad days – when my make-up wouldn't go on right, or I tried on a dress and thought it would look better on someone who wasn't disfigured, or my heated rollers burned my ear and I freaked out – I cried with frustration and would wish I'd known I was going to be attacked. I'd have spent the day before dolling myself up. I'd have slicked on scarlet lipstick and sophisticated eye make-up, and I would have savoured every single second.

At the beginning of April 2010, Mum and I went back over to Istanbul for the second part of my stem-cell treatment. The night we arrived, we went out to a local restaurant for dinner, and we talked like we hadn't done in ages. For the first time ever, I told her about some of the hallucinations I'd had in hospital, though I didn't reveal the full horror of them. Mum had suffered enough, I thought. I didn't want her to hurt any more.

'You and Dad are probably the ones closest to understanding what I went through,' I told her.

'No one understands but you, Kate,' Mum wept, and we held hands across the table. 'You've been so brave, and we're so proud of you.'

When I was taken into surgery the next morning, I whispered a little prayer my nurse friend, Alice, and I had written so many months earlier, when I was in the high dependency room after the attack. 'Please God, guide the doctor's hands and let me wake up again. Don't let me die under the anaesthetic.'

A few hours later, I woke up in recovery and Mum took me back to the hotel to rest. Weak and a bit woozy, I was lying watching CNN when I heard a noise from the room next door. It sounded like a woman crying and, all of a sudden, I had a flashback to the rape. Goosebumps shot up on my skin, my heart pounded, and I remembered how I'd felt when I was at Danny's mercy. How I'd wished someone would hear me and come to my aid. I smelled his stale sweat. I felt the weight of him bearing down on me.

'Is that woman being attacked?' I cried to Mum. 'Maybe we should ring Reception!'

'I'll go and listen at their door,' Mum said, disappearing into the hall. I waited, terrified, until she reappeared a moment later.

'It's okay, Kate. The woman's just laughing,' she said soothingly, and I started sobbing. But I wasn't frightened any more – instead, I was furious. Furious that Danny still had the power to scare me after two long years had gone by. Mr Jawad and a host of other doctors and nurses and therapists had toiled to treat the scars on my body, but what about the scars on my soul? They were still there, no matter how much I tried to ignore them, and they were the deepest ones of all.

I thought about all the other women out there with invisible scars, hiding their pain under smiles. I remembered one lady who'd come up to me in the street one day with tears in her eyes. She'd shaken my hand, and right there and then. I knew she must have been raped, too.

Slowly but surely, as time went on, the bad days were becoming less frequent. At the end of May, I braved the crowds to watch the London Marathon. My trustee, Ros, and my brother, Paul, were both running to raise money for the Foundation, and I couldn't believe I was there to cheer them on. It was the third year Paul had run the marathon – the first time, I was in a coma after the attack, and the second I was housebound with fear. But now, here I was, shouting and waving as he sprinted past. Another milestone had been reached and, in between endless meetings for the charity and operations on my throat, I was starting to think seriously about moving back to London.

'Are you sure that's what you want to do, Kate?' Dad frowned. 'You can stay with us, you know, that don't you? You could get a job in the village, and have a quiet life here.'

'Your dad's right,' Mum added. 'How would you cope there on your own? Wouldn't you be better staying here?'

It was a good question, but I knew moving was the next step. It was something I had to do, if I was ever going to live a normal life again. But there was also another reason: buried deep in my heart was the fear that I only had sixteen years left. Danny would be out of prison in that time. And he'd surely come after me. The clock was ticking, and I had to make sure I was strong enough to cope with what might happen then.

'Maybe I could get somewhere gated, with a concierge,' I mused. 'And with underground parking, so I could park my car and go up to my flat in a lift or something. That way, I wouldn't need to be on the street.' That was what scared me the most. Having to walk from my car to my front door, or vice versa, in the darkness. I'd be a sitting duck, so open to attack.

In March, 2010, two years after the attack, I signed up with a few estate agents and started viewing flats. But those high-security ones were totally out of my price range. I'd received some compensation after the attack, but it was only enough for a modest deposit. And, since the Foundation had launched I'd mostly been working voluntarily. It was so demoralising. I realised I had to radically adjust my expectations. There would be no concierge, no security gates, no underground parking on my budget. But I still needed somewhere I felt completely, 100 per cent safe.

By the end of May, the charity was really taking off. Donations were starting to come in and Simon Cowell had agreed to be a patron, so the trustees and I decided to plan a launch party to celebrate, and drum up more publicity for the Foundation. Simon offered us the use of his Sony offices, and we began drawing up guest lists and sending out invitations. Meanwhile, *Katie: My Beautiful Face* was nominated for a prestigious BAFTA for Best Single Documentary, and I was invited to go to the ceremony at the beginning of June.

The evening was as exciting – and nerve-racking – as going to the Oscars would be for me. I got a spray tan especially, and a stylist dressed me in a gorgeous black strapless gown with gold sandals and a gold bangle. With my hair slicked over to one side, I walked down the red carpet.

The paparazzi flashed their cameras in my face and the crowd cheered, but all I could think was how ironic it all was: '*The old me would've thought she'd died and gone to heaven if this was happening to her.*' I was still star-struck by the constellation of celebs – familiar faces from *EastEnders*, Simon and JLS, big-screen names like Helen Mirren – but it was different now. I was different.

The documentary had meant so much to me, as had the people who had made it and who had become such good friends, and I wanted it to win so badly. When it was time for our category, I crossed my fingers and exchanged a nervous grin with Jessie, the director. First, they showed clips from each nominee. My scarred face flashed up on the huge screen, and I heard my quivering voice say: 'And then I looked in the mirror, and saw my face.' I was used to seeing my injuries – my appearance couldn't shock me any more, but it was still strange to see it up there. Blood rushed to my cheeks as applause rang out.

'And the winner is ...' the presenter said, opening the envelope. I held my breath '*Oh, no!*' It wasn't us, and the cameraman perched beside me got a clear shot as I screwed my face up and rolled my eyes in disappointment.

'How embarrassing,' I giggled to Jessie. 'The losers are supposed to look really gracious and pleased for the winner. I must've looked like a right madam!'

It was still a wonderful night, though. Kara Tointon, who played Dawn in *EastEnders*, came over to say hello to me, and at the after-party I found myself standing next to Helena Bonham Carter. It was surreal, but in a good way.

'*It's a funny old world,*' I thought that night. For so long I'd mourned my old life, but I didn't want it back. Too much had happened, and I had changed too much. I didn't want to be one of those celebrities, idolised and adored. There was much more to life than beauty and fame, I thought, as I drifted off to sleep.

Chapter Twenty-Three
New Beginnings

After the BAFTAs, I started meeting more burns victims, both through the charity and for my second documentary, which was scheduled to air in early 2011. I met a twenty-four-year-old Irish girl called Emily, who had suffered seventy per cent burns in a horrific house fire when she was just seven. A twelve-year-old called Terri, who was badly burned as a baby and still faced years of reconstructive work. A sixteen-year-old boy called Will, his upper body injured by a barbeque. A nineteen-year-old girl called Adele, who'd had an epileptic fit and collapsed under scalding water in the shower. Because we'd all been through the same thing, there was an instant camaraderie between us. We all knew what it was like to endure one operation after another, to hate your reflection in the mirror. I tried to help them in any way I could.

'I've had a boyfriend,' I told them. 'Lots of people won't be bothered by your scars, I promise.' They inspired me, too, though. These were the kind of people I wanted to help through the Foundation, and it seemed like a whole other world was opening up to me. I also met a professional make-up artist called

Katey, who'd emailed me volunteering to help with the charity. Her husband, Simon, who was a successful businessman, became our chairman and gave me lots of practical advice and guidance on fundraising.

At the beginning of July, Mr Jawad and I were invited to a garden party at Buckingham Palace, which was being held to celebrate Princess Anne's sixtieth birthday, for our work with Acid Survivors Trust International. As we mingled with our fellow charity campaigners, I couldn't quite believe I was there.

'You look lovely,' Mr Jawad smiled, and I looked down at my fitted blue dress and pink shoes.

'Thanks! You do, too. Nice suit,' I grinned, popping a *vol-au-vent* into my mouth. Even after all this time, however, my throat still gave me problems, and I was still having to have it dilated every eight weeks. As soon as I swallowed the flaky pastry, I knew it was going to come straight back up again. '*Oh, no. I was going to vomit in the gardens of Buckingham Palace.*'

'I'm going to be sick,' I mumbled, trying to keep my lips clamped together in case any food shot out.

'Use this,' Mr Jawad said, handing me his silk handkerchief.

'No way. Can't use that!' I shook my head. It was much too good to ruin.

'Go on, I don't mind,' he insisted, but thankfully one of the waiters handed me a bit of kitchen roll instead. As discreetly as possible, I spat out the regurgitated food and Mr Jawad disposed of it for me. How mortifying.

'Let's take a walk in the garden,' he suggested, and we headed towards the perfectly manicured lawns.

Away from the crowds, we talked happily. 'How are you doing, then?' he asked kindly. 'Are you happy?'

'Yes, I'm learning how to be,' I smiled, as we took a seat on a bench next to a lake filled with pretty pink waterlilies. 'Thanks to you.'

I thought about how Mr Jawad had worked so tirelessly for me from the beginning. He'd fought for the best treatment for a nameless girl without a face, a girl he'd never met before. He didn't need to do that, but that was the kind of man he was, and he was now like a second father to me. So many times, I'd wanted to give up and I hadn't, because I hadn't wanted to let him down. So many times his phone calls and emails had lifted me and given me the will to fight on.

'*If I ever have a son,*' I thought, '*I'll name him Ali in honour of Mr Mohammed Ali Jawad.*'

'I didn't want to tell you this before,' Mr Jawad now began hesitantly, 'but do you remember I told you that the specialist in Istanbul had treated the Turkish actress, who was acid attacked by her partner?'

I nodded, and he went on: 'When he was released from prison, he killed her.' He paused when he noticed my expression, but pressed on: 'Are you worried about that happening to you?'

No one had ever asked me that outright before, but that was the kind of relationship Mr Jawad and I had. We were completely honest with each other. As I looked at his face, etched with worry, I knew I had to tell the truth. He didn't want me to suffer in silence. He wanted to be there for me, to help me.

'Yes,' I gasped out loud. I doubted Danny would ever change his ways, and by doing the documentary, I had probably incensed him even more. I'd told the police; I'd spoken out about him – just like he warned me not to.

'But he won't be out for sixteen years. That's a long time.' I tried to smile, and Mr Jawad nodded. We sat in silence, and he looked into the distance with sadness in his eyes. I wondered what he was thinking. Did he think Danny would come after me, too? Then he jumped to his feet.

'Take a picture of me on my phone,' he grinned mischievously.

'But we're not allowed to take photos here,' I reminded him.

'Nonsense! I must show my family back in Pakistan that I have made it to Buckingham Palace!'

Afterwards, Mr Jawad refused to leave until he'd put me safely in a taxi. 'A proper taxi, too,' he insisted. 'A black one, not one of those dodgy cabs.' I climbed inside and waved as it pulled away and, once again, thanked God for Mr Jawad.

The next night, it was a dinner for Islamic Help – another charity Mr Jawad was involved in. They helped acid attack victims in Asia who didn't have access to the wonderful treatment I'd received, and I'd become their ambassador to help raise awareness for them.

'I'd like to go to Pakistan one day,' I smiled to Mr Jawad. 'Once the centre is up and running. I want to help acid attack victims from overseas, too.'

The night after, I went to the Police Bravery Awards, where I convinced David Cameron to pose in a photo with me. 'I don't think he had a clue who I was, but he was too polite to tell me to go away,' I giggled to Mum the next day.

The next five days were a whirlwind of activity as we prepared for the launch of the Katie Piper Foundation. By now, a lovely lady called Caroline was working with me in the offices, but we still had a million and one things to organise.

The morning of our bash, I woke up as excited and nervous as if it were my wedding day. My pulse racing and my throat tight, I agonised over making my speech. How would I cope with so many people looking at me? What if it triggered my old anxiety? What if no one even showed up? What if …

Caroline and me made our way to Sony's headquarters, and I started to get ready. As I pulled on a pale pink dress, fierce blue stilettos, chandelier earrings and a pearl cuff, my hands trembled.

We went up in the lift to Simon's office. As soon as he saw me, his eyes widened. 'Wow, Katie, you look amazing,' he whistled, handing me a glass of champagne. 'And have you had your teeth whitened?'

'Yes,' I giggled, and we compared our gnashers. Until then, I'd felt too anxious to think about my appearance, but now I looked at my reflection and smiled. I did look damn good. Burnt and fabulous, that was me.

'I'm pretty nervous, actually,' I confessed, clasping my shaking hands together.

'I get nervous all the time, too,' Simon shrugged. 'I don't like making speeches at all. Just pretend everyone is naked!'

I burst out laughing. 'Ewww, I can't do that! My parents and Mr Jawad will be there!'

Simon smiled and held out his hand. 'Are you ready?' he asked, and I nodded.

'Let's do it!' Hand in hand, we walked into the room. It was already packed with 200 people, including my family and friends; the other burns victims I'd met; the medical people who'd saved my life; Mags and all the documentary crew … Each and every one of them had helped me more than I could ever tell them. They all turned to look at us, and it felt like one of the defining moments of my life. It was magical, it was amazing, unbelievable. It seemed like only yesterday that I'd felt like a monster. That I'd crouched on the floor of the car, terrified of being seen. That I'd been too disgusted to touch my own face. That I'd assumed people were ashamed to be seen with me. Now look at me, holding hands with Simon Cowell, and feeling on top of the world. Nerves tingling, I climbed onto the podium, and adjusted the microphone. A hush fell over the room.

'Good evening, everyone. I would like to thank you all for joining me on this very special evening,' I said, trying to feign confidence. 'As you know, the past two years has been an intense time to say the least, and it's thanks to every single one of you that I'm able to stand here in front of you now … Since my documentary was broadcasted I have been overwhelmed by the support from not just the public, but the media, businesses, and celebrities alike. And, of course, the unconditional love and support my family and friends have always shown me.'

In the sea of faces, I spotted my parents. With her hair and make-up done to the nines, Mum looked so glamorous, and Dad had tears of pride rolling down his cheeks. I knew how special this moment was for them, too.

I talked about my plans for the Katie Piper Foundation and showed a DVD about the treatment I'd received in France. 'In addition to raising enough money to create a centre in the UK like the one in Lamalou, I also feel strongly that it's important that the Foundation helps make some fundamental changes in society. I want to change the way people view and judge those suffering from disfigurement: I am living proof that disfigurement does not mean the end of your life as you know it. We intend to raise awareness, empower people and show that scarring isn't ugly.

'One of the hardest things about being disfigured is getting over how other people view or react to you. If together we can change that, we will take away half the battle that someone like myself would face.'

Applause rang out, then Simon came up onto the podium.

'Katie is one of the most inspiring people I have met,' he said, and I had to remind myself he was talking about me. Me! 'She is brave, talented and determined, and I think what she is doing with the Katie Piper Foundation is incredible.'

I felt like I was floating on air as I walked around the room afterwards, and everyone crowded round to congratulate me. 'Well done, Katie!' they said. 'You look gorgeous!'

I spotted my uncle Richard and made my way over to him. We embraced and, like Dad, he had tears in his eyes, too.

'I remember visiting you when you were in the coma,' he said. 'I didn't think you'd make it. And now look at you. You haven't just survived, you're thriving, too.'

My eyes filled with tears as I thought back to those days. At times, I hadn't thought I'd survive, either. I'd expected my broken heart to just give up at any second, and in my darkest hours, I'd wanted to die. How frightened I'd been back then. How terrified of even looking anyone in the eye. But now, I'd just given a speech to 200 people. I'd stood up, with all those eyes riveted to my face, and I'd spoken about what had happened to me. I'd revealed my hopes for the Foundation, and it was like waking up from a nightmare.

'*If only I could find love and a home of my own,*' I thought, '*then my new life would be complete.*'

'I'm so proud of you,' Dad came over and hugged me. 'I never imagined you'd have any job again, never mind something as wonderful as this.'

Then Mr Jawad appeared at my side. He gave me a hug so big, I almost fell over, then he smiled with satisfaction and said: 'I always knew you could do this. I never doubted you for a second.'

But I knew I hadn't done it on my own. Practically every single person there had helped me in one way or another: Mags, who'd filled in countless forms and done a hundred different things to get the charity up and running; Simon, who'd infused me with confidence and given his unflagging support; my friends, who'd accompanied me to hospitals and seminars all over the country. The list was endless, and each and every one of them deserved to share the triumph.

By the end of the evening, my killer blue heels had cut my feet to ribbons, but I was on such a high, I barely even noticed.

The next morning, I was up at 6 a.m. for a day full of TV and radio interviews, including *BBC Breakfast* and *This Morning* again. I rode it all on a wave of elation.

A few days later, having a drink with a crowd of friends in Camden, north London, I met a guy called Joe. With blond hair and a trendy V-neck top, he looked like a member of a boy band. Still buzzing from the launch and confident thanks to my camouflage make-up and a few drinks, I was in a wonderful mood especially when my friend Darren whispered that Joe fancied me.

'Are you sure?' I gasped in surprised delight.

Darren nodded. 'Yeah, he just told me so himself,' he exclaimed, handing me a drink. I smiled into my glass and enjoyed feeling like a normal girl, who was out in the pub with some friends, flirting with a fit guy who liked her back. At the end of the night, Joe and I had a tipsy kiss and exchanged numbers, and after that he phoned me constantly. There was a definite connection, and I was excited that something special might grow between us.

'You're lovely,' he said. 'Really funny and interesting and sexy. When can we meet up again?'

'Soon. I've just got lots on at the minute,' I told him, not wanting to admit I had to go into hospital for a skin graft. It was too soon, and I wasn't sure how much he knew about what had happened to me. This time, they were taking skin from my groin and sewing it onto my outer eyelids, and skin from my inner lip to sew onto my inner eyelids. This was because my skin had shrunk and their wasn't enough to keep my eyes lubricated and protected.

The operation was a bit of a step backwards, an unwelcome return to the early days, and I felt my euphoria fade away as I was admitted to Chelsea and Westminster Hospital. It was yet another operation – was it my fortieth? Fiftieth? I could hardly keep track there had been so many of them. Having that many general anaesthetics wasn't good for me, either, and I knew it was putting a strain on my liver and kidneys. Mr Jawad had explained it would probably affect my life expectancy, but I didn't dwell on that too much. I couldn't.

Because this operation involved my eyes, I was especially anxious. Blindness was still my biggest fear, and I whispered

Alice's prayer with extra fervour as I was wheeled into theatre. When I woke up afterwards, both my eyes were bandaged and I was flailing around in darkness. Disorientated and doped up on medication, I thought I saw Danny lurking at the bottom of my bed,

'I want my mum,' I cried, and I felt her stroke my hair.

'I'm here, darling,' Mum said.

'Danny's here, too,' I babbled. 'I saw him at the bottom of my bed!'

'He's not. It was just a hallucination.'

No, no it wasn't. He was here. And I couldn't see anything! My greatest fear had come true. I was utterly helpless, trapped in the shadows with him.

'Mum, they've won,' I whimpered.

'What do you mean? Who have won?'

'Danny and Stefan. I'm blind, so they've won.'

'You're not blind. Your eyes are just bandaged over. Shush, it's okay. Just go to sleep. I'm here.' She held my hand, and I drifted back into unconsciousness.

The next time I woke up, I was a lot calmer and more lucid. I wasn't blind; Danny wasn't there. I was safe. The nurse removed the dressing from my good eye, and the world swam into focus. Even though my limbs were floppy and weak, I made my way to the toilet and looked at myself in the mirror. My face was bruised and swollen, but it wasn't too bad.

'I've seen worse,' I smiled wryly to Mum.

I was discharged that evening, but back home the pain in my bad eye became excruciating. It was like a bright ball of agony, pulsating in my skull.

'Mum!' I called, and she ran into my bedroom. 'I can't sleep, it's so bad. You have to help me.'

The painkillers she gave me didn't do a thing, and when we got to hospital the next morning, the doctor said the dressing had been pressing down on the stitches from the graft, causing them to scratch the cornea. He administered anaesthetic eye-drops that numbed the pain, but over the next few days, it kept flaring up again and we had to dash back and forth from A&E.

'*Just a week or so ago, I was standing on that podium with Simon Cowell, feeling fabulous*,' I thought in frustration. It had been so momentous and I had thought it marked a new beginning. And yet here I was again, my injuries dictating my life.

By the time a week had passed, the pain had finally subsided, but then my good eye started hurting. It became bloodshot and swollen, and I really started panicking then. If anything happened to it, I'd be totally blind. '*God, please let it be all right. Please don't let them win. I won't be able to drive or live on my own if I go blind. Or do half the things I do for the Foundation now*,' I thought as Clare, the camera-woman for the new Channel 4 documentary, whisked me to hospital.

'Blood has leaked under the skin graft,' the doctor said. 'We need to drain it and keep the eye covered to reduce the risk of infection.'

Thankfully, it wasn't too serious, but wearing patches over both eyes meant I couldn't see a thing. Clare drove me home, and when we pulled up outside my house, I climbed out like a blind person. Fumbling and stumbling, I had to move with my arms stretched out in front of me.

'I've got you.' I heard Dad's voice as he took my arm and led me indoors.

It was horrible, every bit as frightening as I'd always feared, but I reminded myself it was only temporary. What was the point in crying over it?

'We've cooked a roast,' Mum said, shepherding me into the kitchen and helping me sit down at the table. 'Want me to feed you?'

'No, I want to do it by myself. But I'm going to need some help,' I smiled, feeling for the knife and fork.

'Right, the peas are at one o'clock,' Dad said, and I started laughing. 'The carrots are at three o'clock, and the potatoes are at six o'clock.'

I tried to spear some food, but even when I managed it, actually getting it into my mouth was another struggle.

'Ow!' I yelped when I accidentally jabbed myself in the chin with the fork. It was frustrating, but I was determined to see the funny side.

'No one's allowed to watch TV tonight,' I joked. 'You have to sit and chat to me, instead. And Mum, you're going to have to be my personal stylist until my eyes get better. I'll tell you what clothes I want to wear, and you can help me put them on.'

As we talked and laughed, we pushed the sadness away. I might be helpless and housebound once again, but it was only a hiccup; a walk in the park compared to what I'd already endured. Danny and Stefan hadn't won yet, and they never would.

Chapter Twenty-Four
A Beautiful Life

Within a week, the eye patches were off and I was back in the game, having meetings for the charity, organising camouflage make-up kits for burns victims and viewing flats.

'Talk about resilient. You're like the Duracell bunny,' Suzy whistled.

Joe and I were still talking on the phone a lot, too, chatting about when we could meet again. I wanted to, but I was still worried. It had been really dark inside that pub, and he had no idea what I looked like underneath my make-up. What should I do? Jonathan had accepted me scars and all, and I'd learned to accept myself, too, but I didn't know how Joe would react. Sure, he seemed to like my personality, but I was all too used to people freaking out over my disfigurement.

A week or so later, he invited me to a party at his friend's house. 'I'll pick you up from work and drive you there,' he said, and my heart skipped a beat. He was going to see me in daylight, so I'd have to make sure my make-up was flawless.

That day, I was a bag of nerves. As I started getting ready, my vision suddenly blurred. I was still recovering from the graft, and I could hardly see a thing as I tried to apply false eyelashes. 'Oh, *no*!' I shouted, as glue dripped all over my cheek. The clock was ticking, and Joe was going to be here at any second. Flustered, I jumped into trendy harem pants and a white crop top. I popped some ethnic wooden bangles over my wrists and started frantically curling my hair. This was a disaster. I looked terrible. Then my phone rang. Joe was outside, and I cursed silently then chirped: 'Great. Be right there!'

Grabbing my bag, I tottered downstairs in my brown suede wedges and tried to tell myself everything would be okay. He was really into me, he'd said so himself. He thought I was funny and sexy and smart, so he wouldn't care what I looked like. This would be my fairytale ending, right?

Wrong.

As soon as I got into his car, I could tell it was awkward. He didn't screw his face up or gasp, but his feelings were as plain as day. It was there in his uncomfortable 'Hello', in his subdued demeanour, in the look in his eyes. I wanted to burst into tears.

'*He doesn't fancy me at all any more*,' I thought, masking my sadness with a manic stream of nervous chatter.

'So how was work? I had a hectic day. What's this party for? Is it your friend's birthday or something?' I jabbered on and on. Joe was friendly and polite, but that spark between us had been extinguished. It was excruciating.

At the party, he seemed really distant, and I spent most of the evening chatting to his friend and knocking back drinks, desperate to quell my anxiety.

By the time Joe drove me home again, I was more than a little tipsy. Fired up on Dutch courage, I took a deep breath and turned to him.

'You don't like me any more, do you?' I asked, even though the sensible bit of my brain was telling me to shut the hell up. Right now.

'Don't be daft! 'Course I do,' he exclaimed, but I didn't believe him. 'I'll ring you later,' he said as I jumped out of the car.

When I sobered up, I was mortified. I must have sounded desperate and demented. Why did I open my mouth? Why did I have to be such an idiot? But maybe he had been telling the truth; maybe he did like me and he was just shy or something. But the next week, Joe cancelled our date at the last minute, and a week later, he did the same thing. There was no point hoping or pretending otherwise – he had been attracted to me until he'd seen my face properly. And then he wasn't remotely interested. I started sobbing, haunted by the old fear that I wasn't good enough. Why couldn't Joe give me a chance? Why couldn't he see past my scars? Perhaps if he'd tried, he might've seen some beauty in me still. I was furious at him, furious at Danny and Stefan, furious at myself.

I didn't need a man for validation or completion, but I wanted someone to share my life with. Until that moment,

I just hadn't known how much. My self-esteem, which had grown so much since the horrific aftermath of the attack, was knocked badly.

'*I don't want my disfigurement to matter. Not to me, and not to other people,*' I thought sadly. '*But if men realise how burned I am, they don't flirt with me. They don't fancy me. It's like I'm permanently branded a victim. I'm not a sexual being. I know Jonathan wasn't like that with me, but most blokes are.*'

I was almost twenty-seven, and I wanted love as much as the next girl. I wanted a family one day; I wanted a man to desire me, to support me, to protect me. Even though I'd probably look lots better in a decade, when my injuries had healed more, I wanted to meet someone now, so I knew they loved the real me. The girl beneath the scars. But then, I'd always known I couldn't change attitudes overnight. Disfigurement just had to be normalised and accepted – that was one of the aims of the Foundation, and *that* aim would probably take years and years.

In the meantime, I knew I was a fighter. I was a survivor and, as the weeks went by, I picked myself up once again. Okay, I'd put myself on the line and been knocked back. Fine, it wasn't the fairytale ending I'd dreamed of, and it had shaken my fragile self-esteem to the core. But I'd got through it, just like I always did, and now I realised I was stronger than ever.

Like going blind, being rejected like that was one of my greatest fears. So many times over the last twenty-seven months, I'd agonised about men not wanting me, not fancying me. But in the space of a few weeks, I'd faced both those demons and overcome them. '*Maybe it was the final hurdle,*' I thought. Maybe I'd needed to go through that, to know I couldn't be beaten. Life had been a rollercoaster for so long, and now I knew I could live with the lows as well as the highs. I could roll with the punches and dust myself off as many times as I needed to. It was Joe's loss, I told myself; he didn't deserve me anyway. Sure, I was single, but that was all right. I would just keep on living this life that I had worked so hard to rebuild from the ashes of my old one.

It was a great life, too. The charity was going from strength to strength, and I'd put in an offer on a gorgeous two-bedroom flat on a quiet mews street in a leafy part of London. I was encircled by people I loved, people like Mr Jawad. For his birthday a few days later, I sent him a photo of us together at the launch of the Foundation, with a poem I'd written.

Mr Jawad, you are a hero.

A hero thinks of others before they think of themselves.
A hero is courageous and will take steps that others won't.
A hero will never complain.
A hero can be made in one act of compassion
Or in years of tender loving care.
Some heroes are remembered, whilst many are left forgotten.
Heroes are angels in disguise, saving precious innocent lives.

You helped me see a purpose
when I thought I had no future.
You saved me, and you were my rock.

The thoughtfulness and care
you have shown will never be forgotten.

'Katie, I'm speechless,' my angel-in-disguise phoned to say. 'I have hung the photo on my living room wall, alongside pictures of my wife and children. And the poem; it was wonderful.'

'I'm so happy you liked it.'

The days of me writing angry, heartbroken poems to Danny and Stefan were over. Never again would the ink run in places as my tears fell onto the page. Never again would I feel the need to address either of them.

Now I was full of gratitude and love, instead of hurt and anger.

A few weeks later, the estate agent phoned to say my offer on the flat had been accepted, and I screamed with excitement.

'I got the flat! I got the flat!' I shrieked down the phone to Mum, my mind whirling. I'd banged on about regaining my independence for so long, and now that it was within reach … well, it was a bit scary, too. My mind raced. Fire extinguishers and smoke alarms, I needed them in every room. A rope ladder, so I could escape from my bedroom window in case there was a fire. Locks on every door, but no candles or lighters or matches. Everything electrical would have to be tested. No knife rack in the kitchen, in case anyone broke in and tried to stab me. A baseball bat under the bed to protect myself, and some kind of sophisticated alarm system, too. Non-flammable bedding, I couldn't forget that. I mentally listed all the things I'd need to make myself feel safe. I might be frightened and neurotic, but I'd realised that was how I had to live my life. I didn't know if the fear would ever leave me totally, if I would ever be able to go shopping on my own on the spur of the moment, or not freak out if a guy in a hoody walked in my direction. I might always be hyper-sensitive to danger, always hyper-conscious of risks. But it wasn't going to stop me living. Not for a second.

That night, I lay in the bath and flicked though an Ikea catalogue, fantasising about the different furniture I could get. A big chair I could curl up on after a long day in the office. A stainless steel fridge where I could keep my face creams and nail varnishes without Mum teasing me about all the room they were taking up in hers. I smiled, but then thought about how difficult it would be for her and Dad to let me go. I'd left before, and they'd almost lost me not once but twice. First when I was sucked into that shallow, champagne-fuelled world, and then when Danny tried to destroy me. But the nightmare had brought us all so much closer than we used to be. It had forged new bonds, and I knew they could never be broken. I'd still come home all the time – I'd probably be back every weekend, to help Mum make roasts like I used to. To cuddle Dad on the sofa, to play board games with Suzy and take Barclay for a walk to the park.

Climbing out of the bath, I went into my bedroom and reached up into my wardrobe for a box on the top shelf. I sat on the bed and opened it up. It was my memory box, filled with things from the last couple of years. Letters, cards and poems people had sent me. My hospital wrist band, CDs friends had made and one little newspaper clipping from *The Sun* reporting the attack. I wasn't even named in it, and I didn't know why I'd kept it. A hundred stories had been written since that one, but I hadn't kept any of them. I didn't need to – I'd lived it all, and I remembered every single thing.

I thought about how I was still tied to Danny. In any search engine or news website, our names were linked. Would that ever change? Maybe one day, when we'd built the rehabilitation centre, that association would be severed. Maybe then I'd be Katie Piper, the charity campaigner who changed the way people viewed disfigurement and treated burns victims, not Katie Piper, acid girl. Not Katie Piper, who was raped by Danny Lynch. God, I hoped so. Either way, I could never forgive or forget what he and Stefan had done to me, but I wouldn't allow the bitterness to define me. For so long, I'd thought I was a monster, but I wasn't. *They* were the monsters, not me.

Then I flicked through my modelling portfolio. I hardly ever looked at it any more, and it had lost the power to hurt me. I wondered if my old face was in heaven. Would I see it there when

I died? I imagined walking into a white room, and meeting the old me. I wanted to look into her face, to run my hands over her smooth cheeks, her perfect lips, her strong jawline. I wanted to touch every inch of unblemished skin, and remember what it was like to feel that way. But I didn't long for it any more. I didn't long to go to sleep and wake up miraculously restored. Somewhere over the last six months, I'd learned to love myself again. It was okay to be scarred, and it was more than okay to be me. Any time I faltered, any time I got frustrated or anxious, I just had to think about other people in pain. The soldiers coming back from war with missing limbs. The other burns victims who weren't fortunate enough to get the treatment I'd received. I was surrounded by wonderful people, and I was doing something I felt passionate about. I was one lucky girl.

I put the lid on the box, and placed it back on the wardrobe shelf. Would I take it with me when I moved? I wasn't sure. I knew I would never throw it away – its cargo was much too precious. But maybe it was time to leave those memories where they belonged. In the past.

Walking round the kitchen, Dad knocked on the walls, cocking his ear to listen to the noise it made.

'The building work is sound,' he nodded authoritatively, as Mum and I exchanged affectionate smiles. Why did men always have to do that? As if Dad knew the first thing about building a house! It was September 2010, and I was showing them round my new flat for the first time. The paperwork was being processed and I was due to move in in just a few short weeks. I couldn't wait.

'What do you think, Mum?' I asked, eager for her approval.

'I love it. I can really see you here,' she smiled, and we all traipsed upstairs to look at the room that would be my bedroom.

'I could make you a built-in wardrobe here,' Dad pointed, and I hugged him. I knew it wasn't easy for them, but they were being so loving and supportive. Just like always.

'That would be wonderful, Dad,' I laughed. 'I can help you, like I used to when I was a little girl.'

I looked around the room. I imagined a nice big double bed, covered in scatter cushions in pretty colours, and a dressing table with my jewellery on display. My rows of shoes lined up, and maybe some plants. And a nice big mirror, too.

'It's going to be gorgeous, Kate.' Mum squeezed my hand.

I showed them the bathroom. I pictured myself relaxing in the bath, surrounded by all my creams and toiletries with the radio playing in the background. I could put my Palmer's Cocoa Butter on that shelf; buy some nice new towels for that rail.

'It's so clean, and the whole place is really secure,' Mum nodded.

I grinned. 'I can really make it my own, too, don't you think?' I exclaimed in excitement. 'I want lots of quirky bits and pieces, so it really feels like mine.'

As we wandered back down the stairs, I smiled with satisfaction. This wasn't just a new flat; it was a new chapter of my life. It meant I was back in control, back in the driving seat. I wasn't helpless any more. I was an independent woman again, and it felt amazing.

I wasn't naive enough to think it would be plain sailing from here on in. I would be back in hospital for more treatment, more operations, more consultations, more complications, but that was okay. And I would still have bad days, when I wasn't happy with how I looked – but every girl had those, right? I would still be afraid, but I'd feel the fear and do it anyway. I would embrace my scars, because they were my badges of honour, my war wounds from the battle Danny had waged but hadn't won. He had tried to destroy me, but he had only made me stronger. I was a better person now, less self-obsessed, less superficial. I wanted to help people and make a difference to the world in any little way I could. Who knew where I would be in ten years' time? Married with children? I hoped so, but I wasn't going to sit around obsessing over it. I had so much love in my life already.

As we wandered into the living room together, I thought about how incredible this was. How far I'd come since that day in Lisa's office when I'd seen my new face for the first time. I never thought I'd have anything even vaguely resembling a normal life ever again, never mind one as fulfilling and rewarding as this one. I never imagined I'd be able to leave the burns unit in hospital, let alone live on my own in London – the place where the old me had been raped and murdered. It seemed miraculous, and I remembered what Alice used to tell me:

'This is not the end for you, Katie,' she'd gently insist when I thought about giving up. And she had been right.

'I want a nice big comfy sofa right here,' I grinned to Mum and Dad, who were checking out practical things like the plug sockets and skirting boards. 'Maybe a little coffee table here. And some shelves against the wall, for books and knick-knacks.'

'It really ticks all the boxes, Kate,' Mum said, and I could tell she was thinking the same as me. She'd never dreamed this would happen, either. We smiled at each other, not needing to say a word. Then I looked around the bare walls. They were a blank canvas, a clean slate; just like my future. My old dreams might be dead, but while I was living in this flat I would make new, better dreams that would come true.

'I know! I could hang up lots of photos!' I suddenly cried. In the past, the only photos I'd cared about were the ones in my portfolio. Airbrushed and posed, with perfect lighting and cool styling, they had been proof of my beauty. Tools to help me make it as a model. But I didn't care about those any more.

'I could put new ones on the walls,' I said, imagining the frames arranged in a nice pattern. Mr Jawad, Mum and Dad, Suzy and Paul, and the friends who'd been there for me … I smiled to myself, and thought about how each and every one of them was beautiful. Because beauty wasn't big boobs and hair extensions. It wasn't immaculate make-up and on-trend clothes. It wasn't even a perfect face, with symmetrical features and unblemished skin. It was Mr Jawad, selflessly sacrificing his precious few holidays and spending his own money to come to France with me. It was Mum, offering to give up her career – and her life – so she could sit at home with me every single day. It was Caroline working overtime for free because she believed in the Foundation so much, and it was Mags helping me set it up in the first place. It was Suzy, spending hours downloading music onto an iPod for me, because she knew I couldn't bear to listen to the songs I used to love. It was Paul, giving me the angel and writing to Pam Warren for me. It was Alice, singing Indian lullabies while I prayed for death. It was Rita, feeding me cupcakes and advice. It was Marty bringing me sunflowers, and Kay sending me bouquets every few weeks for months on end. It was Dad, picking me up like a baby and carrying me upstairs to massage my skin as we watched *The X Factor* together. Those moments had helped me to endure the unendurable, to cope with the unimaginable. They had given me hope, and the strength to keep going.

With Mum and Dad behind me, I opened the front door of my new home and stepped outside, into the world I'd hidden away from for so long. I breathed in the fresh autumn air and looked at the people passing by, and I didn't peer over my shoulder for evil lurking in the shadows. The nightmare was really over. I'd woken up. I'd seen what was truly important in life, and found a strength I never knew I had. All the pain and suffering, the horror and the terror, the tears and the screams – I'd survived it all. Yes, I was a new Katie, but that was a good thing. Through it all, I'd learned that kindness and love are the most wonderful things of all, and from that moment on I knew my life was going to be beautiful, in every single way.

Acknowledgements

First and foremost, I would like to thank my loving family. Mum and Dad, thank you for putting your lives on hold to rebuild mine. You are the most selfless and caring parents anyone could ever hope for – plus you are quite humorous and fun to be with!

Thank you to my two best friends: my little sister Suzy and big brother Paul. Dinky, all that Finkle and Inehorn time kept me laughing and down with the kids!

Thank you to all of the Piper family who supported me in a variety of ways: my cousins Tom, Louise, Ross, Conner, Tina, and Philip and my aunties and uncles.

To my new friends: thank you for enriching my new life. And, to my old friends: thank you for staying in my life. I love you all dearly and you help me in ways you don't even know.

There are so many medical professionals who I owe a huge debt of gratitude to:

My surgeon and friend Mr Jawad – you made the impossible possible and gave me hope when I thought there was none; all the staff at the burns unit at the Chelsea and Westminster Hospital;

Dr Lisa Williams; the ICU team; Dr Frasson and all his team at Centre Ster in Lamalou-les-Bains; Dr Benson and his team at the gastroscopy unit; Iain Muir-Nelson; Mr Saleh; Mr Professor Onur Erol and his team at the Onep clinic in Istanbul; Dr Matteo Tretti Clementoni; everyone at Q Med; and all the hospital staff at all the hospitals I have been to for touching my life.

A big thank you is also due to Joy and Polly from Dan's Fund for Burns.

I would like to commend the Metropolitan Police. Our Family Liaison Officer Adam was a great help to me and my family, as was Warren, Paul, Steve, Emma, Mark and many others who I never met, but I know worked hard. Thank you also to the CPS and the rest of the legal team.

Telling my story would not have been possible without the help and guidance of Channel 4 and Mentorn Media. I'm truly thankful for the platform you gave me to benefit other people affected by disfigurement.

I'd like to thank Jessie – not just for making the documentaries, but also for helping me to grow as a person – and the rest of the fantastic team.

I'm also grateful to the British and global media for their positive journalism and raising awareness of my cause.

While setting up the Katie Piper Foundation, I saw the best part of human nature. Thank you to my fantastic, energetic trustees and friends of the charity: Mr Jawad, Ros, Simon O, Pat, Mags, Martin, Hilary, Caroline, Larissa, Simon M and Katey.

A huge thank you to Andrew Birks from Regus – I don't think you realise how big a part you have played in giving me a purpose in life.

The Clearing and Tribal DDB – thanks for giving the charity a clear identity and creating a brilliant website! Thank you to everybody who has donated in some way, without you we couldn't carry out the work I'm so passionate about.

I'd also like to thank those who have helped to make this book happen: Gayle Schoales; my editor, Kelly Ellis, and all the team at Ebury; and Belinda Jones.

One thank you I never thought I would write is to Simon Cowell. Simon, thank you for believing in me and helping me send out the message that disfigurement does not mean the end of your life.

The final, but very important, thank you goes to the general public. I am overwhelmed by the warm, strong, supportive response I've received. I have read messages on the internet, your letters and emails, as well as speaking to people on the street. Your heartfelt words of genuine encouragement have enabled me to get on with my life again. Thank you all for helping me to be part of society again and showing me so much love.

About the Author

Katie Piper was born in 1983 and grew up in Hampshire. She was a model and TV presenter until she was the victim of a vicious rape and acid attack in March 2008. While coming to terms with her own disfigurement, she has been helping countless other burns survivors. The Katie Piper Foundation has been able to provide financial support to individuals and places, such as the specialist burns unit at Chelsea and Westminster Hospital, where Katie was treated herself. The Foundation has also sought ways to help burns survivors feel more confident by offering make-up seminars, where people can learn not just how to camouflage scarred areas, but also how to look and feel great with hair styling, manicures and false eyelashes.

The charity's main vision is to see the pioneering treatment Katie received in France be introduced to the UK, with the creation of an advanced burn and scar management and rehabilitation clinic, which would be accessible to anybody who would benefit from specialised treatments, such as pressure therapy and silicone treatment.

Outside of her foundation work, Katie continues to have regular, intensive surgery. Her bravery has been widely recognised and she has won several awards, including: *The Woman of Courage Award at the Vitalise Women of the Year Luncheon and Awards; Most Inspirational Woman Award at The Inspiration Awards for Women supporting Breakthrough Breast Cancer; The Pride of Andover Award*; and the *Editor's Choice Award* at the *Cosmopolitan Ultimate Women of the Year Awards.* She has also taken part in a Channel 4 documentary, *Katie: My Beautiful Face* and has filmed a four-part follow-up to be aired in 2011.

For more information about The Katie Piper Foundation, or to show your support, visit www.katiepiperfoundation.org.uk.